MY RICE BOWL

MY RICE BOWL

korean cooking outside the lines

RACHEL YANG

and Jess Thomson

Photography by Charity Burggraaf

SASQUATCH BOOKS
SEATTLE

To the boys who keep my plate full

contents

introduction

I was born 양정화, not Rachel Yang. But during the summer between high school and college, when I was eighteen, my mother, younger sister, and I sat around the kitchen table in Westchester County with a book of American baby names. *Rachel*, we decided, would replace the butchered Americanization of Yang Chung Hwa. It was the ninth most popular baby name in 1996, so it felt safe: I'd change my name to Rachel. I could be one of them. Nevermind that Koreans typically have a hard time pronouncing *R*s and *L*s. With an American name and a degree from Brown University, I would surely have a nice cubicle in one of those high-rises in a big city—either in Korea or in America. It didn't really matter where.

Twenty years later, I am now a chef, a restaurateur, a wife, and a mom to two young boys. I always knew I was the marrying kind, and I always knew I wanted children. But I didn't just decide to become a chef in the same way. That part was an accident. I didn't expect to work in some of New York's best restaurants, fall in love with a Midwestern cook in the kitchen, move to Seattle, and open four restaurants. And I surprised everyone—especially myself—by winding up as a Korean chef who doesn't cook Korean food.

But that's exactly what happened. Today, with my husband Seif Chirchi (and with the occasional help of our young boys, Pike and Rye), we run four restaurants: Joule, Revel, and Trove in Seattle, Washington; and Revelry in Portland, Oregon. It works first and foremost because Seif and I are an unbeatable team. It works because we have the kind of dedicated, hardworking, creative staff that help us carry out the challenges we set forth but also challenge us in return. And finally, it works because our food is very unique—different from any other food, yet always reminding our customers of their very favorite things.

I am Korean, but this book is not about how to make Korea's traditional rice bowl, *bibimbap*. As you'll learn in the pages that follow, I learned how to cook Korean food well after I had classical French training and modern American fine-dining experience under my belt. At our restaurants, we create food that is an improbable combination of all those things. It's food without boundaries, made with ingredients from all over the globe, created within a relatively rigid framework built from our understandings of how flavor works. Seif and I love that by pushing away norms about what foods go with what we've been able to change people's expectations. With this book, we're hoping to bring some of our unusual flavors into your kitchen. The food you'll find in the recipes that follow isn't Korean food. Korea is our starting point, but as anyone who has walked into our restaurants looking for traditional *bibimbap* can tell you, we do not run Korean restaurants. But our version of Korean-inspired food is itself akin to that rice bowl. Underneath everything, there's a dependable backdrop—my Korean heritage, made up of my childhood and distant food memories that are engrained in me. It's topped off with a mosaic of flavors seasoned with my cooking experience, informed by Japan, China, France, Italy, Mexico, Spain, Thailand, Vietnam, Mongolia, and India (just to name a few)—the way America is.

This is the authentic food of a Korean immigrant who tried everything she could to become an American but only became one when she realized that her culture—among many—is what makes America so delicious today. Cook it as written or make it yours. Enjoy every bite.

how to use this book*

When you flip through this book for the first time, you'll notice that, while it has undeniable Korean influences, you won't find traditional Korean staples like *bibimbap* or *bulgogi*. You'll also notice that I don't tend to use Korean words for foods. My tendency to give ingredients and my dishes American names reflects my own way of making them more understandable. Often, American chefs who specialize in specific cuisines try to advocate for authenticity, but I'm already Korean. I'm as authentic as it gets, I guess. Also, because Korean words are often very difficult to read and pronounce—even though they are becoming more "mainstream," most Korean foods wind up sounding garbled in American English—I find it most accurate to use my own English descriptions for foods. Since I'm frequently inventing concepts that are riffs on American or European favorites, it would be totally incorrect to use a more Korean name anyway.

No matter what they're called, chances are the recipes that follow will contain combinations that seem a little improbable. Jump in. We think you'll find that, while the recipes could be novel to you, most of them taste familiar because the concepts we use to combine flavors—balancing sweet, salty, bitter, and sour—are usually quite homey and comforting. Below are a few tips that might help you along the way.

EMBRACE YOUR OWN ADAPTATIONS

It's a crazy thing to say in a cookbook, I realize, but here's the truth: all recipes are inherently flawed because no two cooks are using the same set of tools. Every person who looks at a recipe brings to it a different cooking history

*however you want

and a different palate and often their own set of expectations about what constitutes simple descriptives like hot, sharp, spicy, smooth, soft, and salty. They're looking at a different stove and holding a different knife. Each time I open a restaurant, it takes me at least a couple of weeks in a kitchen to train experienced cooks with the new recipes, doing things over again and again to figure out what can go wrong when they apply their skills to new dishes in a new place. Recipes are always a great starting point because they guarantee consistency in how ingredients are first combined. The danger of a recipe, though, is that it doesn't take into account all the variables that the person who writes it can't see—whether it's so humid out that the noodle dough might not need quite as much liquid, as is sometimes the case at Revel and Trove, or whether the meat starts extra cold and might need a bit longer to cook. And when you're running a restaurant, a recipe is never detailed enough to describe exactly how each dish should be plated, or exactly how it should taste, or how each cook can work toward that goal so that every single diner who walks through the door gets the same product I expect to hit the table.

At home, though, things are more relaxed. We can be more human at home. Recipes are more flexible. We can use Chinese broccoli instead of rapini if it's what we have or omit the part of a dish that one diner doesn't eat. While my goal here is to give you the same recipes we use in our restaurants, you won't have the training our cooks have, and you'll have to make your own choices about what to change if your oven is on the fritz or your heirloom tomatoes are looking a little tired. Use this book as a guideline; use its lessons to create something unique. It means that, by definition, the recipes won't be mine but yours. Embrace the little differences. Use common sense—a dish without its sauce won't taste the same—but I encourage you to take the liberty to play with these recipes.

PANCAKE THEORY

While we insist that all our cooks know what each dish should look like as it reaches the pass, we've learned that the best way to achieve success is to teach them what something should look like at each step along the way. Our pancakes (see page 165) are a perfect example: because some of the mung beans that make up the pancake batter are sometimes larger or smaller or have more or less moisture than others, and because the ingredients we put in our pancakes have different moisture contents, the batter itself can be totally different from pancake to pancake. If you add a dry root vegetable like taro, for example (see Taro Pancakes, page 175), the batter will be drier than if you add something like squash, which is naturally higher in water. What's important is that the pancake gets crisp on the outside as it cooks, so we teach everyone on the line how to add a little less of the ingredients that are very moist so the pancake doesn't end up steaming. Our "Pancake Theory" evolved to describe the general process of tinkering with anything you're cooking: No matter how much practice you have in the kitchen, think about what you *expect* out of a dish before you start cooking so you have a goal in mind as you work. (In most cases, this simply means reading the whole recipe through before you start. Pay attention to the cues we give for what something should look and taste like.) Then adjust as you go, depending on what your senses and your cooking experience tell you the dish needs. You might find that you like more or less salt on grilled mustard greens than we call for or that you prefer to make kimchi with more of our potent Kimchi Base (page 149) than we generally use. You are your own best guide in the kitchen.

PRACTICE, PRACTICE

When we compare opening Joule (the first time) to opening Revelry, it's clear to us that opening restaurants takes practice. Cooking is no different—which is why when you're making noodles or dumplings for the first time (or even just grilling meat, for that matter), you should keep in mind that the more you do it, the better you'll get.

FIND YOUR FLAVORS

Our kitchens are places where feel and flavor trump all. Coming from very traditional, sometimes pedantic fine-dining establishments, Seif and I were trained to be very exact. It's an excellent way to learn how to follow directions precisely, but from our perspective, it doesn't actually teach a person to cook—that comes with time, experimentation, and freedom. This book mixes ingredients in ways that are not traditional, but it's about the food, not the concept of fusion. We live in a time where you can go to a grocery store and buy foods from a zillion different cultures. Why would you want to pick just one? Find food you love to cook and love to eat.

the making
of a chef

It was always the plan that once I'd gotten my American education I'd go back to Korea. That—I knew in my bones from a very young age—was the Korean dream: study as hard as humanly possible, attend an Ivy League university, become a doctor or a lawyer, then marry a nice Korean man, and maybe return to Korea. My sister and I attended high school together in the United States, staying with our aunt's family in New York, but we still identified steadfastly as Koreans. Our friends were Korean. Our parents were Korean.

Our parents were *so* Korean. If I came home with a test score of ninety-four, they'd nod their heads gravely. "Better next time," they'd say. In general, Koreans do not do compliments. And there is always, *always* a new challenge. Like so many Korean kids thirty years ago—and (albeit to a lesser extent) today—my sister and I were raised with very little play but a lot of after-school programming. Korea is a densely populated place, which means that when it comes to schooling, competition is crazy. Most kids go to school for six hours each day the way kids do in America, but then they come home and sit with tutors for another handful of hours. In sixth grade, I had a drawing class for four hours after school—I went to an art-focused middle school—and then I had a math tutor group. My mom picked me up at ten thirty p.m. I didn't know anything different, but my mother couldn't bear to watch how I had to spend more time learning outside of school than I did inside just to keep up. That it was normal to pack two lunchboxes every day.

My mother is the liberal parent. She started working after she finished high school, which was very rare for her generation. While my dad, who is more conservative, might have advocated for a Korean education, my mom is a risk-taker, and she was able to convince him that their two girls should branch out. Starting when I was about twelve, my mother would say things like, "Hey, do you want to move to America for high school?" It sounded intimidating but maybe also liberating. I didn't discourage her from applying for a green card for me.

I moved to the States when I was fifteen. I don't quite remember how I said yes, or even what the process was for moving. It was the most natural course of events. My mother is from a family of eight siblings, half of whom came to the United States around marrying age. They married Koreans and stayed here. So my mother came with me the first time, delivering me to her sister's doorstep just outside New York City, and went home by herself to be with my father and sister. It was the family plan.

High school was hard for me. I spoke very little English. Every day felt like a rainy October day; I'd look out the window and dread going to school, knowing that, no matter what I did, I'd get soaked. In my first year, in ninth grade, I remember struggling with social studies class most vividly. I'd come home with my reading and try to highlight every word I didn't know, and the pages would bleed yellow. Once, I showed up to class and the teacher handed out exams. I remember crying silently, sitting there at my desk, because I'd missed that we were having a test at all. It took so much courage to ask the teacher to let me retake it, but I did.

I have always been quiet and reserved. Today being an introvert means you are thoughtful, analytical, and independent, but twenty years ago it meant you were shy and hesitant, and often alone. The combination of a new language and social interaction terrified me.

Rachel's family (father, mother, and sister) when she was seventeen

Being alone a lot wasn't actually a bad thing, if you wanted to read through textbooks and study every afternoon. Naturally, I did best at the classes that required less English skill. I thought the sciences were my path, because if you're doing math or chemistry, you can communicate in numbers. I got into Brown's engineering program understanding probably 70 percent of what was going on at any given time, which was a huge validation for me. All the work I'd done as a kid and in high school, it all made sense, if I could get a glamorous American education.

But when I started at Brown, newly named Rachel and finally relieved of the burden of getting into a good college, I lost purpose and drive. I woke up to the cold reality that, at the college level, I was no longer a math and science whiz. My clear path to success was not so clear any more. So while my friends—I definitely gravitated toward Korean students, whenever I could—drifted toward the majors that would prepare them to be doctors and lawyers, I started tinkering with fine arts classes, feeling culturally lost but happier doing things that were more creative. As a child in Korea, I'd actually been taught how to draw, and the American professors really embraced my technical background. I loved inventing new things, but I also relished following the rules. I retreated into art and stopped trying to become more American. I graduated with only Korean friends and with degrees in fine arts and urban studies, not really knowing what either meant.

In my mind and in my parents' minds, I'd made it. I'd studied so hard in junior high and high school, and I'd graduated from an Ivy League college. But I had no immediate goal. I'd always followed the goals my parents had put forth for me. In the Korea I knew, there was no wandering. You picked a profession early, and you did what it took to get there. The whole concept of finding one's path after college was completely foreign to me. But suddenly, I had choices. And I had parents who were more open-minded than most Korean parents I'd known.

I graduated in 2000 when the economy wasn't stellar. A lot of my friends didn't have jobs, so it felt okay to wander. I applied for all sorts of things. The first summer after school, I interned at Providence, Rhode Island's city hall for the summer. My mom and I would have long conversations about what I really wanted to do. She was spending months at a time in America at this point and had rented a place midway between me and my sister. My mom talked about how she and I would spend time on weekends watching the Food Network together. It was a perfect pastime for the two of us, since it seemed to be a TV channel she could understand. I'd never made the connection that watching cooking shows might mean I wanted to and could cook professionally, but she did. It was a group decision, rather than just mine: *we* decided I'd go to culinary school. (Only years later did I realize that food television fascinated me because it made food a universal language that everyone, including me and my mom, could speak.)

I didn't think twice about what that would mean—about whether it was hard to make a living as a cook or about how the rest of your life might change if you commit to spending every night in a restaurant kitchen. I just jumped in. For the first time in my life, even though I still held the deeply engrained belief that I'd be a failure if I didn't come back to Korea with a big graduate degree or a rich husband, I was living by experiment. I was living without a plan.

At Peter Kump's New York Cooking School—now called the Institute of Culinary Education—I became someone completely different. It felt so easy. Cooking was like math—there was some sort of flavor puzzle to solve, except because there was always more than one solution, it was also creative. I could suddenly communicate better than I ever had, through food. And like art, it allowed inventiveness but within certain guidelines. For the first time, I didn't feel out of place. I wanted to work for the biggest names in the restaurant industry to rack up a pedigree that might make up for my second-rate career choice. (A Korean mind-set is impossible to shake.)

THE NEW YORK YEARS

Your first restaurant really forms how you think about food and how you approach it. After about a year of culinary school, I began a job as a line cook at DB Bistro Moderne, which Daniel Boulud had just opened. It was a very busy restaurant in the city's theater district that served three-hundred-plus covers of the same meticulous, precise food most fine-dining establishments plated out for only sixty diners in an average evening. The two-level kitchen was tiny, so we were constantly figuring out how to fit all the ingredients we'd go through into some semblance of a workspace. We set up tables along the stairs, in spare corners, anywhere that they'd fit. We ran up and down those stairs all afternoon and evening. We were expected to do our jobs in any situation, under any constraints we had. If you didn't do something correctly, it got thrown away. There was plenty of yelling. I think in some ways, having such a structured regimen and such a constant push felt very familiar to me—like being back in Korea. Between the heat, the hours, and the stress, working there was almost sadistic—and I enjoyed it. Being in a rigorous French kitchen felt like home.

The most surprising thing to me was that being with other cooks felt comforting too. I formed friendships in a way I hadn't since I'd left Korea. It

Helping with a dinner at the Beard House in New York City, 2002

was forced by propinquity, I guess. In kitchens, like in armies, you go through enough together that if you don't kill each other, you come out closer. When the rush hits and everyone is juggling multiple orders (not to mention knives and fire), you watch each other's backs. You do everything as a team, because if one of you messes up, you all fail collectively. You are each other's best support systems. However, the daily grind was still brutal. At first, it broke me. I had to learn how to be on my feet twelve hours every day, picking through four cases of chanterelle mushrooms or dicing an entire case of shallots into tiny, perfect *brunoise* squares as part of the multipage prep lists we had to tackle before five p.m. dinner service every evening. Every day, I wondered whether I'd survive, and every day, I did. Suddenly, I felt like a badass New York City cook. I developed the confidence that I could cook anywhere. About two and a half years later, after working my way up to the hot line, I was ready for something new.

Alain Ducasse at Essex House was much fancier than the bistro had been, with an almost one-to-one ratio of staff to patrons. I started on a sweltering summer day. I knew I needed to hand in my paperwork at the human resources office, but I didn't know how to get there. I paced in the loading dock area for a minute, trying to figure out what to do and how not to be late. A tall cook in a chef's coat ambled down the stairs with a cigarette in his mouth. He saw my knife bag and stuck out his hand. "Hi, I'm Seif," he said. I mumbled something about starting as a cook that day, not really understanding his name. He stubbed out his cigarette and showed me up to the office on his break.

The kitchen space was triple the size of what I was used to, with each section of it large enough to hold multiple people—so if you worked at the garde-manger station, for example, there might be three of you in one spot, working as a team. It was totally intimidating, yet Seif Chirchi—the guy from the stairs—made me feel instantly comfortable there. He was totally goofy, and even on that first day, it was clear to me that everyone in the kitchen loved him. Seif (pronounced "safe") could make fun of anything—most frequently, himself—and he talked to anyone and everyone who worked there, completely ignoring any sort of kitchen hierarchy by which most more formal restaurants abide. He wanted to tell me about how his mom raised him and his sister single-handed, about hip-hop and jazz, and about cooking. He asked me about my life, which I'd always found boring and plain, but he seemed genuinely interested—fascinated, even. I talked at him for hours at a stretch, spilling out everything about my family, my studies, and my own passion for food. *In English*. And he listened.

Seif started working in the industry as a college student, first when he had a part-time job as a server at a little restaurant near the University of Illinois at Champagne-Urbana. One day, he overheard an angry phone call. The cook had called in sick for the umpteenth time. Seif walked into the kitchen. "I'm not doing anything tonight," he announced to the chef. "I could cook."

He loved every single thing about cooking—mostly, though, he loved that the kitchen worked as a team. A few months later, he decided to go to culinary school. At the Western Culinary Institute in Portland, Oregon, he learned that the newly opened Alain Ducasse at Essex House was reputed to be the best restaurant in New York City. When the school required he set up an internship at the end of classes, he wrote the restaurant a letter. They didn't usually take *stages* (or interns) because they had plenty of experienced cooks banging down their door, so it was understandable that they didn't reply. Seif then proceeded to send a letter to the restaurant every day for a month. Something in his conviction caused them to offer him the position about six months before I had arrived. By then they'd hired him as a full-time cook.

At first, I didn't think anything of Seif, other than that I respected him a lot as a cook. He was always the first one to volunteer to do anything and everything that Chef needed. His enthusiasm to learn and to do better was infectious. As I became comfortable there and started going out for drinks after work with the rest of the kitchen, I noticed that he really made me feel different about myself. He told me I was doing a good job and that I was an awesome person. It caught me off guard. In Korea, modesty is considered a virtue; it's important not to show off. The downside of that cultural habit is that when people do a good job at something, no one really gets credit. It's a completely different psychology. One very rarely compliments someone else.

Seif was brought up differently. His mom always told him that whatever he did was amazing. He is quite clearly the product of that environment. When he told me exactly what he thought of me—that I was funny, that I was beautiful, and that I was a great cook—I pretty much swooned. From the beginning, Seif infused me with the self-confidence I needed to break the Alain Ducasse glass ceiling, where (in 2003) women typically only did garde-manger and pastry work. He was a consistent positive force as I worked my way up from garde-manger to *entremetier*—breaking into the boys' club—and then to the fish and meat stations. In my head, every day, I heard my parents pushing me, telling me that I wasn't doing well enough, that I could try harder. If I didn't have the drive inherent to a Korean upbringing, I might not have succeeded in a tough kitchen like Alain Ducasse's. But if I didn't have Seif encouraging me, I might not have ultimately succeeded either. He provided the assurance and solidified the confidence that I needed to move forward.

During this time, Korean cuisine stayed in the background. I'd never cooked Korean food—not beyond rice and snacks, anyway. After about a year and a half at Alain Ducasse, I went to work at Thomas Keller's Per Se, and Seif went to Asiate, in the Mandarin Oriental hotel. (They were both in the Time Warner Center at Columbus Circle, at the base of Central Park.) Per Se was more detail oriented than anything I'd ever done before. We weighed every ingredient for every dish down to the gram, even when we were making stock. Watching Keller's food go out, I learned about how he constructed his kitchens so that every plate left the kitchen as if he'd made it himself, even if he wasn't on-site. It was there that I learned the importance of consistency.

Needless to say, the food was incredible. We weren't just reproducing food, we were reproducing art. Like so many cooks, *The French Laundry Cookbook* became a sort of bible for me. I developed a faith in Per Se's perfectionism and worked very hard to recreate it. However, what influenced me the most was not the food. It was a singular moment when I was at The French Laundry, in Yountville, California, working at a wine dinner with Keller himself. At the end of the event, when all the cooks were milling about trying to find the last odds and ends to do, Keller was the one holding a garbage bag, picking up the last stray bits of *mise en place* left on the counter. I was confused and a little horrified. Here was a chef who was arguably the best in the world. Rather than ordering an underling around or waiting for others to do the dirty job, he was doing it himself. His cooks looked embarrassed. Without a word, they followed his lead. I knew, in that instant, what it meant to cook for a living. It was more than just putting great food on guests' tables. It was the before and the after. It was the attitude, the professionalism, the work ethic, and the constant I-give-a-shit mind-set. I knew then that this was the moment I'd come back to again and again if I was ever going to be a chef or own a restaurant.

While I was at Per Se, a wealthy Korean woman in her early thirties approached me about opening a Korean restaurant in Chelsea. She'd come to America to study like I had and thought opening a restaurant might be a cool project. She was smart and committed but had absolutely no experience in anything restaurant related, so she tapped me as a consultant of sorts. She wanted to bring a Korean sensibility to New York but wanted it to be modern and updated—more chic and trendy than typical 32nd Street–Koreatown options. Back then, having a modern Korean restaurant was completely unheard of. I was the Korean face with Per Se on my résumé; I represented what she wanted her place to be. Plus she figured that I'd eaten enough Korean food in my life to have an opinion on the general flavors her kitchen churned out.

But a month before D'or Ahn was slated to open, the person she'd hired to be the chef wasn't working out, and she asked me if I'd consider the position. She wanted someone with a real Korean background and asked me to do a tasting for her. I'd certainly spent some time in kitchens by then, but I didn't know how to cook Korean food. So we compromised, in a way: she loaned me her Korean mother, and in the span of four or five days her mom taught me Korean Food 101. I learned how to make kimchi and tasted the difference between fermented sand lance sauce and fermented anchovy sauce. It surprised me how familiar and instinctive the flavors felt. With the knowledge from my crash course, I searched for the flavor combinations that would fit her idea of "modern Korean," relying on the framework of my fine-dining experience to adjust concepts until I had something I thought was interesting. I did the tasting, and I got the job. I told her I'd stay for six months, just until she found someone to replace me.

What impacted me most was that, out of all the people she interviewed, I was the only one who could do what she wanted. I was the winner. I had the solid Korean flavor background from my childhood, but I also had the chops from high-end restaurants that allowed me to capture the kinds of flavors and textures she wanted, and I could present the food in just the right way. At all my positions until that point, I had been one of many good cooks in every kitchen, but I had always been replaceable. Realizing that I could do something no one else could do gave me a new sort of high. I realized I'd found my path.

Opening a restaurant might have been the first thing in my life that I wasn't prepared for in any way. I had never come close to leading a kitchen. I had never ordered food. I had never hired anyone. I had never written a menu. But I did all of those things in a topsy-turvy whirlwind six-month period in which I went from being a cook to being a chef. I set up a closet-size kitchen in a New York City basement and hired three full-time cooks (two of whom didn't speak much English). For the first time, everyone turned to me for answers. "Is the kimchi ready to serve?" (No, it's only been fermenting for a day.) "Where is the Korean treasure rice?" (You didn't start cooking it when the ticket came in thirty minutes ago?) "We ran out of dish soap! Should I just leave the dishes in bus tubs?" (Shit. No. I'm going to the store right now and will be back to help you do dishes.) I'd find myself at two in the morning staring blearily at the order sheet for the next day in the dim light of the walk-in, hoping someone could just tell me whether I was doing it right. I was a little kid thrown into the deep end of the pool, and somehow, with profuse flapping, I made it to the edge with my head above water.

Meanwhile, Seif and I had been talking about getting married and about moving to Seattle, where someone Seif had once worked with wanted us to help him open a restaurant. I was no longer a cook with fine-dining

experience but a chef doing modern Korean cuisine (as pronounced by a *New York Post* review). We left New York City. In the winter of 2007, we moved to Seattle and helped to open Coupage. The owner had loved what he'd had at D'or Ahn and wanted to feature fusion food with Korean influence. The Seattle dining scene welcomed us with open arms, curious about what two New Yorkers might do in the Pacific Northwest. We celebrated prematurely, thinking we'd made it. We decided we'd get married in April.

SEATTLE

Seif and I were shocked when we moved to Seattle. Restaurant people actually had lives outside of work. We'd spent so many years as deprived New York City cooks who sacrificed everything for their careers. Seattle felt like the city where you could have it all. Also, for the first time, Seif and I worked as partners. We felt invincible. We were young, and we were willing to do whatever it might take to please the Emerald City.

In the beginning, Coupage was busy. We got good reviews and positive feedback. People were curious about the food and about the chefs. Despite its location in an offbeat neighborhood, people flocked when the local newspaper gave it three stars and the fancy-sounding label of "contemporary Euro-Asian cuisine." But then the honeymoon phase ended and so did the business. The owner decided he wanted something different—a different menu and different chefs—so we parted ways. A month after we got married, we were both twenty-nine and jobless. Our families had just visited for our wedding, congratulating us on our success as a husband-and-wife chef duo. But suddenly, just when we were getting used to being considered some sort of culinary force, we were nobodies. It was devastating.

"Open your restaurant," my mom said, watching us suffer, and gave us a loan. Seif's parents helped us too. We started looking for small restaurant spaces, determined to open a restaurant with the food we thought defined us then—contemporary Euro-Asian food with Korean flavors and French techniques. The banks we visited for small business loans suggested we look at a mall food court. They didn't get it. But looking back, I'm not so sure we did either. Eventually, we secured enough money to fund a small space. In November of 2007, and just four weeks after we got the keys to a former Syrian restaurant on 45th Street in Seattle's Wallingford neighborhood, we opened Joule. It had just forty seats and a kitchen that wouldn't fit more than three people, but it was ours.

our restaurants

JOULE

Joule (pronounced "jewel") is a term that you probably learned about in high school physics class, and promptly forgot, for a unit of energy. Seif's mom gave us the name, wishing that the restaurant be filled with energy and shine forever.

It was an exciting time. We planned to have fun with food, mixing up Korean and international flavors—everything from Seif's favorite Korean spicy beef soup to the little tapioca puddings, served with caramelized grapefruit and lime zest, that became known as the "Joule Box" (page 299). The kitchen was as small as many New York kitchens—it had six burners, two refrigerators, prep spaces, and a grill, but not much more. We didn't have room to plate anything formally, and we didn't have the space or money to have a large kitchen staff, so we developed an unconventional style that took our desperate space and budget constraints into account. Ironically, it was that tiny spot that instigated a lot of our initial style. We made pickles and kimchis because they added flavor without taking up any cooking space, and we grilled our greens (see page 110) because often, the grill was the only spot available to cook anything. We compensated for the fancy plating we were used to by adding flavor. We developed sauces that were pungent and powerful. We added smoke and spice and funk.

"Does it taste dirty enough?" Seif used to ask our cooks, when they wanted to know if they'd gotten something right or when I asked him to taste a new dish. Dirty for us was synonymous with big, bold, complex flavors that we didn't see at other restaurants. We were cooking at a time when Northwest cuisine was still about using local ingredients and preparing them simply and cleanly, without a lot of global influence. If Seif said something tasted clean, it wasn't a compliment.

When we realized how many young families were in the area, we started doing something we called "urban barbecues" in an effort to lure them out for easy casual dining. On Sunday afternoons, we literally turned the dining room into a backyard barbecue, complete with fake green turf and children's picnic tables from Ikea. Each Saturday, we'd change the restaurant into something completely different—one week we'd do a Cajun shrimp boil, the next week a Thai-style barbecue, the next week a clambake—entertaining neighbors and amusing kids with the variety of foods they got to try. And then on Monday morning the turf got rolled up and put back on top of the walk-in refrigerator until the following weekend. Looking back, Seif and I can't believe all we did week after week.

Joule gave us the freedom to spin the globe. For both of us, it was an opportunity to learn about foods we'd never tried. Under the vague banner of East-meets-West cooking, we were given free reign to roam. Two years in, we decided to have a baby. There was never going to be a right time. (I'm pretty sure the babysitting situation never occurred to us.) I worked until the day I went to the hospital and went back to working at Joule soon after Pike was born.

We got good reviews. We got national attention. We went on Iron Chef. We had great regulars. But even with all that, we never felt like it was working. The restaurant business proved, yet again, that it's tough no matter how hard you try. We were barely breaking even. One cold Tuesday in the winter—Seif and I always remember this together, even now—we had no reservations on the books. We called off the cooks and our two servers, and then we called off the dishwasher. It was just the two of us. We had one walk-in diner for the entire night.

We didn't make bad food. We didn't work less hard. It was the reality of the restaurant industry and of being a small business. The fear that lurks inside every restaurant owner's heart had come true. We had hit bottom. Tallying that we'd made fourteen dollars that day (a woman came in and ordered our grilled sweetbread dish and a glass of water) was something we couldn't unsee. With nothing to hold fast to, we took a gamble: three local real estate developers had approached us about partnering to open a new restaurant in Seattle's Fremont neighborhood. In the winter of 2010 we opened Revel, not knowing whether we would sink or swim.

REVEL

While Joule served as an experimental lab for Seif and I to find our voice, we set a clear agenda for Revel; we'd serve urban Korean street food with a twist. With a menu anchored by dumplings, pancakes, and rice bowls, Revel's almost-instant popularity took us by surprise. We opened in December, and by summer, we were cooking for 250 people each night in a kitchen not designed to handle half that. So, as we'd always done, we got creative: we bought a few portable burners and installed a grill on the deck, effectively doubling our cooking space. As a result, we became known there for our summer grill menu, and in the winter, for the hot pots we made on the portable burners.

It was at Revel, I think, that we really became full-fledged fusion cooks. Our wacky flavors seemed to find their own homes: they were different and interesting from a culinary standpoint, yet because they were grounded in culinary traditions, they became approachable enough for a weeknight dinner. We started to embrace the term "fusion," even though it was a tricky one to use. After an initial boom in the eighties, "fusion" was so overused to describe poor cross-cultural combinations of flavors that it became a sort of warning—a red flag identifying restaurants that were simply trying to do too much. For a while, fusion meant throwing foods from different cultures together haphazardly, instead of carefully and intentionally melding different foods together.

We set clear boundaries. Our small menu helped us stay within the categories of food that we set out to serve. We were making Korean dumplings with yeasted or egg yolk– or butter-based doughs, instead of the traditional flour-and-oil dough, but they were still dumplings that were delicious. We were incorporating ground seaweed and red curry paste into the noodles themselves, but again, they were still noodles people craved. Five years after learning to cook Korean food in a New York City basement kitchen, we'd learned to make food fueled by my heritage and creativity, Seif's drive for big flavor, and a diversity that only exists in America. And people loved it.

JOULE, AGAIN

In 2013, when we had an opportunity to move Joule to a bigger and newer space, we seized it, taking time after closing the first space to bring home our second boy, Rye. During the move, we transformed the restaurant. Ultimately, the biggest asset of Joule's initial incarnation was also its biggest challenge: we hadn't given Joule boundaries. The original Joule taught us how to be creative with limited resources; Revel taught us how to think outside of the box given a very small, very structured menu. At the new Joule, we reimagined it as a contemporary Korean steakhouse serving nontraditional cuts of beef. The concept gave it the boundaries it had always needed and also gave customers a way to understand it.

Once we set that as our concept, the new menu came naturally. We played with steakhouse favorites like beef tartare (with toasted pine nuts, pickled pear, and spicy cod roe aioli), shrimp cocktail (with Chinese celery pistou, pork belly ham, and ginger beer), and of course our now-signature steaks, from Kalbi short ribs (see page 205) to kombu-cured chuck. In some ways, giving Joule a more specific goal allowed us to have more fun. Soon after we opened, the restaurant landed on *Bon Appetit*'s Hot 10 list, and we were shortlisted for the James Beard Awards' Best Chef Northwest award. Joule was finally filled with its namesake energy and shining with media buzz.

TROVE

At both Joule and Revel, customers used to ask us where to go for Korean barbecue. There aren't great barbecue restaurants in Seattle—you have to drive north or south, and even then, they're not always reliable. It was natural for people to ask, of course—for most people, Korean food means *bibimbap* and grilled meats. Trying our hand at a new take on barbecue seemed like an awesome new challenge.

That said, we aren't the type of people to open a classic Korean barbecue place, so we decided to make it our own. If we were always challenging our staff to outdo people's expectations, why not demand the same thing from ourselves, we thought? In the end, we actually opened four spots under the same lipstick-red ceiling—a casual noodle bar and a walk-up frozen custard ice cream "truck" in the front, a bar in the middle, and a sit-down grill-your-own barbecue restaurant in the back where people can order raw marinated meat and grill it to their liking. It's Korean-style grilling, but instead of traditional kalbi and spicy pork, we had sliced beef belly and kasu-marinated pork loin. Seattle freaked out over the concept, in a good way. Soon after we opened in 2014, we were listed as one of *GQ* magazine's top twenty-five most outstanding restaurants in the country.

REVELRY

Soon after Trove opened, our investment partner (and the CEO of the outdoors goods store EVO) Bryce Philips approached us about opening a restaurant in Portland. "Impossible," we said. But a year later, he came back saying the space was still available. What if we did something like Revel, he asked, but with a Portland twist? He also found business partners for us who enabled us to conceptualize how it might work to own a restaurant three hours from home. We'd been hands-on chefs at every restaurant, even with two kids, and wondered whether we could rise to the challenge of running a restaurant successfully without being there every night. We agreed to meet with Eric and Karen Bowler, who owned a couple of successful music venues in Portland, and knew immediately that we'd be able to trust them when we couldn't be there.

Portland has never been a stranger to us. Seif's parents live there, and we've always spent holidays there. The Portland dining scene was dynamic and exciting, getting national attention. (In 2015, when we were planning Revelry, the *Washington Post* named it the best food city in America.) We loved the idea of being part of it. Even though it was our first restaurant in Portland, it was clear to us that while many new restaurateurs have the luxury of making mistakes—customers and critics are often more lenient for the first couple of months—we had been in business in Seattle for nine years. We had to get it right the first time in Portland.

We opened Revelry in Portland in August of 2016. We imported a few of our favorite dishes from Revel—the short rib rice bowl (see page 205), our kimchi and pork belly pancakes (see page 171), and the crab noodles (see page 243). We gave it a name that echoed its roots but implied something new. We wanted people to know it wasn't a copycat restaurant. We gave Revelry a much different vibe—it has nineties hip-hop-themed décor and a DJ booth that pumps out music late into the night—and set a menu targeted at a late-night crowd, with more small plates and snacks.

Like all our restaurants, Revelry has turned out differently than we expected. The clientele is younger and more adventurous. Our Korean spicy fried chicken (see page 223) has been a runaway hit. We love that the restaurant has its own personality and offers things you can't find anywhere in Seattle. Revelry was crowned the city's Rising Star Restaurant by *Portland Monthly* just after it opened.

MOVING FORWARD

It's not possible for one of us to be in the kitchen every time one of our restaurants opens its doors for the night. The more time we spend in this business, the more we realize that our job is to create a good system—to inspire our cooks to care more about our food and to motivate our servers to be genuinely gracious hosts. Even though I do enjoy teaching all our cooks how to make everything on the menu, we've realized that now it's most important to teach one head chef and have him teach the others how and why things cook the way they do. What we try to do every day, in some way, is to inspire our staff to want to be better at whatever it is they do. We train people to learn what flavors and textures they're looking for when they cook, whether it's a certain noodle doneness or a perfectly tender steak or a chili oil with just the right heat level. Actually, the first thing we train our cooks to do is to cook for the customer, rather than for themselves. When they learn to appreciate the smile on the face of someone eating the food they cook, they begin holding themselves to a higher standard than we could ever evoke ourselves. It's admittedly a little cultish—we are preachy about old-school hospitality—but ultimately we believe that if every employee knows how to challenge themselves, to care for the whole team, and to please customers the way we've learned to do over the years, we'll all succeed.

As we race forward to the next challenge—now as Relay Restaurant Group, instead of a couple that owns a few restaurants—we know we will always function by trial and error to some extent. It's a requirement, actually, because experimenting is the only way we'll be able to exceed our own expectations and create new things. I ask my cooks the same thing Seif and I ask ourselves when we discuss our restaurants: How can we be different? That, I hope, is why you're here cooking—to create something different and discover unique tastes. Let every unfamiliar flavor inspire you. Then make it yours.

in our kitchens

If you inspect the kitchens at Joule, Revel, Trove, or Revelry, you might sense a slightly schizophrenic approach to cooking. You'll find the basic tenets of Korean cuisine, to be sure—buckets full of assorted fermenting kimchis and rice vinegar—but also ingredients from the rest of the planet, like Japanese bonito, Italian white anchovies, Thai tamarind paste, North African sumac, and Mexican guajillo chilies, plus whatever odds and ends we come upon in our explorations. My mother-in-law, Sarah, who has definitely started to eat and to cook more Asian foods since I became her daughter-in-law, always keeps a fully stocked pantry. She will have the American usuals—canned beans, olive oil, and balsamic vinegar—but she'll also have leftover (or more likely six-month-old) dried seaweed, fish sauce, and ground chipotle powder. If you are like her, or like a lot of our customers who like to experiment with different flavors and occasionally cook with foods from other parts of the world, this section might as well be called "In Your Kitchen." The difference between our kitchens and yours is simply that we have more space. Ultimately, though, we're cooking the same way Sarah does: peering behind bottles and boxes to find whatever's lurking in the back and figuring out how things go together. Those corn flakes? They give amazing crunch to Korean pancakes (see page 178). Instant mashed potatoes? They help give our fried chicken its hallmark texture (see page 223).

What follows is a big list of the ingredients I rely on, organized by the tastes we associate with them—umami-rich fish sauces, pungent vinegars, numbing spices, fragrant pastes, earthy fermented products, and everything in between. Because I didn't grow up cooking Korean food, I don't refer to many of these ingredients by their Korean names—so while I've listed the ethnic translations for some ingredients below, in the recipes that follow I refer to them by their most common English names. (This is also because, many times, the English translation of Korean names isn't quite right. Growing up as Chung Hwa, my name meant a certain thing in Korean, but when Americans shortened it to Chung, thinking the "Hwa" portion was just a middle name, it took on a completely different Korean meaning.)

In the pages that follow, you'll also find recipes that show how we tend to tweak common food concepts, translating traditional recipes into our own culinary language to concoct new flavors and textures (see the chipotle fish caramel we use for pad Thai, page 245) or piping Korean influence through recipes often considered to be set in stone (see Mushroom XO Sauce, page 59, and Miso Caramel Chocolate Torte, page 297). As you get to know them, you may find yourself using these elements in your own cooking. Our Chili Oil (page 240), for example, makes an instant sauce for soba noodles, while our Magic Dredge (page 63) makes light, crisp onion rings (hint: add a tablespoon of coarse Korean chili flakes for heat).

At the end of the chapter, you'll find our Mother Sauces (pages 71 to 73). While they're not required, you can serve them alongside everything, as we do at a couple of our restaurants. We'd recommend making a few of them in advance; they make fantastic frequently used constituents of the refrigerator door.

Note that when searching for ingredients whose packages are labeled in foreign languages in a large Asian grocery store, it's often easier to identify what you're getting by reading the small price tag installed on the shelf below each item. Also, don't assume that the store is organized the same way as a standard American grocery store. Ask questions, and if necessary, call in advance to find out if the store you're hitting up has what you want.

JAPANESE MISO PASTE: Found in red, yellow, and white varieties (and usually stronger to weaker in flavor in that order), miso is Japanese soybean paste fermented with a type of mold. Most frequently, we use white miso (which is less fermented) when we want a lighter taste and aged red miso (which packs more punch) when we want a more pronounced miso flavor.

KOREAN ANCHOVY SAUCE: Considered a crucial ingredient when making the base for Korean kimchi (see page 149), anchovy sauce is just that—a translucent brownish condiment made from anchovies. It has a slightly deeper and funkier flavor profile than sand lance sauce, which is why Korean recipes traditionally use both. Look for it in the fish sauce section; you may have to read the English price tag to figure out which bottle is anchovy.

KOREAN COARSE SEA SALT: We find that if we salt vegetables with different-size salt particles to draw out their water, the water comes out at different rates. Using coarse sea salt, which is readily available in plastic bags in the Korean section of most large Asian grocers, encourages the osmosis process to happen more slowly, which means the liquid comes out of the whole vegetable more evenly. (For example, when salted with coarse sea salt, both the crunchier stems and fragile leaves of Napa cabbage release their water.) If you have access to other coarse sea salts, by all means use them. We just find the Korean brands tend to be much less expensive. Also, Korean coarse sea salt is often sweet and not as salty, so we prefer using it as a garnish. The salt crystals themselves hit your tongue, giving you a bigger burst of flavor than table salt or Kosher salt would. Kosher salt, on the other hand, is what we use for general seasoning.

KOREAN FERMENTED BEAN PASTE (*DOENJANG*): Korean bean paste is fermented with a type of bacteria found on rice stalks, and as a result, is slightly more sour and nuttier than miso, which most cooks are familiar with already. It's used in much the same way, as a flavoring agent, in dressings, as a dip, and in soups and stews. Look for the Wang brand in a brown plastic container in the Korean section of a large Asian grocery store.

KOREAN SALTED SHRIMP: These are one of the most common ingredients in Korean cuisine that Americans have never heard of. They're just what they sound like—teeny-tiny shrimp sold in salty brine. Measure them with their liquid. Look for them in the refrigerated section, typically in a transparent plastic jar.

KOREAN SAND LANCE SAUCE: Sand lance sauce, like anchovy sauce, is a translucent brownish liquid made from sand lances, which are tiny slender fish that look like eels (but aren't actually related). Look for it in the fish sauce section; you may have to read the English price tag to figure out which bottle is sand lance.

OIL-PACKED BROWN ANCHOVIES: Commonly used in Italian cuisine, brown anchovies add meatiness and sweet saltiness to a lot of the dishes we make—like bagna cauda (see page 118).

SOY SAUCE: Talking about soy sauce can send chefs down a condiment rabbit hole. It's a big market, and you'll find people have as many opinions as there are brands. We prefer Yamasa's basic version in our restaurants, but you could also substitute low-sodium soy or tamari. In all our recipes, we used Revel's Seasoned Soy Sauce (page 73), but you can substitute regular soy sauce unless otherwise specified.

VIETNAMESE FISH SAUCE: We think of fish sauce (known in Vietnamese as *nuoc mam*) as a unique way to add saltiness and flavor to any food, no matter where it comes from. It's made from a fermented mixture of different fish, often depending on where the sauce is made. Brands can vary widely in taste but always have a pungent fishy smell that translates more as deep umami flavor than as a particularly fishy one once incorporated. We usually buy a Vietnamese brand called Three Crabs.

SALTED SHRIMP VINAIGRETTE

Made with savory sesame oil and salty shrimp, this is a great basic Korean vinaigrette. Serve it on steamed or grilled vegetables, over rice, or as part of the Kalua Pork Stone Pot (page 270).

MAKES A GENEROUS ½ CUP

¼ cup canola oil
2 tablespoons salted shrimp
2 tablespoons rice wine vinegar
1 tablespoon toasted sesame oil
1 teaspoon coarse Korean chili flakes

1 teaspoon toasted white sesame seeds

MAKE THE VINAIGRETTE. In a small bowl, whisk together the oil, salted shrimp, vinegar, sesame oil, chili flakes, and sesame seeds.

HOISIN SAUCE: Most traditionally used in Chinese food, hoisin is a thick, dark-brown, sticky sauce made with soybeans, chilies, and garlic, often with sweeteners and sometimes with vinegar and rice or wheat starch. We usually use it as a sweet and salty flavoring in sauces and dips.

JUJUBES: Also called Chinese, Korean, or Indian dates, these wrinkly dried red dates have a lovely, floral apple flavor. They have pits inside like Medjool dates do, but the flesh is much drier and lighter in color, and it often takes a bit of effort to pry the pit out, so buy them pitted when possible. Our recipes are written for the smaller grape-size jujubes, rather than the larger Medjool-size version. Look for jujubes in transparent plastic bags.

MEDJOOL DATES: Dates are the dried fruit of a specific kind of palm tree native to the Middle East. They're great as a snack, but when they're cooked, they dissolve and lend a mild, earthy sweetness to foods.

MIRIN: Mirin is sweet Japanese rice wine with a very low alcohol content and an almost syrupy consistency. We buy the Kikkoman brand, which usually has a red cap.

SWEET AND SPICY ALL-PURPOSE SAUCE

This is the simple chili paste sauce recipe we use for the rice cakes at Joule (see page 251), which our customers have, over the years, given the eyebrow-raising name "crack sauce." Make sure you grate the ginger and garlic extremely finely with a Microplane-type grater. (If you double or triple the sauce, you can use a blender, mixing it in with the rest of the ingredients.)

MAKES 2 CUPS

½ cup Korean chili paste
½ cup mirin
½ cup sake
3 tablespoons soy sauce
1 teaspoon finely grated peeled fresh ginger
1 teaspoon finely grated garlic

MAKE THE SAUCE. In a medium bowl, whisk together the chili paste, mirin, and sake to blend. Add the soy sauce, ginger, and garlic, and whisk again until smooth. Store in the refrigerator, covered, for up to 1 month.

ACHIOTE PASTE: Often found in small tins packed in a box (like sardines often come), achiote paste is actually a well-packed powder, usually made with a blend of annatto, oregano, cumin, cinnamon, cloves, pepper, garlic, and other ingredients, depending on who makes it. (It can also be made moist with vinegar and sold in blocks, but we tend to use the drier kind.) It's often used as a marinade in Mexican and Central American foods. Try using it as a rub the next time you make tacos or barbecue; it adds an incredible earthiness.

BANANA LEAVES: Giant, smooth banana leaves make the perfect wrapping material for roasting meats that want to be slow-cooked. Buy them in the freezer section of a large Asian grocery store, then thaw them completely before using. Wrap ingredients in banana leaves for steaming or grilling for a sweet, herbaceous note.

CRAB PASTE: Crab paste is made from salted preserved crab, often mixed with garlic, chilies, and ginger. It lends a savory, salty flavor to foods, but you don't need much of it. Look for crab paste in a jar in the Thai section of a large Asian grocery store.

SESAME SEEDS: In Korea, as in cultures all over the globe, black (unhulled) and white (hulled) sesame seeds are used frequently in cooking. Note that they go rancid quickly, so they should be purchased fresh (most grocery stores carry them) and refrigerated if you live in a hot climate. Toast them following the instructions for toasting spices (see page 53), but note that they toast quickly.

MAKING BLACK SESAME POWDER

Also referred to as black sesame flour, this is just what it sounds like—black sesame seeds, ground into a fine flour. It has a nutty, almost peanut-like flavor. Look for it in flat, transparent bags, often in the dessert section near the pudding mixes. If you can't find them, simply whirl the seeds in a heavy-duty blender until fine.

TAHINI: Made from toasted white sesame seeds, this traditionally Middle Eastern ingredient (you might have used it to make hummus before) is widely available. Because sesame is so prevalent in Korean cuisine, we find it's a great way to add traditional sesame flavor without sesame oil's sometimes overbearing flavor. Make sure you stir it before you use it.

WILD SESAME SEEDS (*DEULKKAE*): These little dark-brown seeds, also called oilseeds or perilla seeds, are technically from the perilla plant, which isn't botanically related to sesame. But with their tiny size and nutty flavor, they're used in similar ways—we love to sprinkle them on top of noodles.

THE BEST OF SESAME

The reason we frequently have both *togarashi* and *za'atar* on the menu—both spice mixtures made with sesame seeds, from Japan and North Africa, respectively—is because sesame is a Korean thing. These two things are a great example of how we parlay one supposedly Korean ingredient into totally different flavor profiles. Both the togarashi and the za'atar can be kept on the counter in a sealed container for a week or two.

ORANGE TOGARASHI

MAKES A SCANT ½ CUP

Finely grated zest of 1 medium orange
3 tablespoons black sesame seeds
2 tablespoons coarse Korean chili flakes
1 teaspoon ground ginger
1 teaspoon garlic powder

DRY THE ORANGE ZEST. Preheat the oven to 300 degrees F. Place the orange zest in a small ovenproof dish and bake for about 15 minutes, or until shriveled and totally dry, stirring once or twice. Set aside to cool completely.

MAKE THE TOGARASHI. Transfer the cooled zest to a small bowl and stir in the sesame seeds, chili flakes, ginger, and garlic powder.

ZA'ATAR

MAKES A SCANT ½ CUP

3 tablespoons toasted white sesame seeds
3 tablespoons ground sumac
1 tablespoon ground toasted cumin
1½ teaspoons salt

MIX THE SPICES. In a mortar and pestle, pound the sesame seeds until sandy. Transfer them to a small bowl and stir in the sumac, cumin, and salt.

CHINESE DRIED CHILIES: Similar to many other small dried chilies, Chinese dried chilies add gentle heat to marinades and broths when used whole, and add more heat (especially when rehydrated) when crushed or pulverized. They often come in large bags in the spice section of an Asian grocery, but you could substitute *japones* chilies, which are often available in a grocery store's Mexican foods aisle.

CHINESE MUSTARD: Sometimes sold as "Oriental mustard" or "Chinese-style hot mustard," Chinese mustard is easy to make—you just mix Chinese dried mustard powder (English powders also work) with cold water, which produces a chemical reaction that makes the mustard sharp, with its signature sinus-clearing heat. Because jarred premade varieties (which are what we are calling for in our recipes) are blended with other ingredients to make them shelf stable, they are often less hot than homemade Chinese mustard.

DRY MUSTARD POWDER: English-style dry mustard powder is essential in our kitchens, both because it makes Chinese hot mustard when mixed with cold water, but also because it lends great flavor to marinades. We use Coleman's.

GUAJILLO CHILIES: Frequently used for Mexican *mole*, guajillos are the medium-hot dried chilies we rely on in part for the heat in our Chili Oil (page 240). They usually need to be softened with a soak in hot water before using.

KOREAN CHILI PASTE (*GOCHUJANG*): Entering our common culinary lexicon as *gochujang* more often than not, this hallmark fermented Korean paste is made with dried and finely ground red *gochu* chilies, soybeans, salt, and glutinous rice, which gives it a sticky, almost stretchy consistency. Its sweetness, derived from fermented rice, means you can add it to dishes when you're looking for a strong, sweet heat. Look for it in the Korean section of a large Asian grocery store, often in red plastic flip-top containers. We like a brand called ChoripDong.

COARSE KOREAN CHILI FLAKES (*GOCHUGARU*): Processed differently than the chili flakes most Americans are familiar with, Korean chili flakes, made from Korean *gochu* chilies, are coarser, with flat sides that often make the flakes look like they're glistening. Because each grain is bigger, they are hydratable—which means that when you add liquid to Korean chili flakes, the resulting sauce or soup will change in texture after a few minutes, as the flakes rehydrate (see Kimchi Base, page 149). It's also important to note that the way they taste changes depending on the way you process them. If you stir them into something, for example, the result will be spicier than if you blend them with the same ingredients in a blender, because blending emulsifies ingredients and mellows their flavor. (Takeaway: follow the instructions in recipes that use them.) Look for coarse Korean chili flakes in flat transparent plastic bags. The package sometimes reads "red pepper powder," which is actually a mistranslation if what you see inside is flaked. The important thing is that you buy an ingredient that is flaked, rather than ground. If you can't find Korean chili flakes at all, look for Aleppo pepper flakes—they're the most similar in heat and flavor.

SAMBAL OELEK: This is just chilies ground with water and salt until they form a paste. (For our house version, we ferment fresno chilies with ginger and garlic in a salt brine for about twenty days.) Although it's considered an Indonesian or Malaysian food, we use *sambal oelek* when we want straight spicy flavor with no sweetness. The Huy Fong Foods brand (the same company that makes the sriracha with the green cap) is my favorite.

SZECHUAN PEPPERCORNS: Made from the dried buds of a tree related to citrus (and not, as the name proposes, from any sort of pepper plant), Szechuan (sometimes Sichuan) peppercorns have a bright citrus flavor and cause a numbing, tingling sensation on the tongue when you eat them.

TOASTING SPICES

To toast spices like whole coriander, fennel, and cumin, and peppercorns like Szechuan peppercorns, heat a small skillet over medium-high heat. When hot, add the seeds to the dry skillet, then toast, shaking the pan occasionally, until the seeds are fragrant and a full shade darker. (They may begin to smoke a bit, which is okay.) Transfer the seeds to a plate to cool completely before you grind or crush them. You can toast multiple types of spices in a pan at the same time if the seeds are roughly the same size.

CHIPOTLE CHILI POWDER: Made from jalapeño peppers that have been smoked, dried, and ground, chipotle chili powder has a distinct smoky aroma that other chili powders lack. You'll notice we use it often; we love that it adds a smoky flavor you don't usually get in Korean food, and it plays well with other flavors. Don't be tempted to substitute ancho or another chili powder for chipotle.

SMOKED SPANISH PAPRIKA (*PIMENTÓN DE LA VERA*): Made from chilies that are traditionally dried over a fire, Spanish paprika often comes in mild (sweet), medium, and hot varieties. It has an earthy, smoky, woodsy flavor and often adds a lovely orange-reddish hue to foods.

PEANUT BRITTLE

Peanut brittle is legendary for its addictiveness. Add Korean chili flakes, which have enough power to give the brittle heat but not so much you can't stand at the counter and eat the whole batch, and you've got some next-level candy. We do use it as such on our Milk Chocolate Bingsoo (page 304), but it really shines as the crunchy garnish on Mrs. Yang's Spicy Fried Chicken (page 223).

The yield for the brittle really depends on how you chop it up; it will make about 4 cups of big candy-like pieces, or about 2 cups of finely chopped crumbles. Use something in between for the chicken and bingsoo.

Nonstick cooking spray or canola oil
1 cup sugar
½ cup water
¼ cup light corn syrup
1 teaspoon kosher salt
1 tablespoon coarse Korean chili flakes
1 teaspoon baking soda
2 cups toasted, crushed peanuts

PREPARE A BAKING SHEET. Line a baking sheet with parchment paper, spray or rub the parchment with a thin layer of oil, and set aside.

MAKE THE BRITTLE. In a small saucepan, stir together the sugar, water, corn syrup, and salt to blend. Bring to a boil over high heat and cook, undisturbed, until the mixture is evenly brown, or measures 305 degrees F on an instant-read thermometer. Carefully stir in the chili flakes and baking soda, then the peanuts, and pour the mixture onto the prepared baking sheet, pressing it immediately into a 1-inch layer if possible. (It will begin cooling almost instantly.) Let cool to room temperature until completely hard, and then cut into the size pieces you need.

BLACK VINEGAR: This dark rice vinegar is a great way to add acid and a sweet, smoky profile to foods at the same time. We prefer Koon Chun brand, which has a yellow label and a yellow cap. If you can't find it, use balsamic vinegar.

RICE VINEGAR: Rice vinegar is made by fermenting rice wine. Since it's an essential staple in our cooking (see Pickles, page 125), you'll want to grab a big bottle of rice vinegar when you start digging into our recipes. Don't buy the seasoned kind or anything specially designed for salads. We prefer Marukan brand—the version with the green cap.

SUMAC: This deep-red, fragrant spice has enough tart, sour flavor that if you mix it into a vinaigrette, it can almost stand in for the acid. When you're looking for ways to add it to your food, think of it as a substitute for lemon.

TAMARIND PASTE: We add tamarind paste when we're looking for bright, acidic flavor. Made from the fruit of the pods of a tamarind tree, it's a slightly sticky substance—stir it before you use it. Look for it in the ethnic foods aisle of a large grocery store. We buy the kind with the blue lid. (If you find it in a solid block, soak the block in two cups of hot water for an hour or two, then push the mixture through a fine-mesh sieve to get a smooth, thick puree. Refrigerate any leftover puree, covered, for up to three months.)

PICKLED LEMONS

As with so much of our food, these lemons combine multiple cultural approaches to a given ingredient. Like preserved lemons, they're a great way to enjoy the entire fruit—and because they're cooked with sugar, the pith is less bitter than usual. But because they're pickled using a rice vinegar, the hallmark Korean pickle flavor, they taste very Eastern, which can be unexpected because we so rarely associate lemon with any Asian cuisine. Eat them on their own, as a spunky snack, or scatter them atop some fried cauliflower (see page 118).

MAKES 1 CUP

1 large lemon, ends trimmed, halved lengthwise, cut into ⅛-inch-thick rounds
½ cup rice vinegar
¼ cup sugar
¼ cup water
½ teaspoon kosher salt
3 Chinese dried chilies
2 bay leaves
½ teaspoon fennel seeds

BLANCH THE LEMONS. Bring a small pan of water to a boil over high heat. Add the lemon slices and cook for 30 seconds, then drain and transfer the lemons to a small bowl filled with ice water. When they're cool, transfer the lemon slices to a small nonreactive container.

MAKE THE PICKLES. In a 1-quart pot, stir together the vinegar, sugar, water, and salt. Bring to a boil over high heat, stirring occasionally to help the sugar and salt dissolve, then add the chilies, bay leaves, and fennel. Pour the mixture over the lemons, cover with a paper towel to prevent the lemons on top from drying out, and let cool to room temperature before serving, at least 1 hour. Store the pickles in the refrigerator, covered, for up to 3 weeks.

DRIED MUSHROOMS: Find shiitake, wood ear, and other dried mushrooms in transparent plastic bags in large Asian grocery stores. Recipes using them typically call for the mushrooms to be soaked before using, which makes them tender enough to be sliced or blended, but you may still need to trim off the ends if there are parts of the mushroom that remain tough. Also note that it's important to weigh dried mushrooms as directed, because they're so light that a guess of what constitutes an ounce of, say, shiitake, is often quite incorrect.

HIJIKI: This spiny-looking seaweed, found most often on the shores of Asia, is easiest to buy dried in flat transparent bags. It looks like tiny black sticks and is usually rehydrated before using for its green, briny flavor.

KOMBU: Kombu (sometimes spelled "konbu") is thick, dried, dark-green seaweed usually sold in strips. As it rehydrates in warm liquids, it casts off a sweet, briny flavor, which is why it's used in dashi, the traditionally Japanese soup stock. Try adding it to your chicken stock or rice cooking water, or wrap it around meats as they cure.

NORI: You know nori as the paperlike seaweed that comes wrapped around sushi rolls. Cut into thin slivers, it makes a great crunchy topping; pulverized in a food processor, it makes a flavorful powder. It's available in most regular grocery stores, often in flat plastic packages.

TWO-INGREDIENT DASHI STOCK

While dashi is often made with fish, we typically make ours with a combination of sweet daikon radish and kombu, so it stays vegetarian. In general, anything you want to cook in this—rice, vegetables, shellfish, you name it—will be far more flavorful than if you cook it in plain ol' water. Use any leftovers as a base for soup.

MAKES 2 QUARTS

2 quarts water
4 ounces daikon
  radish (about
  ½ small radish),
  cubed
1 (3-by-3-inch) piece
  kombu

MAKE THE DASHI. In a large saucepan, combine the water, radish, and kombu. Bring to a boil over high heat, then reduce the heat and simmer for 15 minutes. Scoop out and discard the radish and kombu (actually, you should probably eat the radish, because it's delicious this way) and use as directed.

MUSHROOM XO SAUCE

We make our version of XO using dried mushrooms, which gives it the same intensity and spice but a different flavor. Use the sauce as a condiment on grilled meats or fish, over rice, or as part of a dipping sauce for dumplings, such as the Shrimp and Bacon Dumplings (page 191).

MAKES 3 CUPS

2 ounces dried shiitake mushrooms (1 cup)

2 ounces dried wood ear mushrooms (1 cup)

1 quart warm tap water

1 medium yellow onion, diced

¼ cup roughly chopped peeled fresh ginger

10 cloves garlic

½ cup canola oil

½ cup mirin

¼ cup Japanese white miso

1 tablespoon coarse Korean chili flakes (or 1 teaspoon cayenne pepper)

½ cup dry sake

SOFTEN THE MUSHROOMS. In a medium bowl, stir together the shiitake and wood ear mushrooms and warm water, and set aside to soak for about 30 minutes, or until the mushrooms are completely soft. (They should almost double in volume.) Using a slotted spoon, remove the mushrooms, squeezing them to remove as much excess water as possible, and transfer them to a medium bowl. Set aside 1 cup of the mushroom water, and discard the rest (or save it to use in place of stock for a soup.)

CHOP THE VEGETABLES. Using a meat grinder with a medium-size die (or using a food processor fitted with the chopping blade), grind or chop the mushrooms, onion, ginger, and garlic into roughly ⅛-inch pieces. (If you're using a food processor, dump all the ingredients in together and pulse about twenty times.)

MAKE THE SAUCE. Heat the canola oil in a large, heavy high-sided skillet or Dutch oven over medium heat. Add the chopped mixture, then add the mirin, miso paste, Korean chili flakes, and reserved mushroom water, and stir to blend. Bring the mixture to a simmer, then cook at a bare bubble, stirring occasionally, for 15 to 20 minutes, or until the mixture begins to look dry and the ingredients begin sticking to the bottom of the pan. Add the sake, then cook over low heat for another 15 to 20 minutes, stirring occasionally, until the mixture is shiny and chunky but no longer watery.

Use the sauce immediately, or cool to room temperature and store in a well-sealed container for up to 2 weeks in the refrigerator, or up to 3 months in the freezer.

FERMENTED TOFU: We like to compare fermented tofu to feta cheese. Not only does it look similar—and like feta, fermented tofu is typically stored in brine—but it lends the same funky, tangy flavor. Look for it in small jars (often with a red lid) in the refrigerated section of a large Asian grocery store. Use the solid parts, not the liquid.

FERMENTED BLACK BEANS: Traditional Chinese black bean sauces are made with fermented black beans, which are black soybeans that are salted, fermented, and partially dried (think of making a raisin out of a bean). Their flavor profile is similar to that of a kalamata olive, which means they tend to pair really well with Mediterranean flavors. Look for them in transparent plastic bags.

FERMENTED CHINESE MUSTARD GREENS: Similar to how kimchi is sold (and usually in the same section), fermented Chinese mustard greens are greens with a sharp pickled flavor that mellows with cooking and often a yellow hue derived from turmeric. We make our own (see opposite page) for the crispy rice cake dish we serve at Joule (see page 251), but you can also purchase them at a large Asian grocery store.

KIMCHI: Discussed at length in our chapter on kimchi, which begins on page 145, kimchi is a typically Korean genre of fermented vegetables. Sometimes spiced with a chili-based paste—but not always spicy!—kimchi can be made with an almost-infinite varieties of vegetables, proteins, and even fruits.

FERMENTED CHINESE MUSTARD GREENS

Fermented Chinese mustard greens are most well known as a component of homey Vietnamese cooking, but stirred into noodles or chopped and added to a filling for dumplings, they bring a bright, funky flavor. Chop them finely for the rice cake recipe on page 251.

MAKES 1 QUART

1 bunch Chinese
mustard greens
(about 8 ounces),
ends trimmed,
leaves separated

2 tablespoons
Korean coarse
sea salt

2 cups water

2 tablespoons
Korean coarse
sea salt

1 tablespoon juli-
enned peeled fresh
ginger

1 teaspoon ground
turmeric

SALT THE MUSTARD GREENS. Put the greens in a large bowl, sprinkle the coarse salt on top, and mix until well blended. Transfer the greens to a ziptop bag, pressing the air out as you close it, and refrigerate for 24 hours. The salt will draw excess water out of the greens.

MAKE THE BRINE. In a medium saucepan, combine the water, Korean salt, ginger, and turmeric. Bring to a boil, stirring until the salt has dissolved completely, then remove from the heat and let cool. (You can do this when you salt the greens and leave it covered on the counter overnight if you'd like.)

FERMENT THE MUSTARD GREENS. The next day, rinse the greens in three changes of fresh cold water and squeeze them dry. Pack into a quart-size container and pour the brine on top. Cover the greens and let them sit at room temperature (65 to 68 degrees F) for 5 to 7 full days. (You can taste along the way; it will begin to taste a little sour after the first 24 hours or so.) Transfer the greens to the refrigerator, where they will continue to ferment (but much more slowly). Use immediately, or refrigerate for up to 3 weeks.

MUNG BEANS (*nokdu/sukju namul*): Most commonly used in our kitchens to make pancakes (see page 169), mung beans are a type of legume sold both with their skins on (green) and with the skins removed (yellow). We use the yellow kind, because soaked and whirled together with water, they create a flavorful paste that cooks quickly. Note, though, that because purveyors and provenance may change the quality of the beans, some bags may be drier than others, and thus result in a slightly different yield when you make the pancake batter. (See Pancake Theory, page 14.) Look for mung beans (sometimes labeled "meng beans" or "yellow dal") in transparent plastic packages in the bean section.

PANKO BREAD CRUMBS: Made by shredding snow-white bread into large shards, these Japanese-style bread crumbs add more crunch and texture than the typical kind.

PINK CURING SALT: Curing salt is used to prevent meat from spoiling while it's being corned, such as with the corned lamb (see page 106). The sodium nitrite (and sometimes nitrate) in it helps prevent botulism. It's important to note two things: First, pink curing salt (which is only pink to discern it from table salt more easily) is not the same as Himalayan pink salt. Second, pink curing salt comes in two strengths. The first is called Prague Powder #1 (or InstaCure #1), which is intended for food that will be eaten within a week or so, and the second is called Prague Powder #2, and is intended for food that will cure for weeks or months. For our purposes, we use Prague Powder #1, which can be found in large grocery stores or online.

POTATO FLAKES: Used to both thicken and add texture to coatings, these little white mashed potato pieces add crunch to our Magic Dredge (page 63), which is the secret behind the texture of Mrs. Yang's Spicy Fried Chicken (page 223). We call them "potato pearls" in the kitchen, but it's a bit of a misnomer—we're just talking about instant mashed potatoes.

TAPIOCA: Often used in South American kitchens, tapioca is a starch from the cassava plant that we use both in powder form (in our Magic Dredge, page 63) and in pearl form (for our Joule Box, page 299). The pearls are opaque when dry but become translucent when you hydrate them. Look for both in the baking section.

MAGIC DREDGE

This dredge is an example of how we often mix flavors and cooking techniques from around the world. We wouldn't call it "magic" if it weren't the best way to fry food since, well, flour. It's light, crisp, and holds up well like many Korean fried foods, and the potato flakes give it occasional bits of bigger crunch, which is a lovely textural surprise. (It also happens to be gluten-free, which many of our customers appreciate.)

In our restaurants, we rely on this simple mix of dry ingredients to coat foods quickly without the sometimes-overwhelming taste of a floury dredge. Use it for the fried cauliflower (see page 118), double this recipe for Mrs. Yang's Fried Chicken (page 223), or use it wherever you might typically use a seasoned flour mixture. Try it for a unique take on eggplant Parmesan or onion rings (in which case, adding a tablespoon of Korean chili flakes to the mixture is delicious). It fries up best at about 375 degrees F.

I'd add the potato flakes if you can—they give a sweet, almost French fry–like flavor.

MAKES A GENEROUS 1¾ CUPS

½ cup tapioca flour
½ cup rice flour
½ cup cornstarch
¼ cup potato flakes (optional)
1 tablespoon kosher salt

MAKE THE DREDGE. In a medium bowl, whisk together the tapioca flour, rice flour, cornstarch, potato flakes, and salt. Use immediately.

BEAN SPROUTS: Mung bean sprouts and soybean sprouts are both used in Korean cooking, in cooked foods (such as soups and pancakes) and as a topping. Be sure to buy fresh, firm sprouts; the leafy portions of each sprout should be lively.

BURDOCK ROOT: Although burdock is often used in traditional Chinese medicine for detoxification and the treatment of digestion, we think of it as a simple root vegetable with great bitter, earthy flavor. It looks like a long, skinny carrot-shaped stick. Peel off the thick brown skin with a sturdy vegetable peeler before you use it.

CHINESE BROCCOLI: Chinese broccoli (sometimes labeled *gai lan*) looks like a combination of broccoli and spinach, and has a stronger, slightly more bitter flavor than Western broccoli. The bottom stalks are sturdy but thinner than broccoli's, and the leafy section, instead of having florets, has smooth green leaves with just small bunches of flower buds here and there. You can cook it all at once, but since the stalks take longer than the leaves and buds, we usually separate the top and bottom sections and then blanch the stalks first, before grilling both parts together. Look for specimens with fresh-looking green stem ends, without any white portions (which could indicate age and bitterness).

CHINESE CELERY: Like Chinese broccoli, Chinese celery has a stronger and slightly more bitter flavor than its American cousin and looks and tastes more like lovage. The stalks are also thinner and longer, and usually end in leaves that are used right along with the stalks. Look for bunches with fresh, healthy-looking leaves.

CHINESE MUSTARD GREENS: Mustard greens are the leafy part of the plant that produces mustard seeds. Like the seeds, the greens have a slightly spicy flavor. Look for bunches whose ends look fresh (instead of dried and split). They tend to be less bitter than other sturdier greens like chard or kale. In the kitchen, they're sometimes treated like lettuce and sometimes more like their brassica cousins. Note that there's a difference between Chinese mustard greens and larger regular mustard greens, which we only use in the pesto on page 249.

CURRY LEAVES: These are the fresh, green leaves of a curry tree, used frequently in Indian (and especially Sri Lankan) cooking. They look rather like lime leaves, but their flavor is floral in a different way. Store them in the freezer, well wrapped, for up to six months.

GARLIC: Koreans use more garlic than Chinese, Italian, or Spanish cooks for good reason: garlic is in our blood. According to traditional myths, the history of Korea itself dates back to 2333 BC, when a bear appealed to Hwanung, the son of heaven, to turn her into a human. Hwanung asked the bear to fast on only garlic and mugwort for one hundred days. She did, and so became a woman and Hwanung's wife, and gave birth to Dangun, the first human ruler of Korea. If you're cooking three or four recipes out of this book at once, consider buying containers of pre-peeled garlic for ease and speed. In general, I don't take out the germ unless I want a milder garlic flavor with less bitterness.

GINGER: Ginger is a Korean staple. I look for ginger knobs with smooth, tight skin, and I usually cut the skin off with a knife, peel it off with a vegetable peeler, or scrape it off with the edge of a spoon before using it. For most recipes, I cut ginger into roughly half-inch pieces before measuring it and adding it to a blender. Ginger keeps best in the produce drawer in your refrigerator, unwrapped.

DAIKON RADISH: Daikon looks like an elongated turnip (with a green hue instead of purple). It varies in size from the size of a carrot to the size of a baseball bat, so don't be shy to ask the produce department to cut a piece off for you, depending on how much you need. Daikon gives our vegetarian dashi (see page 58) a sweet flavor. Try steaming or boiling it for an easy, delicious dinner vegetable that kids tend to love, or pickle it (see page 129) and toss it in sambal oelek, like we do for our short rib rice bowl (see page 205) at Revel.

KOREAN CHILIES: Long, grass green, and thin, Korean chilies look like long green Serrano peppers and have a similar heat level. Korean peppers are often available at large Asian grocery stores, but you can substitute Serrano peppers (or, if you want something less spicy, Anaheim peppers) in a pinch.

LEMONGRASS: Lemongrass plants make twelve- to eighteen-inch stalks that add a powerful green, lemony flavor to foods. Choose stalks that are firm on the bottom. To grate them, peel away any dry outer layers, cut off the bottom root until you see white and purple rings, then grate the cut side on a fine grater or Microplane. You want to use just the tender insides. Lemongrass is now widely available at large grocery stores, in the produce section. It will keep in the refrigerator for two or three weeks.

LIME LEAVES: The roundish, waxy leaves of the bumpy tropical Asian lime known as the makrut or kaffir lime flavor liquids the same way bay leaves do. Look in the herb section for taut-looking leaves with no brown spots. Store them in the freezer, well wrapped, for up to six months.

SHIITAKE MUSHROOMS (FRESH): Cultivated with pretty brown tops and firm white stems, shiitake (also spelled "shitake") mushrooms are usually easy to find in any large grocery store. To use them, hold the stem near where it meets the cap and give it a firm tug; the stem and the tough part of the stem just inside the cap will come out.

TARO: White-fleshed, purple-speckled taro is a root vegetable with a sweet, mildly nutty flavor. Fresh out of the ground, it can be giant, so you may want to buy it in hunks if you don't want to bring home a vegetable the size of your forearm. Peel off the bumpy brown skin. Above all, don't eat it raw, because it is toxic if it isn't cooked.

TATSOI: Tender, spoon-shaped tatsoi are Asian greens frequently used fresh, often in salads. If you can't find them, substitute spinach.

THAI BASIL: Like basil with purple and black stems, Thai basil is clearly related to Mediterranean basil but has a much more pungent, anise-like flavor.

THAI CHILIES: Also known as Thai bird chilies or bird's eye chilies, these tiny, thin, sharp-looking fresh peppers have great bite and are used across Asia to add a clean heat and a slightly fruity flavor to a huge variety of preparations. They can be either green or red, depending on their ripeness.

YUCCA: Cassava, manioc, and yucca—all the same plant from which tapioca starch is derived—are long, tapered brown tubers that, like taro, can be toxic if consumed uncooked. Choose specimens that you can smell or see the inside of; fresh yucca is snowy white and doesn't smell much, whereas old or decaying yucca can be brownish inside and may smell of mothballs. Peel off all parts of the waxy exterior before using.

REVEL'S GREEN CURRY PASTE

While green curry does have a little bit of heat, its best asset is its bright, citrusy flavor. We make ours with a hefty dose of lemongrass.

MAKES 1 GENEROUS CUP

1 cup packed chopped cilantro (leaves and stems, from 1 small bunch)

2 jalapeño peppers, seeded

½ cup chopped peeled fresh ginger

1 medium shallot, chopped

4 medium cloves garlic

¼ cup water

¼ cup chopped lemongrass (from the tender insides of 2 large stalks)

5 lime leaves

¾ teaspoon Madras curry powder

¼ teaspoon ground turmeric

⅛ teaspoon ground toasted cumin (see Toasting Spices, page 53)

⅛ teaspoon ground toasted coriander (see Toasting Spices, page 53)

⅛ teaspoon freshly ground black pepper

MAKE THE CURRY PASTE. In a heavy-duty blender or the bowl of a food processor, whirl together the cilantro, peppers, ginger, shallot, garlic, and water until it forms a smooth green paste, stopping to scrape down the sides of the bowl with a flexible spatula as necessary. When smooth, add the lemongrass, lime leaves, curry, turmeric, cumin, coriander, and black pepper, and whirl until smooth again (may take a minute or two). Transfer the paste to a small container and store in the refrigerator, covered, up to 2 weeks.

THE MOTHER SAUCES

In classic French cuisine, there are five so-called mother sauces,
the knowledge of which purportedly provides the basis for all
of the sauces in French food. We laugh sometimes at how our
sauces—most famously the four served in DIY containers on
each table at Revel and Revelry—are often what make the dish,
but they're always added *after* the food hits the table. So rather
than controlling the sauces very carefully as the foundation of
each dish, as cooks must in French cuisine, we give up control
and let the diner guide the final flavor at the end. It's the ultimate
flip-flop (which is often how we roll).

When you work the garde-manger station at Revel, you grow
to hate the mother sauces. You make huge batches. The job
sort of hovers in the background—our cooks always know they
need to be making them continuously, but people often forget
to report from station to station how much is actually needed,
so we wind up in dipping sauce emergencies. At Revelry, we
learned how to manage our inventory better by putting the
sauces in squeeze bottles.

At home, you can put all four in mason jars and store them in
the refrigerator for months. And when you run out, you can have
your own little emergency sauce-making binge.

REVEL'S SPICY DIPPING SAUCE

When you're blending up the ingredients for this spicy, ginger-and-garlic-scented hot sauce, make sure you blend until completely smooth or the mixture will get grainy. Resist any temptation to add the chili paste to the blender; blending will aerate the sauce and turn it pink.

MAKES 1 GENEROUS CUP

¼ cup roughly chopped peeled fresh ginger
2 large cloves garlic
¼ cup rice vinegar
¼ cup sugar
⅔ cup Korean chili paste

MAKE THE SAUCE. In a heavy-duty blender or the bowl of a food processor, whirl the ginger, garlic, vinegar, and sugar until completely smooth. Transfer the mixture to a small container and stir in the chili paste until smooth. Serve immediately, or store in the refrigerator, covered, for up to 2 months.

REVEL'S NAM PRIK SAUCE

Thai by tradition, this chili-infused blend of fish sauce and lime juice is a lovely way to liven up steamed rice. At home, it's an easy process; you just stir a few ingredients together. But because we go through so much of it in our restaurants, most of our chefs loathe making it. Antonio de Anda, who is now our chef at Revelry in Portland, spent his first day in the kitchen at Revel thinly slicing Thai chilies, which is about as close to hazing as our kitchens get. It's not a fun job—especially when you start with a full gallon of the things—because the skins of the chilies dull a sharp knife blade very quickly. Luckily, you'll start with only two or three chilies at home.

MAKES 1 GENEROUS CUP

1 cup fish sauce
2 teaspoons lightly packed lime zest
Scant ¼ cup freshly squeezed lime juice (from 2 small limes)
1 tablespoon thinly sliced Thai chilies

MAKE THE SAUCE. In a small bowl, stir together the fish sauce, lime zest, lime juice, and chilies to blend. Serve immediately, or store in the refrigerator, covered, for up to 2 months.

REVEL'S SAVORY CHILI SAUCE

If you read Korean, you know that when you peruse the different Korean chili pastes at an Asian grocery store, the containers tell you different things about the products. But if like most Americans, you don't read Korean, you might come home with something slightly spicier or less spicy than the average box—or, more likely, you will buy exactly the right thing and it will be more or less spicy than usual, depending on the brand or the chilies that particular batch was made with. The lesson is this: because chili pastes differ from brand to brand and batch to batch, you'll want to taste this as you make it and add more chili paste or bean paste to taste. It should have a good balance of spice and funk.

MAKES A SCANT 2 CUPS

1 cup Korean bean paste
½ cup Korean chili
  paste
2 tablespoons water
1 tablespoon sesame oil

MAKE THE SAUCE. In a small mixing bowl, stir together the bean paste, chili paste, water, and sesame oil until smooth. Serve immediately, or store in the refrigerator, covered, for up to 3 months.

REVEL'S SEASONED SOY SAUCE

One of the four sauces we serve at Revel with every meal, this seasoned soy sauce has a bit of heat, a bit of citrus, a bit of floral flavor, and—because it's cut with mirin and sake—a bit less saltiness than straight soy. We use it in all the recipes in this book that call for soy sauce.

MAKES 2½ CUPS

1½ cup plus 1 table-
  spoon soy sauce
½ cup mirin
½ cup sake
2 Chinese dried chilies
1 (1-inch) piece lemon-
  grass (from the tender
  inside of a large stalk),
  thinly sliced
1 lemon wedge
1 orange wedge
1 (2-inch) section peeled
  fresh ginger, cut into
  ¼-inch-thick coins

1 bay leaf
1 sprig fresh thyme
1 teaspoon whole cori-
  ander seeds
1 teaspoon whole black
  peppercorns

MAKE THE SAUCE. In a large saucepan, stir together the soy sauce, mirin, and sake, and bring to a boil over high heat. Add the chilies, lemongrass, lemon, orange, ginger, bay leaf, thyme, coriander, and peppercorns; remove from the heat; and let cool to room temperature. Strain and serve immediately, or store in the refrigerator, covered, for up to 2 months.

dumpling and noodle basics

At Revel, we've been doing dumpling and noodle classes for years. And for years, it's been the same: spots for fifteen participants sell out with in a matter of hours. On the day of the class, I give all fifteen people the same recipes and demonstrate how to make the dough. And every single time, we wind up with fifteen different doughs.

It's not because they're not all great cooks. It's because everyone works the dough a little differently. And like all of us, doughs are affected by everything around them—by the weather, the warmth of your hands, and the ingredients you use, just to start. In the pages that follow, you'll find step-by-step instructions that give intricate detail to the directions in the chapters on noodles (pages 227 to 253) and dumplings (pages 181 to 195). Please take the time to read them before making noodles or dumplings for the first time. The best noodles come from practice.

THE DOUGH

making dough by hand

The major advantage of making dough by hand is that you can feel what the dough is doing more easily. If it's too moist, it will stick to your hands, whereas if it's too dry, you'll have trouble holding it all together. Personally, I think mixing by hand is just easier.

When you make noodles or dumplings for the first time, it may seem strange to plunge your hands into the mess in the bowl, but that's exactly what you do. Start by swirling the fingers of your dominant hand in a circle

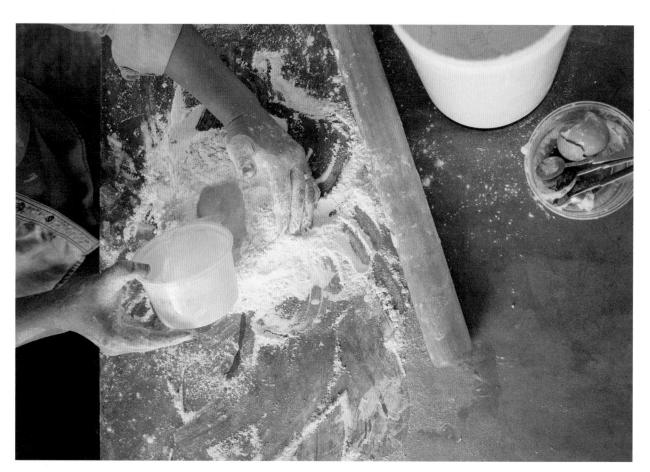

around the bowl, which will distribute the wet ingredients into the dry. Swirl and stir and press, scraping the inside and outside edges of your hand along the sides of the bowl as needed, until you've incorporated all the dry ingredients. At first, the dough will stick to all your fingers, but as you work, the dough will form a big, shaggy mass. (You can rub your hands together over the bowl to rid them of any stubborn bits.) Once the dough starts to hold together, knead it a few times in the bowl (at this point, you want a slightly rough dough that feels a little tacky), then transfer it to a clean countertop dusted with flour and begin to knead it there.

Note that you can also make dough directly on a countertop, rather than in a mixing bowl; simply mix the dry ingredients on the counter, then gather them up in a heap, make a well in the center, add the wet ingredients, and start to knead once the dough comes together.

mixing with a machine

In the bowl of a stand mixer fitted with the paddle attachment, blend together the dry ingredients on low speed for just a few seconds. In a separate bowl, whisk together the wet ingredients until they are uniform in color. With the mixer on low speed, add the liquid to the dry ingredients in a slow, steady stream. Let the paddle work the ingredients together for about 30 seconds, then switch to the dough hook, scraping all the dough on the paddle back into the bowl. If necessary, push the dough into a ball with your hands, gathering up any little pieces on the bottom of the bowl. Increase speed to medium and knead for 1 minute. The dough should be soft and tacky. (If the dough isn't smooth, knead it on the counter for 1 to 2 minutes.) Note that while it can be tempting to let the machine knead away for a few minutes the way it might for bread, it's not good to overwork our doughs because it makes them hard to roll out.

You can also mix the dough together in a food processor fitted with the chopping blade until it comes together, and then complete the kneading process by hand.

kneading dough

In all our dough recipes, when we say "knead until smooth," here's what we mean: the dough should feel smooth, like the skin on the inside of your forearm. You'll likely notice that it doesn't start this way; only with kneading does the glutinous structure of the dough organize itself and get stronger, which changes its texture.

Our cooks use a fold-and-turn method, kneading with the heel of one hand while the other hand does the turning. If you're right handed, start by placing the heel of your right hand in the center of the dough. Push the dough into the counter and away from you, then with your left hand, move the dough a quarter turn clockwise, folding the dough now at the 12 o'clock position into center of the dough. Use the heel of your right hand to push the folded-over piece away from you, then repeat, turning with the left hand and pressing with the right. You'll note that you're only working with about a quarter of the dough at a time this way. As you work, the dough will become smoother and springier. Continue kneading for about 5 minutes. When you turn the dough over and the side that was on the surface is smooth, you're done. (The dough should also spring back when you poke it in a smooth spot.)

TROUBLESHOOTING DOUGH TEXTURE

The most important thing to remember when making noodle dough is that there are a huge variety of factors that can affect it. I often love taking a cognitive approach to cooking; I always want to know why noodles do what they do. But anyone who makes noodles and dumplings every day begins to notice different things—cold flour absorbs cold liquid more slowly than room-temperature flour absorbs room-temperature liquid, for example.

There is no God Recipe for dumpling and noodle doughs. While it's not crucial to study the temperature of your ingredients before using them or to get out your micrometer ruler to measure the dough's thickness, it is useful to know that, because things like temperature and humidity can affect every dough, the same recipe might yield slightly different noodles every time you make them. While you may need to add a little flour or water one day, it might not be necessary the next. Conveniently, there's also a pretty wide window for success, so even if your dough doesn't look or feel exactly like mine might, it will probably still make good noodles. Use your judgment.

If you're kneading dough by hand and the dough seems too wet and sticks to your hands or your work surface, you can keep adding a bit of flour to the surface, kneading your dough directly in the flour, adding more little by little until the dough no longer sticks. If the dough seems too dry, do the same thing with water—using a fine mist from a spray bottle works best. It's always easier to fix a wet dough than a dry dough. If your dough is so dry you can't knead it, wrap it and let it rest for about 10 minutes. You'll be surprised how much resting the dough facilitates kneading.

If you're using a stand mixer and, after the first minute, the dough has not begun to clean the sides of the mixing bowl and make slapping noises against the edges of the bowl, the dough is too sticky. Add a bit more flour, about a tablespoon at a time, until the dough cleans the sides of the bowl. If, on the other hand, the dough doesn't seem to want to stick together and appears powdery or breaks up easily, it may need more liquid. Add a bit of water, a teaspoon or two at a time while the mixer is running, until the dough comes together.

resting the dough

Before rolling your dough into thin, elegant sheets, it needs a rest so the gluten that developed during kneading has a chance to relax. We suggest covering the dough with plastic wrap during the 30-minute rest to prevent the surface from forming a crust, which will interfere with the rolling process. Keep the dough covered, whenever possible, to prevent it from drying out.

Keep in mind that your dough might need some R&R more than once. If you notice, as you roll it, that it begins to spring back into a smaller form after you roll it out, it needs a few minutes to hang out. Cover it with a towel or plastic wrap and find something else to do for 5 minutes.

refrigerating and freezing dough

When you've kneaded a dough but want to wait more than an hour before rolling it out, you should refrigerate it. (You can keep doughs in the refrigerator up to 48 hours before they start to discolor, unless they don't contain eggs, in which case they last 3 or 4 days.) Let your dough come back to room temperature before rolling, because cold dough is hard to roll out.

You can also freeze dough, well wrapped in plastic and sealed in an airtight bag, for up to 2 months in the freezer. Before using it, let it thaw in the refrigerator for a full 24 hours, and then proceed to bring it up to room temperature before using.

rolling the dough into sheets

Once your dough has rested, you'll need to get it ready to go through a pasta-rolling machine. For making pasta at home, we recommend using a rolling attachment that works with a stand mixer, which typically has a thickness scale that goes from 1 (thickest) to 9 (thinnest). (Level 5 allows you to just see your hand through the dough when you hold it up to the light, whereas level 6 is slightly thinner—which makes for a silkier, although less sturdy, noodle.) You can play with whatever machine you're using to determine what thickness you like.

Typically, we roll dumpling doughs to thickness level 4 and noodle doughs to thickness levels 5 and 6.

But first, you need to get the dough into the machine. Cut the dough into thirds and roll it out into a strip about 4 inches wide and as thick as a deck of cards. (As you get better at working with the dough, you can try cutting it into halves or using it as a whole.) While most machines are indeed made to smash the dough into submission, it's common to have trouble with the very first roll. Before you begin, use a rolling pin to roll one short side of the dough into a little ramp, so there's one short edge that's very thin. Lightly flour the dough with all-purpose flour if it feels tacky. Starting with the flattened edge, feed the dough into the pasta maker on the thickest setting (1 for the stand mixer attachment) at low speed. (You can increase speed as you become more comfortable with the dough.) Fold the resulting strip of dough into thirds or quarters, pat it into roughly the same shape you started with, and press it firmly with your fingertips to get the layers of dough to adhere. Then use the rolling pin to create another little ramp, this time on one of the sides where you see three or four layers of dough stacked up. Feed the dough ramp-first into the machine, flouring the dough first again if it feels tacky.

Now your dough is ready to expand. Run it through the machine at increasingly thinner intervals, until you reach the desired thickness, dusting the dough on both sides with all-purpose flour as needed wherever it's tacky. As you roll it, you can either feed the dough with one hand and catch it with the other, stretching it away from the machine as it comes out, or simply allow the dough to stack up on its own underneath the machine. The latter approach requires a lot less work, as long as you don't leave it in a pile for too long, in which case it may stick together.

Once you have long sheets of dough, you can move on to Making Dumplings (following page) or Making Noodles (page 89).

Photos on left:

1. Start with a piece of dough no thicker than a deck of cards.

2. Fold the dough into thirds after the first roll.

3. When you fold, press your fingers into the dough to encourage the layers to adhere.

4. Handle the dough with the backs of your hands as you roll it out.

MAKING DUMPLINGS

You'll notice that while our noodle doughs often have eggs in them, the dumpling doughs (which begin on page 184) are usually made with water. This allows
the dumplings to be soft on top but still crunchy on the bottom and cooked
throughout. We use warm water because it relaxes the gluten in the dough,
which makes it easier to work with when filling and forming the dumplings.

preparing the dough sheets

Once you've rolled your dough into long sheets on thickness level 4 of a
pasta-rolling machine, allow the sheets to dry on a clean, lightly floured
surface for 5 minutes on each side. (We use all-purpose flour at all stages with
dumpling dough.)

filling and forming dumplings

When you're ready to fill the dumplings, place one sheet of dough on a clean
work surface. Dust off any excess flour with your hands or a pastry brush.
Using *the dull marking side* of a 3-inch round cutter (or the open end of a
wide-mouth canning jar), mark out as many circles as you can on the strip of
dough, flouring the cutter if necessary, leaving about ½ inch between each
circle. (The goal here is to stamp the place where your dumplings will be but
not actually cut them out.) In the center of each circle, place a scant tablespoon of the filling.

Spray the surface of the dough lightly with water to encourage the two sides
of the dumpling to stick together. (You can also do this by dipping your fingers
in a bowl of water and lightly tracing the outer edge of the dough circle, but
take care not to put too much water on the dough or it will become gummy and
stick to the counter.) Fold the entire length of the dough sheet in half lengthwise, over the bumps of filling, so the long straight edges eventually meet. Use

Photos on right:

1. Place filling in the center of circles marked with the dull
   side of a round cutter. Fold dough over the filling lengthwise
   so the long ends meet.

2. Seal the dough together around each pile of filling with the
   dull side of a small round cutter. Cut dumplings with the
   sharp side of a large round cutter.

your fingers to gently press the dough together around each bump, so there is as little air as possible between the filling and the dough. Using the floured dull marking side of a 2-inch round cutter (a narrow-mouthed half-pint jar also works), gently pull the filling toward the folded edge of dough so the filling is also forced into a semicircular shape, then make a gentle half-circle indentation around each lump of filling with the cutter, sealing the two sides of dough together but not actually cutting through the dough. Then, using the floured *cutting* side of the 3-inch round cutter (or a round cookie cutter), cut out each dumpling into a half-moon shape.

Repeat with the remaining dough and filling, making sure to flour the board and the cutting tools lightly for each batch, transferring completed dumplings to a lightly flour-dusted cloth or baking sheet and covering them with a cloth as you work. As long as they are still clean, dumpling dough scraps can be rerolled to make additional dumplings.

panfrying the dumplings

At our restaurants, we cook dumplings on a flat-top grill, snuggled up against each other, so that they come out like little siblings, all lined up in a row. But it really doesn't matter how you cook them, as long as you achieve two things: first, you need to brown them on their undersides; and second, you need to steam them long enough that the top layer collapses and the filling cooks through.

When all the dumplings are assembled, heat a 10- or 12-inch skillet over medium-high heat. Add 1 to 2 tablespoons of canola oil (or enough to coat the *entire* bottom of the pan with a thin layer of oil), then add as many dumplings as will fit in the pan without touching, likely about a dozen, flat sides down, brushing off any excess flour before you add them to the pan. Cook, undisturbed, for about 1 minute, or until golden brown on the bottom. Add ¼ cup water to the pan, cover, and cook for 6 to 8 minutes, without turning; add another 2 or 3 tablespoons water (more for a larger pan) after 3 or 4 minutes, when the first batch of water evaporates and the skins of the dumplings have started to collapse onto the filling underneath. When all the water has evaporated and the dumplings begin to shine from the oil, transfer them to a plate. (It's pretty cool to watch the transformation as wet, steamy dumplings get crunchy, nicely browned bottoms as they crisp in the oil.)

If you don't have specialized circular dough cutters, you can improvise—the tops of water bottles and lids from mason jars work well.

MAKING NOODLES

The most frequent mistake new noodle cooks make is allowing the dough to stick together. Drying the sheets of dough thoroughly and dusting both the dough sheets and completed noodles with flour prevents this. While flouring noodles as you cut them prevents them from sticking, having too much flour on each noodle can make them gummy, and can turn the cooking water cloudy. You can use all-purpose flour to prevent sticking if you use it judiciously, but since white rice flour's gluten-free properties means it doesn't cause any stickiness, we powder our completed noodle sheets and noodles with a thin layer of rice flour.

cutting noodles

Cut the prepared dough strips into 12- to 16-inch-long sections (depending on how long you want your noodles to be), dust with rice flour, and set aside to dry for 10 minutes on each side, or until the dough no longer feels tacky on either side. (Drying dough sheets for noodles means they don't need as much flour after they've been cut, which saves them from getting gummy. And as long as they don't begin to get hard or crisp, drier noodles are often easier to cut.) When the dough sections are no longer tacky, use a pasta machine to cut into noodles of desired thickness.

———

"Be kind to your dough," Seif tells the kids. When you're working with sheets of noodle dough after they come out of a pasta machine, use the palms and backs of your hands, rather than your fingers, to avoid tearing the dough.

thickness guide

When we talk about cutting dough into "thin" or "thick" noodles, we're referring to the two most typical settings on the kind of pasta machine that attaches to a stand mixer. The contraptions are designed cut the dough into spaghetti or fettuccine, respectively, but in general, we aim for noodles between ⅛ and ½ inch thick. You can cut yours by hand, of course, if you don't like the thicknesses available on your machine.

The moisture in a dough also affects its ultimate thickness. A wetter dough is heavier, so when you roll it, the resulting sheet of dough or batch of noodles often stretches out more and results in a thinner product.

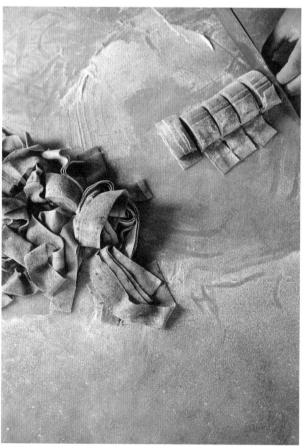

hand-cutting noodles

Because hand-cutting noodles requires rolling sheets of dough up into a spiral and cutting through multiple layers of dough at once, it's best to make sure the dough is quite dry before cutting; we often wait 15 minutes per side, turning occasionally. To hand-cut the noodles, first make sure the dough is evenly dusted with rice flour, so the layers don't stick to one another. Starting with one short end, roll the dough into a tight spiral. Trim the ends, then, using a large, sharp knife, cut the dough into noodles of desired thickness—1 inch thick for the Black Sesame Noodles (page 239), for example. Unroll the noodles and separate them, then dust them again with rice flour so the edges don't stick together and set aside until ready to cook.

cooking noodles

It's hard to uncook a noodle. That said, what's important about cooking our noodles isn't the amount of time they spend in boiling water (2 to 3 minutes, or until they float to the top of the water and puff up a little), but the amount of time they have to sit between being cooked and being sauced. Since you can always add a little water to a sauce to buy it time on the stove, consider the noodles your first priority. Ideally, the noodles will go directly from their cooking water into the sauce.

banchan

When most people imagine Korean food, they picture volume— plates and plates of wildly colored foods, sometimes stacked multiple dishes high, with bowls resting on other bowls. There is no coursing in Korean food, the way there is in other parts of the world. Instead, side dishes, or *banchan*, come as a series of small plates, often eight or ten on the table at a time. They're sometimes just enough for a few bites per person, but their size often reflects how much you're expected to eat—small dishes are typically salty and spicy, while larger *banchan* are more saladlike. Traditionally, they're meant to be served with rice, but in our restaurants they're refreshing salads, perfect starters, or simply vessels that transport interesting flavors. Trove is the only restaurant where we really serve side dishes that resemble *banchan*, but even there, we don't really follow the rules of traditional Korean cuisine. We don't dole out the same complimentary *banchan* with every meal, but instead offer a series of options that demonstrate the fine line we walk between being Korean and decidedly un-Korean. Make one, or make them all. Just don't expect anything you've tasted before.

KALE SALAD

octopus, white bean, miso

Although this miso-rich salad has hunks of tender octopus and a smattering of earthy white beans, it is, at its heart, a kale salad.

Because there are a few steps in this recipe, I like to poach the octopus and soak the beans the night before I plan to serve it. You could use canned beans, of course, but I usually take this recipe as an excuse to make beans to keep around for something else since it seems silly to cook a half cup's worth of beans.

MAKES 4 TO 6 SERVINGS

FOR THE BEANS:

1 cup white beans, such as cannellini
 or navy beans, soaked overnight in
 cold water
1 quart cold water
½ medium carrot, cut into 3 pieces
½ celery rib, cut into 3 pieces
1 yellow or white onion, quartered
¼ teaspoon kosher salt

FOR THE VINAIGRETTE:

1 tablespoon drained capers, rinsed
1 tablespoon drained fermented
 soybeans, rinsed
1 tablespoon Japanese white miso
1 tablespoon sherry vinegar
1 tablespoon water
1½ teaspoons tamarind paste
⅛ teaspoon red pepper flakes
3 tablespoons canola oil

FOR THE SALAD:

1 bunch green kale (about 8 ounces), ribs
 removed, torn into large bite-size pieces
 (about 4 well-packed cups)
2 to 4 poached octopus tentacles
 (about 4 ounces) from Poached
 Octopus (recipe follows)
¼ fennel bulb, cut into ⅛-inch-thick
 slices crosswise

fermented soybeans + miso = umami punch!

1. **PREPARE THE BEANS.** Drain the soaked beans, then transfer them to a medium saucepan. Add the water, carrot, celery, and onion, bring to a boil over high heat, then reduce the heat and simmer until the beans are completely tender, stirring occasionally to make sure the beans are submerged. (It will take 30 minutes to 2 hours, depending on the size of your beans.) Drain the beans and transfer them to a medium bowl, removing the vegetables. Season the beans with salt and set aside.

2. **MAKE THE VINAIGRETTE.** Chop the capers and soybeans together on a cutting board. (You want them to be small, but not actually pasty.) In a small mixing bowl, stir together the miso, vinegar, water, tamarind, and red pepper flakes with a fork until the miso is evenly distributed. Add the oil in a slow, steady stream, whisking to combine as you go, then stir in the chopped mixture. (The vinaigrette won't be completely blended, which is fine.)

continued

3. **ASSEMBLE THE SALAD.** Dump the kale into a large bowl and drizzle about ¼ cup of the vinaigrette on top. Using gloved hands, massage the dressing into the kale leaves, making sure each piece is well coated. Cut the octopus tentacles into ¼-inch slices diagonally (for about 1 cup's worth of meat) and add to the kale, along with ½ cup of the drained beans (reserve the rest for another use) and the fennel. Mix the ingredients to blend, and add additional vinaigrette to taste, if needed. Serve the salad at room temperature. (It will hold on the counter for 1 to 2 hours without suffering.) Store any leftover salad in the refrigerator, covered, for 1 to 2 days.

poached octopus

Since freezing is effectively a tenderizing method, we actually prefer not to get fresh octopus at our restaurants; we also choose Filipino octopus, as opposed to Pacific octopus, because the former is often much smaller (only about four to six pounds each), so the tentacles are more manageable, and it has a great ratio of beautiful purple surface to tender internal meat.

When you buy a frozen raw octopus, it sometimes comes in a cylinder or another shape that seems antithetical to the wild, far-reaching shape a live octopus takes. Thaw it slowly in the refrigerator, in a large bowl, over the course of a day or two, so there's no chance of ripping the tentacles, which can happen if you pry the legs apart before they're fully thawed.

The trickiest part of cooking octopus, if there even is one, is rinsing it, because when it's raw, the long, smooth tentacles have a habit of escaping down the drain if you're not careful. If you have a big sink with a tall faucet, this should be easy, but even with a small octopus, it's often difficult to fit the entire thing under running water. I like putting my octopus in the strainer portion of a salad spinner or pot insert designed for cooking pasta, and putting that in a big bowl of water, which I use as a rinsing pan, changing the water until I'm sure the octopus is well rinsed.

This recipe makes one octopus. Theoretically, you could use it to make both the barbecued octopus (see page 219), using four to six tentacles, and Kale Salad, using two to four tentacles, so plan accordingly.

MAKES 1 POACHED OCTOPUS

3 quarts water

¾ cup sake

½ small daikon radish (about 4 ounces), cut into 1-inch pieces

5 cloves garlic

1 large carrot, cut into 1-inch pieces

1 celery rib, cut into 1-inch pieces

1 medium yellow or white onion, cut into 1-inch pieces

1 teaspoon whole black peppercorns

1 teaspoon whole coriander seeds

1 sprig fresh thyme

1 bay leaf

1 tablespoon kosher salt

½ cup Korean coarse sea salt, or more as needed

1 (4- to 6-pound) octopus, fully thawed if frozen

1. **MAKE A COURT BOUILLON FOR POACHING THE OCTOPUS.** Cut a round of parchment paper as big as the inside diameter of a 5-quart pot and set aside. In the pot, combine the water, sake, radish, garlic, carrot, celery, onion, peppercorns, coriander, thyme, bay leaf, and kosher salt, and stir to combine. Bring to a boil over high heat, then reduce to a bare simmer and cook for 45 minutes.

2. **PREPARE THE OCTOPUS.** In a large bowl, vigorously rub the octopus on all sides with as much of the sea salt as you need to cover the whole body, as though you were washing your hair or washing laundry by hand. (Don't be delicate. Scrubbing the octopus like this removes its outermost layer, which can have a slimy texture. It will foam up a bit—that's normal. You'll know you're done when the water looks soapy and you're starting to sweat a little.) Thoroughly rinse the salt off the octopus.

3. **DUNK THE OCTOPUS.** Fill a separate pot large enough to fit the octopus about three-quarters full with water and bring to a boil. When the court bouillon is ready, carefully holding the octopus with tongs, dip the entire octopus in and out of the boiling water 3 to 5 times, or until the tentacles begin to curl. (The dunking process ensures that the skin stays attached to the rest of the meat during poaching, and shrinks the octopus considerably.)

4. **POACH THE OCTOPUS.** Transfer the octopus to the court bouillon, then place the parchment paper over the top of the liquid, and put something heavy on top (such as a plate) to keep the octopus submerged. Bring to a boil, then reduce the heat and cook at a strong simmer for about 2 hours, or until the octopus feels completely tender when pierced with a knife and when you pull at one leg near where it attaches to the body with tongs, it looks like it wants to fall off. Transfer the octopus to a parchment-lined baking sheet to cool completely. Use when cool, as directed, or store cooled octopus in an airtight container for up to 1 day before using.

RED POTATO SALAD

chinese celery, za'atar

One of the things we pride ourselves on at our restaurants is our ability to remake very traditional foods with completely new ingredients without really changing why they work. Take this potato salad: At face value, it's a Middle Eastern dish with a bit of cumin, lemony sumac, and plenty of sesame. But when you taste it, it has all the elements of a classic potato salad—potatoes, celery, acid, and salt.

MAKES 4 TO 6 SERVINGS

FOR THE SALAD:
1½ pounds small red potatoes, quartered
   or cut into bite-size pieces
3 stalks Chinese celery (stems and leaves),
   cut into ½-inch pieces (for 1 loosely
   packed cup)
1 cup canola oil
⅓ cup Za'atar (page 51)

Kosher salt
1 recipe soy-pickled celery
   (see page 129), drained

FOR SERVING:
Kosher salt
½ cup picked celery leaves

1. **BOIL THE POTATOES.** Put the potatoes in a medium saucepan. Add cold water to cover, bring to a boil, then reduce the heat and simmer for 10 minutes, or until the potatoes are tender. Transfer the potatoes to a colander to drain.

2. **MEANWHILE, MAKE THE VINAIGRETTE.** In a medium bowl, whisk together the Chinese celery, oil, za'atar, and salt to taste until well blended, and set aside.

3. **ASSEMBLE THE SALAD.** In a large bowl, combine the potatoes with the soy-pickled celery, vinaigrette to taste, and additional salt, if necessary. Transfer the potato salad to a platter and garnish with the celery leaves. Serve warm or at room temperature.

no vinegar? use sumac!

TATSOI AND EGG

chinese sausage, smoked tea egg

You could call this salad a lot of things: It's a take on a traditional steakhouse spinach salad, with crisped Chinese sausage standing in for the bacon and the bold flavor of smoked tea eggs playing the part of the bleu cheese. Or it's an Asian version of a French frisée salad, with the egg's yolk just barely loose atop the greens. Or it's a great way to define what we do at our restaurants: we find a theme, and we twist it. But as always, every twist has a very careful method.

In this case, our focus is on the smoked tea egg, which tends to make people very excited at Joule. Instead of actually smoking the egg, which gives it an objectionable texture, we steep it in soy sauce infused with Lapsang souchong—a type of Chinese tea dried over a fire, which gives it a smoky flavor. As the egg steeps in the soy, it takes on a gorgeous mahogany color and that same smoky flavor but retains the texture of a perfectly boiled egg.

MAKES 4 SERVINGS

FOR THE EGGS:

1 cup soy sauce
1 tablespoon ground smoked tea
 (such as Lapsang souchong)
4 large eggs

FOR THE VINAIGRETTE:

2 Chinese dried chilies
2 allspice berries
1 star anise pod
¼ teaspoon fennel seeds
¼ teaspoon whole coriander seeds
8 ounces Chinese sausage, sliced into
 ⅛-inch-thick rounds
½ cup canola oil
¼ cup sherry vinegar
¼ cup soy sauce

FOR THE SALAD:

4 ounces tatsoi, baby spinach, or mixed
 greens (about 4 packed cups)
½ cup drained soy-pickled leeks
 (see page 129)
¼ cup picked fresh dill

serve the sausage vinaigrette warm

1. **MAKE THE SOY TEA.** In a small saucepan, bring the soy sauce to a boil. Remove the pan from the heat, add the tea, and set aside to cool.

2. **COOK THE EGGS.** Fill a medium saucepan about halfway with water, and bring the water to a boil over high heat. Add the eggs and cook for 8 minutes. Transfer the eggs to an ice water bath to cool for about 10 minutes, then carefully peel.

3. **STEEP THE EGGS.** Transfer the soy mixture to a tall, narrow container (such as a quart-size jar). Add the cooled eggs to the soy mixture and let sit at room temperature for 3 hours.

4. MAKE THE VINAIGRETTE. In a mortar and pestle, crush the chilies, allspice, star anise, fennel, and coriander until fine but not powdered. In a large skillet over medium heat, combine the sausage, oil, and crushed spices, and cook, stirring frequently. When all the fat is rendered and the sausage begins to crisp, after about 5 minutes, transfer the mixture to a medium bowl and whisk in the sherry vinegar and soy sauce.

5. ASSEMBLE THE SALAD. To serve, place the greens in a large bowl. Whisk the vinaigrette again and add it to the salad to taste (you may not need all of it), then toss with the leeks and transfer the salad to a serving plate. Garnish with the dill, then halve or quarter the eggs and nestle them into the top of the salad. Serve immediately.

HEIRLOOM TOMATO PLATTER

olive gremolata, fermented black beans

When you think about greens that have deep flavor, there aren't many that are common to both Eastern and Western food cultures. In this salad, we use one of the few—mustard—as a bridge between two cultures. Instead of appearing as part of a vinaigrette on a Mediterranean tomato and olive salad, we use it in the form of baby greens, tossed with a bright rainbow of tomatoes under a bread-crumb topping studded with chewy dried kalamatas. (If you can, find purple mustard, because the overall effect is quite pretty.)

MAKES 4 SERVINGS

FOR THE GREMOLATA:

3 cloves garlic

1 cup panko bread crumbs

1 cup pitted kalamata olives

½ cup extra-virgin olive oil

FOR THE VINAIGRETTE:

¾ cup canola oil

¼ cup fermented black beans

1 large shallot, finely chopped

¼ cup soy sauce

¼ cup rice vinegar

¼ cup black vinegar

2 Chinese dried chilies

3 tablespoons finely chopped peeled
  fresh ginger

FOR THE SALAD:

1½ pounds mixed heirloom tomatoes
  (a mix of colors), cut into wedges,
  rounds, or bite-size halves

Chunky sea salt

2 ounces baby mustard greens
  (about 2 lightly packed cups), cut into
  bite-size pieces

1. **MAKE THE GREMOLATA.** Preheat the oven to 375 degrees F. Line a baking sheet with parchment paper. In the bowl of a food processor, whirl the garlic until chopped. Add the bread crumbs, olives, and oil and pulse until the olives are very roughly chopped and the crumbs are evenly moistened, about 10 quick pulses. Transfer the mixture to the baking sheet and bake for 15 to 20 minutes, stirring once or twice, or until the bread crumbs are browned and crispy. Set aside to cool.

2. **MAKE THE VINAIGRETTE.** In a blender, whirl the oil and beans together for just a few seconds to break up the beans. (The mixture shouldn't be smooth.) Heat a medium saucepan over medium heat and add the bean oil. Add the shallot and cook, stirring occasionally, until the shallot just begins to soften, about 3 minutes. Add the soy sauce, vinegars, chilies, and ginger and remove the pan from the heat.

3. **ASSEMBLE THE SALAD.** Arrange the tomatoes on a large platter. Shower with sea salt, then drizzle with the vinaigrette to taste. In a separate bowl, toss the mustard greens with a little more of the vinaigrette, then add the greens to the salad, tucking them in between and under the tomatoes. Top the salad with a few handfuls of the gremolata (you'll use about half of it) and serve.

ARUGULA AND CORNED LAMB

spicy nuoc cham

We've had this salad on the menu at Revel since opening day. It's a hugely flavorful savory pile, made with house-corned lamb and a salty-sweet-sour dressing you'll want to put on anything and everything. (That's why there's extra.) Like many of the Vietnamese salads it's modeled after, it's a perfect appetizer—it opens up your palate in a huge way.

Since the lamb will need to cure for five full days before you braise it, start this salad well ahead of when you plan to serve it. Leftover corned lamb also makes excellent hash for brunch or an atypical Rueben sandwich, so you can double the lamb, if you wish, keeping all the other brine measurements the same.

MAKES 4 SERVINGS

FOR THE LAMB BRINE:
⅓ cup packed light brown sugar
½ cup kosher salt
1½ teaspoons pink curing salt
  (see page 62)
3 cups water, divided
⅔ cup lager or pilsner beer
1 teaspoon whole coriander seeds
1 teaspoon whole black peppercorns
1 bay leaf
3 juniper berries
2 whole cloves
2 star anise pods
3 large dried Thai chilies
1 pound lamb leg or top round

FOR BRAISING THE LAMB:
1 carrot, chopped
1 celery rib, chopped
½ yellow onion, chopped
4 ounces daikon radish
  (about ½ small radish), cubed
2 cloves garlic

FOR THE *NUOC CHAM*:
5 cloves garlic
2 tablespoons sugar
2 fresh Thai chilies
¾ cup canola oil
½ cup rice vinegar
2 tablespoons fish sauce
1 tablespoon freshly squeezed lime juice

FOR THE SALAD:
4 ounces arugula (about 4 packed cups)
¼ cup packed thinly sliced fresh mint
3 radishes, cut into ⅟₁₆-inch-thick slices on
  a mandolin

1. **BRINE THE LAMB.** In a small saucepan, combine the brown sugar, kosher salt, curing salt, and 1 cup of the water. Bring to a boil, stirring occasionally to encourage the sugar and salts to dissolve. When the mixture is clear, remove the pan from the heat and let cool to room temperature. Add the remaining 2 cups water and the beer, then the coriander, peppercorns, bay leaf, juniper berries, cloves, star anise, and chilies. Transfer the brine to a ziplock bag, add the lamb, close the bag with as little air inside as possible, and brine for 5 full days, refrigerated.

bright Vietnamese salad — my way

2. **BRAISE THE LAMB.** Remove the lamb from the marinade and transfer it to a heavy braising pot or Dutch oven with a lid. Add the carrot, celery, onion, daikon radish, and garlic, plus enough water to cover the lamb completely (about 6 to 8 cups). Bring the mixture to a boil, then reduce to a strong simmer and cook, covered, until the lamb is tender at the center, 1½ to 2 hours. (You can use the lamb immediately or let it cool to room temperature and then refrigerate it in the liquid up to 3 days, and reheat it in the liquid before serving.)

3. **MAKE THE DRESSING.** In a mortar and pestle, crush the garlic, sugar, and chilies together until the sugar is dissolved and the mixture is pasty. (Depending on the size of your mortar, you may need to do this in two batches.) Transfer the mixture to a small bowl and whisk in the oil, vinegar, fish sauce, and lime juice.

4. **ASSEMBLE THE SALAD.** In a large bowl, combine the arugula, mint, and radishes. Cut about ½ pound of the lamb into ¼-inch-thick slices and add to the salad, along with about 6 tablespoons of the *nuoc cham*, or to taste. Pile the salad onto plates, top with some of the garlic and chilies floating in the dressing, and serve immediately.

CHARRED CHINESE MUSTARD GREENS

shiitake mushroom pickle, nigella seeds

In the beginning at Joule's first location, we had extremely limited stovetop space. For that reason—and because we are smitten with how leafy greens sweeten and caramelize when charred over a hot flame—we grill a lot of our vegetables and make a lot of warm salads like this one. At a restaurant, the grill is always on, but at home it's often just as easy to throw vegetables on the grill as it is to cook them on the stove.

Chinese mustard—whose stems collapse under heat, so don't need to be removed—has a flavor slightly more pungent than its American cousin. Blended with pickled mushrooms, seasoned with black vinegar, and showered with a crunchy nigella and garlic chive gremolata, the greens turn almost candyish. Serve this salad on small plates as a warm appetizer.

MAKES 4 SERVINGS

FOR THE PICKLE:

6 ounces shiitake mushrooms, stems
    removed, cut into ¼-inch-thick slices
1½ cups rice vinegar
¾ cup sugar
¾ cup water
1 teaspoon Chinese mustard

FOR THE GREMOLATA:

2 tablespoons nigella seeds
2 tablespoons finely chopped
    garlic chives
¼ teaspoon kosher salt

FOR THE SALAD:

2 bunches Chinese mustard greens (about
    8 ounces), ends trimmed
2 tablespoons canola oil
Kosher salt and freshly ground
    black pepper
¼ cup black vinegar

nigella seed gremolata!

1. **PICKLE THE MUSHROOMS.** Put the sliced shiitake mushrooms into a medium non-reactive container. In a small saucepan, combine the rice vinegar, sugar, and water. Bring to a boil over high heat, stirring occasionally to help the sugar dissolve, then whisk in the mustard. Pour the liquid over the mushrooms and set aside to cool to room temperature, at least 1 hour.

2. **MAKE THE GREMOLATA.** Combine the nigella seeds, chives, and salt in the bowl of a mortar and pestle, and grind until fine. (You can also put the ingredients in a small ziplock bag and crush them with a rolling pin.) Set aside.

continued

3. GRILL THE GREENS. Preheat a gas or charcoal grill over medium-high heat, about 425 degrees F. Cut the mustard greens in half where the stems meet the leaves, then cut the leaves crosswise into 3-inch strips. (The strips should be big enough to be grillable.) In a large bowl, combine the greens with the oil and season with salt and pepper. Working in batches, grill the greens for about 1 minute per side (the stems may take a little longer), until wilted and charred in spots. (It will take less time if you cover the grill for a moment.) Transfer the grilled greens to a large nonreactive bowl as you go. You can continue with the warm mustard greens or let the greens come to room temperature before serving.

4. PLATE THE GREENS. Drain the mushrooms and combine them with the mustard greens. Toss the mixture with the black vinegar, pile onto plates, and top with the nigella gremolata. Serve immediately.

GRILLING GREENS

Grilling greens gives them a completely different texture and flavor profile than they have when cooked other ways. As the leaves hit the grill, the sugars in each leaf caramelize, adding sweetness and, because the leaves often brown and crisp, a little crunch. (Leaves with oil on them will turn brown, whereas naked leaves will turn black, so coat the leaves evenly.) Grill greens quickly over the hottest part of the grill, so they char in spots, and take them off when they seem about two-thirds of the way done since the residual heat will continue to wilt the greens. If you're grilling greens for the first time, babysit them a little. You'll notice that thinner, drier greens like kale and mustard greens crisp up a little more quickly than sturdier greens with a higher moisture content like collard greens.

BUTTERNUT SQUASH GRATIN

chipotle, lentil, feta

On the surface, there's very little about this dish that's Asian. Built like a gratin, with a loose layer of feta on top, it's a squash dish with Mexican accents from smoky chipotle pepper, cloves, and coriander. The lentils, with their slightly floral curry flavor, make it feel French. But ultimately—in part because it's got great heat—it eats like Korean *banchan*. When we serve it at Joule, it's fun to see what people get out of it; while some people love the textural contrast between the soft squash and the firm lentils, others really revel in the spice. We feel like we've created a great fusion dish when everyone can find a way to relate to it. This is certainly a mishmash, but it still connects—and that, in the end, is what we're always about.

We don't bake this like a gratin but instead finish it in a pan on the stove, adding the cheese right at the end. (You can make all the components a day or two ahead and store them in the refrigerator, covered, until you're ready to serve the gratin.) Use a pan with flared sides, so you can slide the ingredients right into a serving dish, keeping the cheese on top. If you'd like, top it with the Delicata Sour Pickles (page 142).

MAKES 8 SERVINGS AS** BANCHAN, **OR 4 TO 6 SERVINGS AS A SIDE DISH

FOR THE SQUASH:

1 packed tablespoon light brown sugar

1 tablespoon ground toasted coriander
  (see Toasting Spices, page 53)

1 teaspoon cayenne pepper

½ teaspoon ground allspice

½ teaspoon ground cloves

½ teaspoon ground star anise

1 pound butternut squash (from the long
  part), cut into 1-inch chunks

1 tablespoon canola oil

Kosher salt

FOR THE LENTILS:

½ cup lentils

5 curry leaves

¼ small onion

1 piece carrot (about 3 inches)

1 piece celery (about 3 inches)

3 cups cold water

FOR THE VINAIGRETTE:

½ cup sake

¼ cup mirin

¼ cup toasted pumpkin seeds (see
  Toasting Nuts and Seeds, page 288)

2 tablespoons chipotle puree (see Making
  Chipotle Puree, page 113)

4 cloves garlic

FOR SERVING:

1 tablespoon canola oil

3 tablespoons unsalted butter

Kosher salt and freshly ground black pepper

⅓ cup crumbled feta cheese

2 tablespoons thinly sliced Italian parsley
  leaves

continued

curry leaves make lentils taste extra savory

1. **ROAST THE SQUASH.** Preheat the oven to 500 degrees F. Line a baking sheet with parchment paper.

In a small bowl, stir together the brown sugar, coriander, cayenne, allspice, cloves, and star anise. Put the squash in a medium bowl, drizzle with the oil, then add the spice mixture and toss to coat. Season the squash with salt, then transfer to the baking sheet and roast for 15 to 20 minutes, turning the squash pieces once or twice during cooking, or until the squash is fork-tender and beginning to brown. Transfer to a plate and set aside.

2. **COOK THE LENTILS.** In a small saucepan, combine the lentils, curry leaves, onion, carrot, and celery. Add the cold water, bring the liquid to a boil over high heat, then reduce the heat to low and simmer the lentils until cooked but still firm, 15 to 20 minutes. Drain the lentils, pick out and discard the aromatics, and set aside.

3. **MAKE THE VINAIGRETTE.** In a heavy-duty blender, whirl together the sake, mirin, pumpkin seeds, chipotle puree, and garlic until smooth. Set aside.

4. **ASSEMBLE THE GRATIN.** Heat a large skillet over medium-high heat. Add the oil, then the squash, and toss to coat. Add the butter and cook for 2 or 3 minutes, turning the squash occasionally, until the butter has melted and the squash is brown on all sides. Add the lentils and ½ cup of the chipotle vinaigrette, season with salt and pepper, and cook for 1 to 2 minutes to warm the lentils. Sprinkle the feta on top, then immediately slide the squash and lentils onto a serving dish, keeping the feta on top, if possible. Garnish with parsley and serve warm or at room temperature.

MAKING CHIPOTLE PUREE

Make chipotle puree by blending the contents of a 7-ounce can of chipotle peppers in adobo sauce until smooth. Store the sauce in a sealed container in the refrigerator for up to 2 weeks or freeze for up to 3 months.

MISO-CUMIN GRILLED EGGPLANT

crispy chickpeas

When you brush grilled eggplant with a glaze made by blending spunky black vinegar with oil, miso, garlic, and toasted cumin, it caramelizes into a thick, sticky sauce that almost candies the eggplant. The result: eggplant for noneggplant-eaters. I always make extra of the glaze and the chickpeas because the combination is infinitely translatable—try it on other grilled vegetables, like zucchini or asparagus, or on firm fish fillets.

MAKES 4 SERVINGS

FOR THE CHICKPEAS:

1 (15-ounce) can chickpeas,
  rinsed and drained

3 tablespoons canola oil

1 teaspoon ground sumac

½ teaspoon kosher salt

FOR THE GLAZE:

½ cup black vinegar

4 cloves garlic

1 tablespoon toasted whole cumin seeds
  (see Toasting Spices, page 53)

½ cup canola oil

¼ cup Japanese white miso

FOR THE EGGPLANT:

4 Japanese or Chinese eggplant (about
  1 pound), cut into ½-inch-thick
  slices lengthwise

2 tablespoons canola oil

Kosher salt and freshly ground
  black pepper

¼ cup packed picked Italian parsley leaves

Crunchy sea salt, for garnish

1. **DRY THE CHICKPEAS.** Pat the chickpeas dry with a clean towel, then transfer them to the bowl of a food processor and pulse until all the chickpeas are broken into ragged pieces and some have turned to dust, about 10 times. Dry the chickpeas in a food dehydrator for 3 hours at 115 degrees F. (If you want to dry in an oven, preheat the oven to 170 degrees F. Spread out the chickpeas in an even layer on a parchment-lined baking sheet, and dry for approximately 3 hours, stirring the chickpeas twice during drying.) When they're done, they should be crunchy and crumbly. Set aside to cool.

2. **MAKE THE GLAZE.** In a blender, whirl together the vinegar, garlic, and cumin until the garlic is very finely chopped. Add the oil and miso and blend until smooth. Transfer the glaze to a small bowl and set aside.

3. **FRY THE CHICKPEAS.** Heat the oil in a medium skillet over high heat. Add the chickpeas and cook for 1 to 2 minutes, stirring, until they become crispy and begin to brown. Transfer the chickpeas to a paper towel–lined plate to drain, then transfer to a small bowl, and stir in the sumac and salt. Set aside.

take miso to the next level by adding CUMIN

4. GRILL THE EGGPLANT. Preheat a gas or charcoal grill to medium-high heat, about 450 degrees F. In a large bowl, toss the eggplant with the oil until coated, and season with salt and pepper. Grill the eggplant for 2 minutes, or until well marked, keeping the lid closed as much as possible, then flip each piece over and brush with the reserved glaze. Cook for 2 minutes more, then turn again, changing the angle of the eggplant so the grill creates a crisscross pattern on the eggplant's flesh, brushing the second side with a layer of the glaze. Cook 1 minute, flip again, and cook 1 minute more. Transfer the eggplant to a serving platter, garnish with the parsley and sea salt, plus a small handful of the chickpeas. Serve hot.

GRILLED CHINESE BROCCOLI

walnut pesto

Often presented as the token vegetable at Asian restaurants, Chinese broccoli is usually prepared very simply, and is too often quite boring. As with most vegetables, adding a charred flavor changes the profile considerably, introducing both sweetness and bitterness that we play up by lacing it with a vinegar-forward pesto, which acts more like a vinaigrette. Szechuan peppercorns throw in some heat. But don't confine this preparation to Chinese broccoli; the same nutty drizzle would be delicious on grilled zucchini, kale, or asparagus.

We usually cook this by cutting the broccoli in half first, separating the thick stalks from the leafy portions. For a more dramatic presentation, you can keep them whole—just prepare a bigger pot with as many inches of boiling water as the stalks are long, and set the broccoli upright in the pot for the first three minutes of cooking time before folding the tops in as well.

MAKES 4 SERVINGS

FOR THE PESTO:

1 cup walnuts, toasted and
  crushed, divided
¼ cup sherry vinegar
1 cup canola oil
1 teaspoon crushed toasted Szechuan
  peppercorns (see Toasting Spices, page 53)
½ teaspoon kosher salt

FOR THE BROCCOLI:

2 medium bunches Chinese broccoli
  (about 1½ pounds), thick stems peeled
2 tablespoons canola oil
Kosher salt and freshly ground black pepper

FOR SERVING:

6 cloves confited garlic (see Quick Garlic
  Confit, page 172)

1. **MAKE THE PESTO.** In a blender, whirl ¼ cup of the walnuts with the vinegar until the walnuts are just roughly chopped. Transfer the mixture to a medium bowl and whisk in the oil, Szechuan peppercorns, and salt, then stir in the remaining ¾ cup crushed walnuts. Set aside.

2. **BLANCH THE BROCCOLI.** Fill a medium saucepan with water and bring to a boil. Cut the broccoli in half where the stalks meet the leaves. Cut any stalks thicker than about ½ inch in diameter in half lengthwise. When the water boils, add the stalks, and cook for 3 minutes. Add the tops, cook for 2 minutes more, then drain the greens in a colander and set aside to cool slightly. (If you want to blanch the broccoli ahead of time, dunk it in ice water here to stop the cooking entirely, and then drain it and refrigerate until you're ready to grill it.)

3. **GRILL THE BROCCOLI.** Preheat a gas or charcoal grill to medium-high heat, about 425 degrees F. In a large bowl, toss the broccoli pieces with the oil and season with salt and pepper. Grill the broccoli for about 2 to 3 minutes per side, or until wilted and charred in spots. (It will take less time if you cover the grill for a moment.)

4. ASSEMBLE THE DISH. Transfer the broccoli a large platter. Using a spoon so you get a mixture of big and small walnut pieces, dress the broccoli with pesto to taste. Add the garlic and serve.

CRISPY CAULIFLOWER

bagna cauda

Our best-selling dish at Trove, hands down, is fried cauliflower. Even with the upswing in popularity of cruciferous vegetables like cauliflower, kale, and broccoli over the last decade, people don't expect it on the menu at a Korean barbecue restaurant. But chefs are realizing—and diners are loving—that when you find new ways to fry or char vegetables, their natural sweetness comes through, and you get so many new flavors and textures. If you caramelize chunky florets in a fryer and serve them with a bagna cauda accented with miso sauce for a salty, briny flavor, you get something completely unique. Plan to eat these standing up, huddled around the plate, scooping pieces of pickled lemon onto each bite with your fingers. It's the perfect way to start an evening.

MAKES 4 TO 6 SERVINGS

FOR THE CAULIFLOWER:
1 cauliflower head (about 2 pounds),
   cut into 2-inch florets
2 cups buttermilk
1½ cups Magic Dredge (page 63)
1 teaspoon dried oregano
Canola oil, for frying

FOR THE BAGNA CAUDA:
1 (4.2-ounce) jar oil-packed anchovies,
   drained

4 cloves garlic
½ cup sherry vinegar
¾ cup extra-virgin olive oil
1 tablespoon Japanese white miso
1 teaspoon coarse Korean chili flakes

FOR SERVING:
¼ cup packed picked Italian parsley leaves
4 slices Pickled Lemons
   (page 57), halved

1. **BLANCH THE CAULIFLOWER.** Fill a large saucepan about two-thirds of the way with water and bring to a boil over high heat. Add the cauliflower and cook for 1 minute, then drain the cauliflower and transfer it to a large bowl of ice water to cool. Transfer the cool cauliflower to a colander and let drain.

2. **MAKE THE BAGNA CAUDA.** In the bowl of a heavy-duty blender, whirl about half the anchovies with the garlic and vinegar until smooth, and transfer to a large mixing bowl. Whisk in the oil, miso, and chili flakes, then chop the remaining anchovies and stir them into the mixture. (The liquid won't quite be smooth or uniform, which is fine.) Set aside.

3. **PREPARE FOR FRYING.** In a large, wide bowl, combine the Magic Dredge with the oregano and whisk to blend. Dip a few pieces of cauliflower in the buttermilk, then add them to the dredge, tossing the florets to ensure each piece is coated on all sides with the dredge. Repeat until all the cauliflower is coated.

how to make a bagna cauda better: ADD MISO

4. FRY AND SERVE THE CAULIFLOWER. Preheat the oil in a deep fryer or a large, heavy pot filled with about 3 inches of oil to 375 degrees F. When the oil is ready, add a few handfuls of the coated cauliflower and fry until golden brown, about 3 minutes. (Only add as much cauliflower as will fit comfortably in your fryer or pot; the florets cook best if they have plenty of space.) Transfer the fried cauliflower to the bowl with the bagna cauda and toss to coat. Repeat with the remaining cauliflower; then serve piping hot, garnished with some of the parsley and pieces of pickled lemon.

SMOKED TOFU

honshimeji confit, truffle vinaigrette

Meat-eaters don't typically order tofu in restaurants. But as any one of our employees will tell you, a good tofu dish can be as addictive as great steak—when we take a poll, our staff always vote this their number one favorite dish. More than one of our cooks has told us that this was the dish that made them decide to come work with us. In fact, this smoky appetizer and our Joule Box dessert (see page 299) are the only dishes we've carried over from Joule's opening day.

To be clear, it's not baked tofu. Starting with medium-firm organic tofu, we marinate it in soy (which you can reuse for cooking after marinating); then we cold smoke it. What you wind up with are silky, umami-packed slabs with just a whisp of smoke flavor, topped with a rich mushroom confit and a truffled vinaigrette that always reminds me of walking into a forest. At the restaurant, we often have tiny pieces of truffle we can't use elsewhere, which we blend into our vinaigrette in addition to the ingredients below. Do the same, if you have extra truffle bits on hand.

If you want to work ahead, you can make the confit up to a week in advance and store it in the refrigerator, covered. You can also smoke the tofu a day ahead. Let both come up to room temperature before serving.

MAKES 6 SERVINGS

FOR THE TOFU:

2 (14- to 16-ounce) packages medium-firm
  tofu, drained
1 to 2 cups Revel's Seasoned Soy Sauce
  (page 73)
3 cups applewood chips

FOR THE CONFIT:

1 cup canola oil, divided
2 (3.5-ounce) packages *honshimeji*
  mushrooms, bottoms trimmed off
Kosher salt and freshly ground black
  pepper
1 sprig thyme
3 medium shallots, cut into ⅛-inch-
  thick slices

FOR THE VINAIGRETTE:

¼ cup canola oil
3 tablespoons soy sauce
3 tablespoons rice vinegar
1 tablespoon black truffle oil

FOR SERVING:

2 green onions (green parts only),
  thinly sliced
Chunky sea salt

1. **MARINATE THE TOFU.** Cut each tofu block into thirds (the short way), arrange it in a square container the flattest way in a single layer, and add enough soy sauce to cover. Let marinate in the refrigerator for 1 hour.

continued

2. SMOKE THE TOFU. Put the wood chips in a disposable metal pan or metal pie plate. Pre-heat a gas or charcoal grill to high heat with the plate of wood chips over the hottest part of the grill. Once the chips are burning and the grill has reached about 500 degrees F, turn the heat down to medium (about 400 degrees F) and grill the chips for another 15 minutes or so, until the chips are completely black and are smoking vigorously. Turn the gas off (or let the fire die) with the grill's lid closed.

Drain the tofu and transfer it to a heatproof container, such as a pie plate. When the grill has cooled to 200 degrees F, add the tofu to the grill, closing the lid as quickly as possible to keep the smoke in. Let the tofu smoke for 10 minutes, then remove and set aside.

3. MEANWHILE, CONFIT THE MUSHROOMS. In a large saucepan, heat ¼ cup of the canola oil over medium-high heat. Add the mushrooms, season with salt and pepper, then cook, stirring occasionally, until the mushrooms begin to brown, about 5 minutes. Add the remaining ¾ cup oil, the thyme, and the shallots, reduce the heat to medium-low, and cook, stirring occasionally, for another 15 minutes, or until the shallots are completely soft. Transfer the mushrooms and oil to a small bowl and set aside.

4. MAKE THE VINAIGRETTE. In a blender, whirl together the canola oil, soy sauce, vinegar, and truffle oil until smooth. Set aside.

5. ASSEMBLE AND SERVE. To serve, slice each piece of tofu into ½-inch squares (like large pats of butter) and arrange the slices from each on separate small plates. Divide the mushroom confit between the plates, leaving any excess oil in the bowl as you go. Drizzle each with some of the vinaigrette, shower with sliced green onions and sea salt, and serve.

HOT POTATOES

kalamata olives, soy sauce

For me, the best moment of cooking our food is when I catch a customer trying to figure out what's happening in their mouth. They take a bite and chew thoughtfully, but they either don't find the flavors they expected, or they can't identify what they're tasting. They bite again. And in a storm of discovery, they chat with their fellow diners about what they are tasting. They're hooked—there are smiles and nods and reaches for more.

These potatoes are a prime example. Tossed with a blend of kalamata olives and soy, they look like they've been coated in barbecue sauce (see page 94)—only somehow, the combination of salt, butter, and deep umami flavor comes across as dark chocolate in the first bite.

But don't take my word for it.

MAKES 4 TO 6 SERVINGS

FOR THE POTATOES:

2 pounds fingerling potatoes

1 tablespoon kosher salt

1 teaspoon whole coriander seeds

1 teaspoon whole black peppercorns

1 bay leaf

FOR THE SAUCE:

½ cup pitted kalamata olives

½ cup soy sauce

¼ cup mirin

1 tablespoon coarse Korean chili flakes

FOR SERVING:

3 tablespoons canola oil

4 tablespoons (½ stick) unsalted butter, divided

½ cup packed Thai basil leaves

1. **COOK THE POTATOES.** Put the potatoes, salt, coriander, peppercorns, and bay leaf in a large pot. Add cold water to cover, bring to a boil, then cook for 10 to 12 minutes, or until a fork pierces the fattest potato easily. Drain the potatoes, halve lengthwise, and spread on a baking sheet, flesh sides up, to cool.

2. **MAKE THE SAUCE.** In a blender, whirl together the olives, soy sauce, mirin, and chili flakes until smooth. Set aside.

3. **FRY THE POTATOES AND SERVE.** Heat a large skillet over high heat. Add 1½ tablespoons of the oil, then half the potatoes, cut sides down, and cook for 2 to 3 minutes, until browned and crisp. Turn the potatoes and cook for another minute, then pour off the excess oil and add 2 tablespoons of the butter. When the butter has melted, add about half the sauce and cook, stirring and turning the potatoes, until the sauce has reduced and the potatoes are well coated. Stir in half the basil, transfer the potatoes to a serving plate, wipe out the pan, and repeat with the remaining oil, potatoes, butter, sauce, and basil. Serve warm or at room temperature.

pickles

When we opened Joule, our tiny kitchen forced us to relearn how to cook within special limitations. Pickles emerged as one of our specialties because they were a way to add bright, interesting flavors without taking up space on the stove while we were cooking. Because pickling foods extends their shelf life, pickles were also an economical way to waste less, so in the beginning, they helped us survive. Today, almost everything we serve has a pickled component, because the more we cook, the more we appreciate what they can offer every dish. (Pickles, like salt, bring out the flavors in other foods.) And now, we always make a point to embrace our boundaries. Use our Pickle Basics (following page) to pickle what you want, or use the following recipes to explore the pickles we serve at our restaurants every day.

PICKLE BASICS

Pickles, like kimchi, are technically part of the class of Korean foods known as *banchan*. Eaten as a snack or as part of a larger meal, they're ubiquitous on Korean tables, both at home and in restaurants. Typically, people make simple pickles quite frequently at home, but you can also purchase them premade at most grocery stores.

I think in pickles as though they were another language. For me, pickling is automatic—I know that I always use two parts rice vinegar to one part sugar and one part water to make my brine, and that if the pickles refuse to stay under the liquid, I can use a plastic bag filled with water to weigh them down. I know that I can use the brine cold for vegetables that don't need cooking, or hot, if I want them to soften a bit. But what's most important is that, deep down, I know that you can pickle anything, in any way, with any flavor you feel like using. This is why, even though they start with a pretty formulaic brine, pickles can be a great creative outlet.

THE GREAT CARROT PICKLE EXPERIMENT

During Revel's cooking classes, we induct our participants to the wonderful world of pickles by doing something we call The Great Carrot Pickle Experiment. We chose carrots first because you can eat them raw and second because they get sweeter once cooked. We then taste carrots pickled seven different ways to explore how each variation affects the carrot's flavor in the end. In class, everyone is hooked after tasting the pickles and eager to dig into the world of pickling.

1. **COLD PICKLING LIQUID** (cooled Basic Pickle Brine, opposite page): pretty, raw carroty flavor with a crunch

2. **HOT PICKLING LIQUID** (hot Basic Pickle Brine, opposite page): softer and a bit sweeter than cold-pickled carrots but infused with a stronger pickle flavor

3. **SAVORY HOT PICKLING LIQUID** (carrot is sautéed in oil, then cooled in hot Basic Pickle Brine, opposite page): sweeter carrot flavor, with a more mellow pickle flavor

4. **SPICY HOT PICKLING LIQUID** (hot Basic Pickle Brine, opposite page, with spices like Chinese five spice or Madras curry powder): alters the pickling flavor greatly, depending on the spice

5. **NON-VINEGAR PICKLE** (instead of vinegar, using other souring agents like tamarind and citrus juice to pickle): the carrots take on the flavor of the souring agent

6. **SALT BRINE** (by fermenting over time in about 5 percent salt brine, you get sourness like you would get when you pickle using vinegar): fermented flavor

7. **MISOZUKE** (by fermenting in miso and sake mixture over time, as on page 141): carrots with salty, sweet, and sour flavors all at once

BASIC PICKLE BRINE

korean giardiniara

This basic brine makes enough liquid to cover about four cups of vegetables. Choose just one of the vegetable options below, or make a mix of vegetables with similar textures.

MAKES 4 CUPS

FOR THE BRINE:

2 cups rice vinegar
1 cup sugar
1 cup water
2 teaspoons kosher salt

VEGETABLE OPTIONS:

1½ pounds daikon radish, cut into
¾-inch chunks

3 bell peppers or 8 Korean chilies,
cut into ½-inch strips or rings

2 medium red or white onions,
halved and cut into ¼-inch slices

2 (8-ounce) thumbs ginger, peeled
and julienned

1 pound shallots, thinly sliced

4 large carrots, peeled and cut into
½-inch slices

2 medium leeks, halved lengthwise
and cut into ¼-inch half moons

5 celery stalks, trimmed and cut
diagonally into ½-inch pieces

1. **MAKE THE BRINE.** In a 2-quart pot, stir together the vinegar, sugar, water, and salt. Bring to a boil over high heat, stirring occasionally to help the sugar and salt dissolve.

2. **ADD YOUR VEGETABLES TO THE HOT LIQUID.** If you're making something that doesn't take long to cook (like ginger, shallots, or leeks), transfer the vegetables and liquid to a nonreactive container and let cool to room temperature. If what you're pickling requires longer cooking (think carrots, beets, or other root vegetables), simmer the vegetables for a few minutes—longer for larger pieces—before cooling, remembering that they will continue to cook as they cool down.

3. **STORE THE PICKLES.** Always cool your pickles to room temperature and then store them submerged in their brine in the refrigerator, covered, for up to 3 weeks.

VARIATIONS WE LOVE

GRILLED PICKLES: Grill vegetables first, then cut and pickle. For the peppers used in Cold Red Curry Noodles (page 233), oil and grill the Korean chilies listed above before slicing and pickling.

SPICY PICKLES: Toss drained pickles with ¼ cup sambal oelek. For the spicy sambal daikon we use in our short rib rice bowl (see page 205), use the daikon radish listed above.

SOY PICKLES: Replace the water in the brine with soy sauce and omit the salt. Use this method for the pickles in Red Potato Salad (page 101), Tatsoi and Egg (page 102), and Mushroom Noodles (page 235).

SUMMER GRILLED PICKLES

squash, eggplant, coconut

This quick summer pickle gets its name because its main ingredient is just that—pure summer. Make it using your favorite summer produce but don't limit yourself to the squash and eggplant varieties below. (I love the texture of these small round eggplants' popping seeds, but okra, tomatoes, cucumbers, and peppers also make great pickles.)

Whatever you use, the method stays the same: first, you char the vegetables, so they take on that quintessential summer grilled flavor; then, you pickle them in a sweet, almost tropical mixture of coconut milk and rice vinegar. It's a quick pickle process, but it's best to allow the vegetables to hang out in the pickling liquid for a few hours before serving. And to be sure to save any leftover brine to use as a sauce over rice; it's liquid gold.

MAKES 2 QUARTS

FOR THE VEGETABLES:

4 golf ball–size Thai eggplant (about ½ pound total), trimmed and cut into ½-inch rounds
4 golf ball–size Indian eggplant (about ½ pound total), trimmed and cut into ½-inch rounds
4 tablespoons canola oil, divided
3 teaspoons kosher salt, divided
Freshly ground black pepper
1 medium zucchini (about 8 ounces), trimmed and cut into ½-inch rounds
1 medium yellow squash (about 8 ounces), trimmed and cut into ½-inch rounds
1 cup loosely packed fresh basil leaves

FOR THE PICKLING LIQUID:

2 cups rice vinegar
1 cup coconut milk
½ cup sugar
1 teaspoon kosher salt

rich coconut milk in the pickling liquid

1. **GRILL THE VEGETABLES.** Preheat a gas or charcoal grill to medium heat, about 400 degrees F.

In a large bowl, drizzle all of the eggplant with 2 tablespoons of the oil, season with 1½ teaspoons of the salt and the black pepper to taste, and gently mix to coat all the vegetables. Grill the eggplant, either directly on the grill's grates or in a preheated vegetable grilling basket, for 7 to 10 minutes, turning the vegetables once when they are well caramelized on the bottom and release easily from the grill, after 4 or 5 minutes. Repeat with the zucchini and squash, adding the remaining 2 tablespoons oil, 1½ teaspoons salt, and pepper to taste in the mixing bowl, and grilling for about 5 minutes total, turning after about 3 minutes. Note that the discs will essentially get cooked again when you pour the pickling liquid over them, so they should be fork-tender but not limp.

Transfer the grilled vegetables to two 1-quart glass jars or a large heavy-duty plastic container, stuffing basil leaves between the vegetables as you add them.

2. MAKE THE PICKLING LIQUID. In a 2-quart pot, stir together the vinegar, coconut milk, sugar, and salt, and stir to blend. Bring to a boil over high heat, stirring occasionally to help the sugar and salt dissolve, then reduce to a simmer.

3. PICKLE THE VEGETABLES. Remove the liquid from the heat and carefully pour it over the grilled vegetables. Let the pickles cool to room temperature, then close the container(s) and refrigerate until ready to use, at least 2 hours, or up to 2 months, well sealed. To serve, use tongs or a large fork to pile some of the pickles into a bowl, bringing some of the liquid with you.

PICKLED BEEF TONGUE

chinese celery, turnip

Jangjorim, a Korean soy-braised beef dish with rich sweet and salty flavors often served over rice, was traditionally a way of making a small amount of meat go a long way. It's served as *banchan*—like so many classic Korean dishes, it's more of a side dish than a main course. This is our take on *jangjorim*, made with slow-braised beef tongue instead of the more traditional shank or brisket, and pickled along with turnips, celery, and thin slivers of candied ginger. Eat it as is or stuff it into lettuce wraps.

Because tongue is usually difficult to purchase in small pieces, I recommend braising an entire tongue (the soy-caramel braising liquid gives it a lovely flavor) and reserving the rest for Korean tacos, served in corn tortillas with Korean Taco Pickles (page 139). You can also slice the excess tongue into three-quarter-inch slabs; toss them with canola oil, salt, and pepper; and grill them quickly over high heat just before serving as small steaks, with Grilled Chinese Broccoli (page 116) alongside.

If you're faced with diners who are unsure about eating beef tongue, spare them the preparation process but save them a few cubes of the warm, cooked tongue to try. It has a texture similar to pork cheek or the softest portion of brisket, with a rich, sweet flavor.

MAKES 1 QUART

FOR THE BEEF TONGUE:

1 cup sugar

1 cup soy sauce

1 cup sake

3 celery stalks, cut into 1-inch pieces

2 medium carrots, cut into 1-inch pieces

1 medium white onion, cut into 1-inch pieces

3 small dried chilies, such as *japones*

¼ teaspoon celery seeds

10 cups water

1 (3-pound) beef tongue

FOR THE PICKLING LIQUID:

1 cup rice vinegar

½ cup sugar

½ cup water

1 teaspoon kosher salt

FOR PICKLING:

1 (4-ounce) turnip, peeled and cut into ¼-inch slices, then quartered

3 stalks Chinese celery (stems and leaves), cut into ½-inch pieces (for 1 loosely packed cup)

5 pieces candied ginger (about 1 ounce total), cut into ¼-inch strips

1. **MAKE THE SOY CARAMEL BRAISING LIQUID.** Pour the sugar into the bottom of a 3-quart (or larger) soup pot. Place the pot over high heat and melt the sugar, undisturbed, until it turns a dark amber color, 3 to 4 minutes. Immediately add the soy sauce and sake in a slow, steady stream, whisking as you go, until the mixture is smooth. Add the celery, carrots, onion, dried chilies, celery seeds, and water, and bring to a boil.

2. BRAISE THE TONGUE. Add the tongue to the braising liquid, reduce the heat, and simmer, covered, for about 3 hours, or until the meat is tender enough to be pierced easily with a regular spoon, turning the tongue over about halfway through. (If necessary, add enough additional water to make sure the tongue is completely submerged at all times.) When the meat is tender, remove the pot from the heat and let the meat cool in the liquid until the tongue is comfortable to work with, about 2 hours.

3. MAKE THE PICKLING LIQUID. While the tongue cools, in a 2-quart pot, stir together the vinegar, sugar, water, and salt. Bring to a boil over high heat, stirring occasionally to help the sugar and salt dissolve, then remove the pot from the heat.

4. PREPARE THE TONGUE. Transfer the tongue to a cutting board, reserving the braising liquid. Using gloved hands, peel the skin off the tongue (it often comes off in one piece). Cut about 4 ounces (about 2 heaping cups) of the tongue into ¾-inch cubes, reserving the rest for another use. (It's best to store it, either whole or cut, in the braising liquid.) Place the cubed tongue in a medium nonreactive container, along with the turnip, Chinese celery, and ginger.

5. FINISH THE PICKLE. Add 2 cups of the braising liquid to the pan with the warm pickling liquid, and bring the mixture to a boil over high heat. Pour the hot liquid over the tongue and vegetables, let cool to room temperature, and serve. Store the tongue in the refrigerator for up to 1 week, covered.

YELLOW CURRY PICKLED BEETS

figs, kalamata, pistachio oil

You know pickled beets. But at Joule, our hope is to take a dish you think you know and do something unexpected. This unusual version—curried and pickled yellow beets, paired with kalamata olives and Mission figs—is a longtime favorite. Because both turmeric and beets have a distinct earthiness to them, they're a natural match, especially combined with the saltiness of the olives and the sweetness of the figs. Topped with a pistachio-studded oil touched with heat, each bite is novel but perfectly balanced.

At Joule, we plate these pickles as *banchan*, garnished with cilantro and a sprinkling of chunky sea salt. If you want something a little fancier, you could slice the beets very thinly with a mandolin and simply pour the pickling liquid over them to soften them, instead of letting them cook in the liquid.

MAKES 1 QUART

FOR THE PICKLING LIQUID:

1 cup rice vinegar

½ cup sugar

½ cup water

1 teaspoon kosher salt

3 (4-ounce) yellow beets, peeled and cut
 into ¼-inch slices, then quartered

10 dried Mission figs, stems removed
 and halved

¼ cup kalamata olives, halved and pitted

FOR PICKLING:

2 teaspoons Madras curry powder

1 teaspoon ground turmeric

1 teaspoon ground toasted cumin
 (see Toasting Spices, page 53)

FOR THE PISTACHIO OIL:

½ cup shelled pistachios

2 small Chinese dried chilies, stems
 removed

1 teaspoon kosher salt

½ cup extra-virgin olive oil

1. **MAKE THE PICKLING LIQUID.** In a 2-quart pot, stir together the vinegar, sugar, water, and salt. Bring to a boil over high heat, stirring occasionally to help the sugar and salt dissolve, then reduce to a simmer.

2. **PICKLE THE BEETS.** In a small bowl, stir together the curry powder, turmeric, and cumin. Add the spice blend and the beets to the pickling liquid, and simmer for 5 to 8 minutes, or until the beets are softer but still have some bite to them. (Remember that the beets will continue cooking in the hot liquid, and you want them to still have some crunch at the end.)

Put the figs and olives into a medium nonreactive container. When the beets are ready, add the beets and their liquid to the container. Let cool to room temperature, at least 1 hour.

continued

earthy spices match earthy beets

3. MAKE THE PISTACHIO OIL. While the beets cool, combine the pistachios, chilies, and salt in a ziplock bag. Using a rolling pin or the bottom of a heavy pan, crush the mixture until the chilies are well pulverized and all the pistachios are crushed into roughly quarters or smaller. (Some chilies won't break up as easily; it's fine to keep some pieces larger and just pick them out before serving.)

In a small saucepan, heat the oil over medium heat, until a larger piece of pistachio sizzles when you add it to the oil. Carefully pour the crushed pistachio mixture into the oil, remove from the heat, and let cool to room temperature.

4. SERVE THE PICKLES. To serve, divide the beet mixture between four or more small plates. Stir the pistachio oil to blend, then top the beets with a few spoonfuls of pistachios each, being generous with the oil as well. Store the pickles and the pistachio oil separately in the refrigerator, covered, for up to 3 weeks.

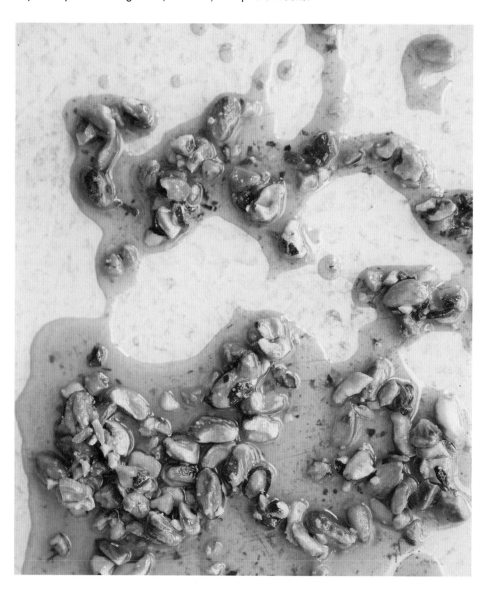

KOREAN TACO PICKLES

carrots, korean chilies

Inspired by the ingredients you'd normally see at a taco stand salsa bar—humble pickled carrots, onions, jalapeño peppers, and limes—this pickle is a simple, spicy mixture of a few things with a ton of natural flavor. Searing the carrots brings out their sweetness (see The Great Carrot Pickle Experiment, page 128), which adds another dimension to the acidity and spice, making this the ultimate taco topping. At home, I serve it with beef tacos (the pickling liquid doubles as a perfect flavoring for taco meat) but also over fried rice or with grilled steaks.

I use thin-fleshed Korean chilies, which are more like serranos than anything else found in most American grocery stores, but jalapeño peppers also work. Ditto for the onions: if you can't find pearl onions, a small chopped white onion works in a pinch.

I usually recommend people avoid eating the limes, but if you prefer a little extra hit of sourness, slice them as thin as you can and chop each slice into a few pieces, so the lime peels have a chance to soften a bit in the pickling liquid.

MAKES 1 QUART

FOR THE PICKLING LIQUID:

1 cup rice vinegar

½ cup sugar

½ cup water

¼ cup soy sauce

¼ cup Korean chili paste

1 tablespoon dried oregano

FOR PICKLING:

1 tablespoon canola oil

2 large carrots, peeled and cut into ½-inch rounds or half moons

6 ounces pearl onions, peeled and halved (see note)

6 cloves garlic, halved lengthwise

6 large green Korean chilies, cut into ½-inch rounds

1 small lime, cut in half lengthwise, then cut into ¼-inch-thick slices

1. MAKE THE PICKLING LIQUID. In a 2-quart pot, stir together the vinegar, sugar, and water. Bring to a boil over high heat, stirring occasionally to help the sugar dissolve, then whisk in the soy sauce, chili paste, and oregano, and remove from the heat. Let cool to room temperature.

2. SEAR THE VEGETABLES. Heat a large skillet over high heat, add the oil, then the carrots, cut side down. Cook for 1 to 2 minutes, or until the carrots are nicely browned, then carefully turn the carrots and cook for a minute or so more, until the second sides are browned. Add the onions and garlic, and cook the mixture, stirring occasionally, for 2 minutes more. Add the chilies, stir to blend, then transfer the vegetables to a medium nonreactive container.

continued

3. PICKLE THE VEGETABLES. When the pickling liquid has cooled completely, add it to the vegetables, along with the lime, and let sit for at least 1 hour. Store the pickles in the refrigerator, covered, for up to 3 weeks.

Note: To peel pearl onions, first trim the ends. Cook them in boiling water for a full minute, then quickly transfer them to an ice bath. After you let them sit for a minute in the ice water, the peels should slip off easily.

ROOT VEGETABLE MISOZUKE

sake, white miso

Misozuke are traditional Japanese miso-cultured pickles. Allowed to ferment at room temperature for five days, root vegetables take on an even earthier flavor, along with some sweetness and tang. At Joule, we serve them as part of our take on dan dan noodles—with ground, fermented root vegetables standing in for the traditional pork—but they're actually best to enjoy as a simple snack. Use this recipe as a jumping off point; you can make misozuke out of almost anything.

It's important to cut thicker vegetables like turnips and rutabaga into chunks so they ferment all the way to the center, but feel free to leave thinner vegetables like carrots and parsnips whole.

MAKES 1 QUART

2 cups Japanese white miso

2 cups sake

1½ pounds root vegetables (such as carrots, parsnips, turnips, rutabaga, or yellow beets), peeled and cut into 2-inch chunks

1. MAKE THE MISOZUKE. In a 2-quart container or medium bowl, whisk together the miso and sake until smooth. Add the vegetables and stir to coat. Press a layer of plastic wrap directly on the surface of the vegetables to prevent any air from reaching them, cover, and let sit at room temperature (65 to 68 degrees F) for 5 days. (You can leave it to ferment for longer, if you prefer. You'll get a funkier flavor and softer texture.) Rinse the pickles and slice them into bite-size pieces, and serve. Store the rinsed pickles in the refrigerator, covered, for up to 1 week.

COVER IT UP

When you're pickling, it's important to keep the ingredients fully submerged. For lighter ingredients, placing a folded paper towel directly on the surface of the liquid does the trick. For heavier or larger pieces, fill a small ziplock plastic bag with water and place that on top of the ingredients to submerge them until the pickling liquid has cooled to room temperature.

DELICATA SOUR PICKLES

chili, coriander

Instead of using a vinegar brine, we make some of our pickles by souring them—that is, allowing them to ferment in the natural lactic acid that a vegetable's sugars produce when left to hang out in a salty brine for a few days. We have the most fun souring unexpected things; when cut almost paper-thin, delicata squash turns sweet as it ferments, which makes it great as a snack or piled on top of the gratin (see page 111).

Delicata squash is often difficult to find out of season, but butternut squash is also delicious made this way. Using the bulb side of a roughly two-pound butternut squash, seed and peel the squash and then cut it into one-sixteenth-inch slices with a mandolin.

MAKES 1 QUART

FOR THE SPICE MIXTURE:

1 bay leaf
1 dried Thai chili
¼ cinnamon stick
1 tablespoon ground coriander
½ teaspoon ground cloves
¼ teaspoon ground allspice

FOR FERMENTING:

3 cups ice water, divided
1 tablespoon kosher salt
1 large delicata squash (about 1¼ pounds), peeled, halved, seeded, and cut into ¹⁄₁₆-inch slices with a mandolin

1. **MAKE THE SPICE MIXTURE.** In a spice grinder or heavy-duty blender, whirl together the bay leaf, chili, and cinnamon stick until ground to a powder. Transfer the spices to a small bowl and stir in the coriander, cloves, and allspice. Transfer 1 teaspoon of this spice mixture to a quart-size container with a lid, and reserve the rest for another use. (It makes a great rub for grilled meats.)

2. **SOUR THE SQUASH.** In a small saucepan, combine about ¼ cup of the water and the salt. Bring to a boil over high heat, stirring just until the salt has dissolved completely. Add this mixture to the remaining cold water, and stir to ensure all the liquid is cool. (You don't want to cook the squash.)

Put the squash in the container with the spice mixture. Add the cool liquid, and stir to make sure all the squash is coated. Press a layer of plastic wrap directly on the surface of the liquid to prevent any air from reaching the squash (it's important that all the pieces are submerged, so the vegetables sour instead of spoil), cover, and let sit at room temperature (65 to 68 degrees F) for 3 days. (You can leave it to ferment for longer, if you prefer. You'll get a funkier flavor and softer texture.) Transfer the pickles to the refrigerator, covered, and store for up to 3 weeks.

kimchi

Kimchi brought Seif and me together. When we were both working in New York, he wanted to impress me. His mother bought him a Korean cookbook for Christmas that year, thinking he might want to know more about my background. From it, he made kimchi, which at the time I had never made by myself. I was working in one of the top kitchens in the world, but the idea of making kimchi was completely daunting. It was one of the sweetest things a person had ever done for me. But more than that, it revealed the idea that, as a trained chef, I could probably learn how to cook Korean food. I realized that I'd been so focused on the Ivy Leagues of fine dining that it had never occurred to me to make the food I grew up eating.

When I was little, the family kimchi-making date was announced weeks in advance. My mom, my sister, and I would go to my aunt's house, where several other relatives would be gathered. We would all sit around the kitchen floor with specific tasks, kids often peeling daikon or garlic while the grown-ups chopped vegetables and grated all the ingredients for the flavorful kimchi base by hand. I remember being so bored. Today, whenever my mom visits one of my restaurants and watches our cooks turn a hundred pounds of Napa cabbage into kimchi every week, she's always stunned by how we make the process look so easy. (Thank God we have very powerful blenders.)

Kimchi is the single ingredient that often identifies Korean restaurants as such. So I guess, in that sense, we have Korean restaurants. But strangely, looking back, I see kimchi as the reason I ended up with Seif. Kimchi is what made me become an American.

KIMCHI BASE
traditional

Making kimchi consists of two basic steps: salting the ingredient you're using, which softens it and rids it of excess water, and layering it with a chili paste, which flavors the ingredient and provides nutrients for the healthy bacteria that help the fermentation process.

Our chili paste is fairly traditional; each component serves a specific role. The pear and the onion, which are both inherently sweet, serve as food for the bacteria that give kimchi its hallmark fermented flavor. The ginger and garlic provide flavor and funk, and the salted shrimp, sand lance sauce, and anchovy sauce balance the paste with their deep, earthy flavors. The chili is, of course, for heat and color. In general, kimchi gets spicier as you move southward in Korea. Since I grew up in Seoul, I got used to something in the middle of the Korean spice range.

This recipe makes enough base to use for the Spicy Napa Kimchi (page 151), Wrinkly Chayote Kimchi (page 162), and Cucumber Kimchi (page 160). If you're not making all three and have extra, smear the base on meats as a blackening rub before grilling. You can double this recipe if you want to make bigger batches of kimchi, but you need about this much volume to make it mix up properly in a regular-size blender, so don't be tempted to halve it.

Anchovy sauce has a deeper flavor than the sand lance sauce, so do try to find that, but you can substitute your favorite Thai or Vietnamese fish sauce for the sand lance sauce if necessary—just make sure you add a little at a time and taste as you go, because some fish sauces are saltier than others. You want the base to be well seasoned but not salty.

MAKES 1½ CUPS

2 tablespoons anchovy sauce
2 tablespoons sand lance sauce
½ peeled Asian pear, diced
½ yellow onion, diced

1 (1-inch) section peeled fresh ginger, sliced into ¼-inch-thick coins
3 cloves garlic
½ teaspoon salted shrimp
¾ cup coarse Korean chili flakes

1. **BLEND THE BASE.** In a heavy-duty blender or the bowl of a food processor, whirl together the anchovy sauce, sand lance sauce, and pear until smooth. Add the onion, and pulse until finely chopped. Add the ginger, garlic, and salted shrimp, and process until as smooth as possible, pausing occasionally to scrape down the lid and sides of the bowl. (It will be quite thick.) Add the chili flakes, and whirl until well blended. Let sit for 30 minutes for the chili flakes to become hydrated, then use immediately, or store in the refrigerator, covered, up to 1 month.

SPICY NAPA KIMCHI

everyday staple

If there's one kimchi that has overtaken the world's perception of Korean food, this is it: hearty Napa cabbage, fermented with a garlicky chili paste that has plenty of kick. Ours has the perfect textural ratio of crunchy cabbage stem, which winds up slightly sour, and leafy greens, which taste slightly more bitter.

While most kimchis are only fermented for a few days, this is the kind that in generations past was often stored in crocks underground to prevent spoilage in the summer and freezing in the winter. Over time, that practice has evolved into a whole industry devoted to proper temperature-controlled kimchi refrigeration, which leads to more predictable fermentation results. Today in Korea, folks often have either a dedicated chest freezer–style refrigerator for kimchi or a separate, specific section of their refrigerator for it, the way many American refrigerators have crisper and meat drawers. In either case, kimchi is usually kept long-term just above freezing, around 35 degrees F.

For our restaurants, we ferment our Napa kimchi for five to seven days at room temperature (65 to 68 degrees F) if it's going to be eaten straight up, but when we're going to use it in cooking, we ferment it for seven to ten days, because it gains a stronger flavor over time, which translates into sweetness once it's cooked. If you're making this for Revel's Funky, Spicy, Porky Pancakes (page 171) or Pork Kimchi Ragout (page 287), ferment it at least a full week before using.

You can press a piece of plastic into the top layer of kimchi after making it, as directed below, or follow tradition and cap the top layer of fermented cabbage with a thick smear of the kimchi base and a few stray softened cabbage leaves before covering.

MAKES 1 QUART

1 Napa cabbage (about 2 pounds)
¼ cup Korean coarse sea salt
½ cup Kimchi Base (page 149)

1. CUT THE CABBAGE. Slice the cabbage into quarters lengthwise, then trim the corner off the core of each cabbage, so you have about ¼ inch of core keeping all the leaves together.

2. SALT THE CABBAGE. Place one of the cabbage wedges pointy side up on a large cutting board. Using one hand to manage the cabbage and one hand to hold about a tablespoon of salt, flip through the cabbage leaves like pages of a book, depositing a bit of the salt on the white parts (but not the green leaves) of each and every leaf, all the way into the core. (As a general rule, if you're making a large batch of kimchi, you'll need

continued

about 2 tablespoons coarse salt per pound of cabbage.) Repeat with the remaining cabbage quarters and salt, then stuff the cabbage quarters into a large ziplock bag and seal.

3. LET THE CABBAGE SOFTEN. Let the cabbage rest in the bag at room temperature for about 4 hours, turning every hour or so. The salt will draw excess water out of the cabbage. Over time, the green parts should turn yellowish and the white stem portions should soften.

4. RINSE THE CABBAGE. Rinse the cabbage carefully in cold water, using your hands to make sure the salt is rinsed off both sides of every leaf. (The cabbage is clean enough when it tastes seasoned, instead of salty.) Using your hands, fold one cabbage quarter in half, leaf tip to core, with the largest leaves on the outside, and squeeze the excess water out with your hands. (You will crush the cabbage a little, which is fine.) Repeat with the remaining quarters, then place the cabbage in a colander set over a bowl and let drain for about 30 minutes.

5. SMEAR THE LEAVES WITH KIMCHI BASE. Place one cabbage quarter back on the cutting board, again with the inside of the cabbage facing up. Page through the cabbage again, this time using your working hand to smear a little of the kimchi base onto the top side of each leaf. (If you have sensitive skin, it's good to do this with gloves on.) Repeat with the remaining cabbage quarters and base.

Pack the kimchi carefully into a sealable quart-size container. Working with one quarter at a time, fold the cabbage in half, leaf tip to core, with the largest leaves on the outside, and pack it into the bottom of the container, pressing it in with your hands, so no air pockets remain between the leaves. Repeat with the remaining quarters, leaving about 1 inch of space at the top of the container. (The kimchi will expand as it ferments.) Cover the top layer of cabbage directly with a piece of plastic wrap to prevent air from getting to the kimchi, and put the lid on the container.

6. FERMENT THE KIMCHI. Let the kimchi sit at room temperature (65 to 68 degrees F) for 5 to 10 days—less time for a slightly milder flavor, or more for a stronger, more fermented flavor. (You can taste it along the way and decide how long you want it to ferment.) Transfer the kimchi to the refrigerator, where it will continue to ferment (but much more slowly). Serve after the first 5 days, or store it in the refrigerator, covered, for up to 1 year.

USING KOREAN COARSE SEA SALT

We use large flaked sea salt because it has better flavor than kosher salt and because the large flakes allow vegetables to give up their water more slowly, instead of all at once. The vegetables keep their shape better this way.

TURNIP WATER KIMCHI

mint, radishes

More akin to an American half-sour pickle than to what we think of as classic Korean kimchi, water kimchi is made by fermenting sturdy root vegetables with garlic, chilies, ginger, and salt in—you guessed it—plain old water. In Korea, it's a winter food, always served very cold in small bowls as a course on its own. (Sometimes, in Korea, you'll see it served with the liquid in frozen slush form on the bottom of the bowl, as if someone dumped out a kimchi snow cone.) You can serve it as is, with both the vegetables and the liquid in the bowl together, so you eat the solids and sip up the liquids, or you can serve it with cold somen or buckwheat noodles—just pour the liquid over the noodles and scoop the vegetables right on top.

The garlic, ginger, and chili flavors will come out a bit over time, but this isn't meant to be a particularly spicy dish. In fact, it's often how Korean kids learn to eat kimchi.

MAKES 1 QUART

1 large turnip (about 10 ounces), peeled, quartered, and cut into ¼-inch slices
1 tablespoon Korean coarse sea salt
Leaves from 3 big sprigs mint (about 15 leaves)
¼ cup julienned peeled fresh ginger

6 cloves garlic, sliced as thinly as possible
4 radishes, cut into ¼-inch rounds
1 Fresno chili (with the seeds intact), halved and cut into ¼-inch half moons
3 tablespoons fish sauce
2 tablespoons rice vinegar

1. **SALT THE TURNIPS.** Place the sliced turnips in a large bowl, sprinkle the salt on top, and mix until well blended. Set the turnips aside for 30 minutes; the salt will draw excess water out of the turnips.

2. **RINSE THE TURNIPS.** After 30 minutes, rinse the turnips in three changes of fresh cold water. (The turnips are clean enough when they taste seasoned, instead of salty.) Place the turnips in a colander set over a bowl and let drain for about 30 minutes.

3. **MAKE THE KIMCHI.** Transfer the turnips to a quart-size container, and add the mint, ginger, garlic, radishes, chili, fish sauce, and rice vinegar. Add water until it comes to about ½ inch below the rim of the container. (We usually ferment the kimchi in layers, and mix everything together before serving.) Press a layer of plastic wrap directly on the surface of the liquid to prevent any air from reaching the vegetables.

4. **FERMENT THE KIMCHI.** Cover the kimchi and let it sit at room temperature (65 to 68 degrees F) for 3 days. (You can taste it along the way; it will begin to taste a little sour after the first 24 hours or so.) Transfer the kimchi to the refrigerator, where it will continue to ferment (but much more slowly). Serve after the first 3 days, or store it in the refrigerator, covered, for 1 to 2 months.

WHITE STUFFED KIMCHI

pine nuts, currants

While kimchis have been around for literally thousands of years, made with salt and fermented soybeans well before refrigeration, today's chili-loaded version, which is often the kimchi stereotype, is only about five hundred years old. (That's when chilies were introduced to Korea). White kimchis—so called because they contain no chili—don't last as long, and they became considered royal cuisine because only those wealthy enough to buy food that might spoil could purchase it.

Today, spoilage is of course much less of an issue, but white kimchi still tends to be seen as a fancier dish, made with more expensive ingredients. At Joule, we make a version with pine nuts and black currants and ferment it in a little cabbage-wrapped package (with just a hint of fresh green Korean chili, because the spice adds a nice balance). It has a bright, tart flavor that surprisingly pairs quite well with champagne when served cold. As it warms to room temperature, the flavor becomes deeper and funkier, which makes it a good match for heavier main courses.

Although you technically only need a half pound of cabbage for this recipe, using a larger cabbage, around two pounds, yields enough whole leaves that are long enough to form the package more easily, so it's what we prefer using. You can use any leftover cabbage to make Spicy Napa Kimchi (page 151) or sauté it.

The short, wide, half pint–size containers sour cream or cottage cheese come in are perfect for these.

MAKES 2 FOUR-INCH KIMCHI CAKES FOR 8 SERVINGS

FOR THE KIMCHI:

1 Napa cabbage (about 2 pounds),
  cut into quarters

¼ cup Korean coarse sea salt

1 small carrot, finely shredded or julienned
  and cut into 1-inch sections

1 large green Korean chili, seeded, finely
  shredded or julienned and cut into 1-inch
  sections

2 tablespoons (2-inch sections) garlic
  chives

1 tablespoon toasted pine nuts

1 tablespoon black currants

FOR THE BASE:

1 tablespoon anchovy sauce

1 tablespoon sand lance sauce

¼ peeled Asian pear, diced

¼ yellow onion, diced

2 large cloves garlic

1 (½-inch) section of peeled fresh ginger,
  cut into ¼-inch-thick coins

½ teaspoon salted shrimp

½ teaspoon rice vinegar

continued

cut into the stuffed kimchi in front of guests for a big reveal

1. **SALT THE CABBAGE.** First, trim the corners off the cores of the cabbage quarters, so you have about ¼ inch of core keeping all the leaves together. Place the cabbage wedges pointy side up on a large cutting board. Using one hand to manage the cabbage and one hand to hold the tablespoon of salt, flip through the cabbage leaves like pages of a book, depositing a bit of the salt on the white parts (but not the green leaves) of each and every leaf, all the way into the core. Stuff the cabbage quarters into a large ziplock bag and seal. Let the cabbage rest in the bag at room temperature for about 4 hours, turning every hour or so. The salt will draw excess water out of the cabbage. Over time, the green parts should turn yellowish and the white stem portions of the cabbage should soften.

2. **RINSE THE CABBAGE.** Rinse the cabbage carefully in cold water, using your hands to make sure the salt is rinsed off both sides of every leaf. (The cabbage is clean enough when it tastes seasoned, instead of salty.) Using your hands, fold each cabbage quarter in half, leaf tip to core with the largest leaves on the outside, and squeeze the excess water out with your hands. (You will crush the cabbage a little, which is fine.) Place the cabbage in a colander set over a bowl and let drain for about 30 minutes.

3. **MAKE THE KIMCHI BASE.** In a heavy-duty blender or the bowl of a food processor, whirl together the anchovy sauce, sand lance sauce, and pear until smooth. Add the onion, and pulse until finely chopped. Add the garlic, ginger, salted shrimp, and vinegar and process until as smooth as possible, pausing occasionally to scrape down the lid and sides of the bowl. (It will be quite thick.) Transfer the base to a small mixing bowl.

4. **MAKE THE FILLING.** Cut the core off the cabbage quarters so all the leaves are free. Starting with the smallest leaves of one quarter, julienne enough cabbage to measure about ⅓ cup and add it to the base. Stir in the carrot, chili, garlic chives, pine nuts, and currants, and set aside.

5. **FORM THE PACKAGE.** Working with the prettiest big cabbage leaves you can find in each cabbage quarter, line two half pint–size sealable containers with cabbage, fanning out the leaves to cover the bottoms and sides of the containers. (It's fine if the cabbage pieces overlap and best if they hang over the edges by a few inches in all directions, so they can be wrapped over the filling.) Divide the filling between the two cabbage packages, pat it into a flat disc, and fold any extra cabbage back over the filling, so you're effectively wrapping the filling like a present, again fanning the leaves out where you can. Add as many additional cabbage leaves as necessary to cover the filling completely. Cover the top layer of cabbage in each container directly with a piece of plastic wrap, to prevent air from getting to the kimchi, and put the lids on the containers.

6. **FERMENT THE KIMCHI.** Let the kimchi sit at room temperature (65 to 68 degrees F) for 3 days, letting any built-up gas out daily if the lid looks puffy. Transfer the kimchi to the refrigerator, where it will continue to ferment (but much more slowly). Serve as soon as it's chilled, inverted onto a plate and cut into quarters (like cutting into a wedge of cheese), or store it in the refrigerator, covered, for up to 1 month.

CHICORY AND APPLE KIMCHI
golden raisin

This sweet, garlicky quick kimchi is probably more aptly described as a salad; you can serve it as a small bite at the beginning of a meal or as a palate cleanser at the end. At Revel, we put it on top of a fennel salad, but at home I eat it straight out of the container. The mixture of tart apples, sweet pickled golden raisins, and bitter chicory leaves seems to encapsulate everything I want in a snack.

Serve it as a salad, or as a pickle with grilled meat or even fish, like the Broiled Mackerel (page 217).

MAKES 8 CUPS

FOR THE RAISINS:
½ cup rice vinegar
¼ cup sugar
¼ cup water
½ cup golden raisins

FOR THE KIMCHI:
3 Granny Smith apples
1 bunch chicory (about 8 ounces),
   cut into bite-size pieces (about 4 cups)
8 cloves garlic, very thinly sliced
¼ cup roughly chopped peeled
   fresh ginger
1 tablespoon anchovy sauce
1 tablespoon sand lance sauce
1 teaspoon chipotle chili powder

1. **PICKLE THE RAISINS.** In a 2-quart pot, stir together the vinegar, sugar, and water. Bring to a boil over high heat, stirring occasionally to help the sugar dissolve. Add the raisins, then transfer the mixture to a small nonreactive container. Let cool to room temperature.

2. **MAKE THE KIMCHI.** Cut the apples into quarters, cut out the cores, then cut each quarter into 4 slices. In a large bowl, place the apples along with the chicory, garlic, ginger, anchovy sauce, sand lance sauce, and chipotle powder. Pour the raisins and their liquid on top, and massage the ingredients together until well blended. (Donning gloves will prevent your hands from smelling fishy.) Pack the kimchi into a large sealable container, pressing gently as you go, leaving about 1 inch of space at the top of the container. Cover the top layer of kimchi directly with a piece of plastic wrap to prevent air from getting to the kimchi, and put the lid on the container.

3. **FERMENT THE KIMCHI.** Let the kimchi sit at room temperature (65 to 68 degrees F) for 1 to 2 days—less time for a slightly milder flavor, or more for a stronger, more fermented flavor. (You can taste it along the way and decide how long you want it to ferment.) Transfer the kimchi to the refrigerator, where it will continue to ferment (but much more slowly). Serve immediately, or store it in the refrigerator, covered, for up to 1 week.

CUCUMBER KIMCHI

grilled shiitake mushrooms

Kimchi is always fermented and is spicy more often than not, but there's a whole sector of Korean side dishes that, unlike traditional kimchi, contain Korean chili paste, or *gochujang*, which makes them much spicier but also a little sweeter. This version, a take on Korean cucumber kimchi, gets its smokiness from grilled fresh shiitake mushrooms. It's great made with any thin-skinned cucumber. Use smaller varieties labeled Persian, Korean, or Kirby cucumbers when you can find them—because they retain their crunch—or regular seedless English cucumbers if you can't.

MAKES 1 QUART

1½ pounds seedless cucumbers

2 tablespoons Korean coarse sea salt

1 pound fresh shiitake mushrooms, stems removed

2 tablespoons canola oil

Kosher salt and freshly ground black pepper

⅓ cup Kimchi Base (page 149)

2 tablespoons Korean chili paste

1 cup (2-inch pieces) garlic chives

1. **SALT THE CUCUMBERS.** Slice the cucumbers in half lengthwise and scoop out the seeds (a spoon, ice cream scoop, or melon baller works well). Cut the halves into 2-inch sections, then cut each section into ½-inch slices lengthwise. Place the sliced cucumbers in a large bowl, sprinkle the sea salt on top, and mix until well blended. Set the cucumbers aside for 30 minutes; the salt will draw excess water out of the cucumbers.

2. **MEANWHILE, GRILL THE SHIITAKE.** Preheat a gas or charcoal grill to medium heat, about 375 degrees F. In a medium bowl, toss the mushrooms with the oil and kosher salt and pepper. When the grill is hot, add the mushrooms, and grill for 4 to 6 minutes, turning once or twice, or until the mushrooms have lost some of their water and are marked on each side. Transfer the mushrooms back to the bowl and set aside to cool.

3. **RINSE THE CUCUMBERS.** After 30 minutes, rinse the cucumbers in three changes of fresh cold water. (The cucumber is clean enough when it tastes seasoned, instead of salty.) Using your hands, working with a small handful of cucumbers at a time, squeeze the water out of the cucumbers (you will crush the cucumber sticks a little, which is fine) and transfer them to the mixing bowl with the mushrooms.

4. **MAKE THE KIMCHI.** In a medium mixing bowl, whisk together the kimchi base and the chili paste, then add the garlic chives. Add the cucumbers and shiitake, stir to blend, then pack the kimchi into a quart-size container, tapping the container on the counter as you go to prevent the kimchi from having large air pockets, leaving about 1 inch of space at the top of the container. Cover the top layer of vegetables directly with a piece of plastic wrap, to prevent air from getting to the kimchi, and put the lid on the container.

5. FERMENT THE KIMCHI. Let the kimchi sit at room temperature (65 to 68 degrees F) for 2 days. (You can taste it along the way; it will begin to taste a little sour after the first 24 hours or so.) Transfer the kimchi to the refrigerator, where it will continue to ferment (but much more slowly). Serve after the first 2 days, or store it in the refrigerator, covered, for 1 to 2 months.

WRINKLY CHAYOTE KIMCHI

thai basil

In Korea, there's a long tradition of drying vegetables at the end of harvest time—par-drying, really, because they're dried until they're compact and chewy but not actually hard like a banana chip. Take chayote: when you dehydrate thick slices (either in a food dehydrator or in a low oven) each bite has deep, green flavor, with much more sweetness, and the texture becomes something like a dried apple's. Smothered in kimchi base, the chayote rehydrates with intense flavor while still maintaining a pleasantly chewy texture.

While kimchi is usually left to ferment for a few days at room temperature, "quick kimchi" usually refers to the type of kimchi you consume immediately, before fermentation. This is technically quick kimchi, but, because it takes a few hours to dehydrate the chayote, it's a bit of a misnomer. In any case, it's delicious.

To prep the chayote, peel it under cold running water to rinse away the sticky juices that leak out when you cut it, then slice it in half and cut out the seed and any white or woody parts. Cut the remaining flesh into slices, like you would an apple.

MAKES 2 CUPS

4 chayote (about 2½ pounds total), peeled, halved, seeded, and cut into ½-inch slices

2 tablespoons Korean coarse sea salt

½ cup packed chopped Thai basil (from about ½ bunch)

1 jalapeño pepper, seeded and julienned

⅓ cup Kimchi Base (page 149)

2 tablespoons rice vinegar

1. **SALT THE CHAYOTE.** Place the sliced chayote in a large bowl, sprinkle the salt on top, and mix until well blended. Set the chayote aside for 30 minutes; the salt will draw excess water out of the chayote.

2. **RINSE THE CHAYOTE.** After 30 minutes, rinse the chayote in three changes of fresh cold water. (The chayote is clean enough when it tastes seasoned, instead of salty.) Let the chayote drain in a colander for a few minutes.

3. **DRY THE CHAYOTE.** Dry the chayote in a food dehydrator for 3 hours at 115 degrees F. (If you want to dry it in an oven, preheat the oven to 170 degrees F, or as low as it goes. Arrange the chayote slices in a single layer on a cooling rack set over a baking sheet, and dry for approximately 6 to 8 hours, flipping the chayote slices once about halfway through. They should be shriveled and dry to the touch but still flexible.)

4. **MAKE THE KIMCHI.** In a medium mixing bowl, add the basil, pepper, kimchi base, and vinegar to the chayote, and stir to blend. Serve immediately, or pack the kimchi into a quart-size container and store it in the refrigerator (where it will ferment slowly), covered, up to 1 month.

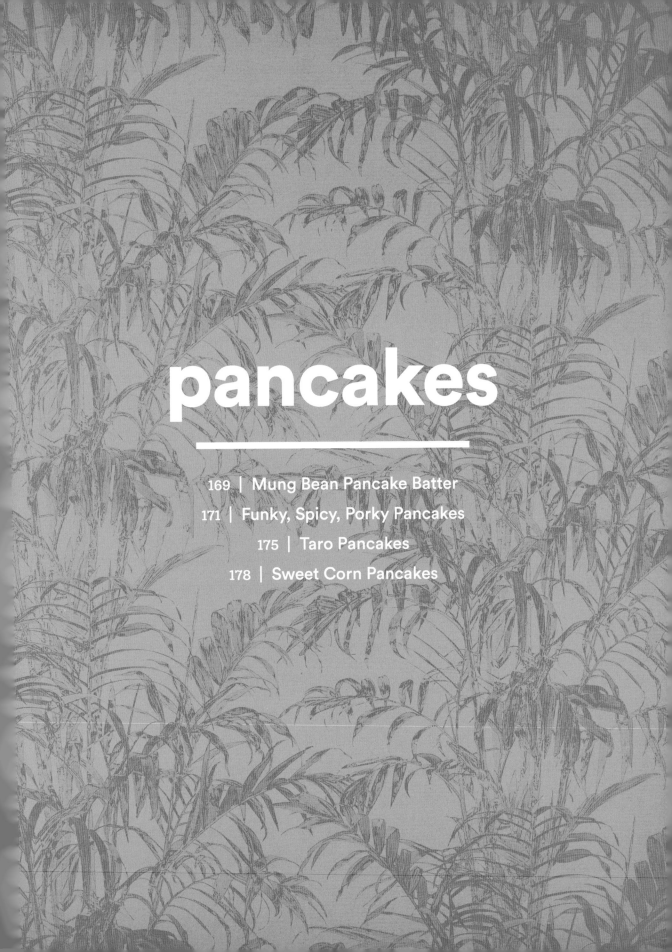

pancakes

My family is gigantic. When we go to Korea, we have to see everyone. My mom has every meal planned out before we get there, so from the time we arrive, we are herded from meal to meal on her clock. Seif calls it the hardest marathon there is—and that's coming from a guy who runs them regularly. We eat mostly in the type of monster mall restaurants Koreans tend to love for big gatherings. It's always delicious. But no matter where we take Seif, his favorite food is always the last stop we make, late into the night, when dinner sometimes fades into karaoke. The dirt-cheap street meals—often simple scallion or seafood pancakes—are always his favorite. It's Korean food at its best, he says.

Modern cooking is usually a study in components. But unlike most of our food—where things are layered on top of each other in carefully executed contrasts—pancakes are one of the few dishes we make where the flavors are mixed together ahead of time. The goal, besides their glistening crisp exterior, is to taste everything in one bite. In that sense, it can be the hardest dish for new cooks to get right (see Pancake Theory, page 14), and it's always the hardest seasonal dish for us to conceptualize. Ultimately, it's simple food, but the balance within is crucial. Maybe that's why I like them so much; they are an edible representation of how we have to balance our restaurants, our marriage, our kids, and our crazy families without necessarily having the luxury of compartmentalizing each aspect of our lives. It's a hot mess, but if it tastes good, you know you got it right.

MUNG BEAN PANCAKE BATTER

Mung beans—the small precursors to the bean sprouts common in many Asian cuisines—make the batter for the flavorful Korean-style pancakes, called *bindaettuck*, that bring regulars back to Revel week after week. Those pancakes are hallmarks of our cooking with their nutty, savory flavor and crisp exterior, but at their heart, they're shockingly simple. Use this recipe to make the batter used in the pages that follow. Note that this makes just over two cups of batter, which should be the right amount for any of the other recipes.

Not all mung beans are created equal. Some will soak up more water than others, which is why when you soak and blend them as directed here, you might not always end up with the same amount of batter. This is fine; all the recipes are designed to work with whatever batter you get starting from one cup of raw beans.

Look at your batter before you use it. It should look like thick pancake batter with a slightly yellow hue. If it looks grainy or chunky, let it sit for another thirty minutes or so for the beans to hydrate more, and then reblend it until smooth. A heavy-duty blender works best.

Make sure you find dried yellow mung beans (often labeled *moong daal* in Asian or Indian grocery stores), which are peeled, rather than the unpeeled green kind, which won't work well for this recipe.

And to answer a question we are asked every single lunch and dinner service at Revel: yes, these are gluten-free.

Note: We like to serve all our pancakes piping hot, but if you'd prefer, you can cook them all ahead. If you're going to serve them immediately after cooking, keep the first pancakes warm in a 300-degree-F oven until serving time. If you cook the pancakes the day before, they can be reheated in a single layer on a baking sheet in a 400-degree-F oven for five to ten minutes before serving.

MAKES A GENEROUS 2 CUPS

1 cup split yellow mung beans
2½ cups cold tap water, divided
1 teaspoon kosher salt

our savory pancakes start with this!

1. **SOAK THE BEANS.** In a medium bowl, soak the beans in 2 cups of the cold water for 1 hour. They should increase in volume by about 50 percent. Drain off any excess water.

2. **MAKE THE BATTER.** In a heavy-duty blender or the bowl of a food processor, combine the beans and the remaining ½ cup cold water. Blend for 15 to 30 seconds on high speed, or until the batter is very smooth.

FUNKY, SPICY, PORKY PANCAKES

pork belly, kimchi

When Seif and I were getting to know each other in New York, we lived very predictable lives. We usually spent twelve to sixteen hours a day, every day, in the kitchen. Then when we got off work, usually around one in the morning, we'd take the train together to Koreatown, near the Garment District. There I introduced him to some of the foods I missed from my upbringing—foods like rich pork belly pancakes, which have full slices of tender, braised meat embedded into one side of each pancake. Today, they're staples at both Revel and Revelry and might be the one dish on our menu that is closest to what you might find on a street corner in Seoul today.

MAKES 4 (6- TO 7-INCH) PANCAKES

FOR THE BATTER:

1 cup loosely packed bean sprouts

1 recipe Mung Bean Pancake Batter (page 169)

1 cup packed roughly chopped kimchi, such as Spicy Napa Kimchi (page 151)

4 green onions (white and light-green parts only), chopped

2 tablespoons fish sauce

2 tablespoons coarse Korean chili flakes

1 tablespoon finely chopped confited garlic (see Quick Garlic Confit, page 172)

1 teaspoon kosher salt

FOR FRYING:

½ cup canola oil, plus more if needed

FOR SERVING:

8 slices Braised Pork Belly (recipe follows)

1. **MAKE THE BATTER.** First, bring a small saucepan of water to a boil. Add the bean sprouts, cook for 15 seconds, drain, and transfer to a medium bowl. Add the mung bean batter, kimchi, green onions, fish sauce, chili flakes, garlic, and salt and mix to blend thoroughly. (If you'd like to make the batter ahead of time, you can make it up to 24 hours ahead and store in the refrigerator, covered, but add the salt just before frying.)

2. **PANFRY THE PANCAKES.** Heat an 8-inch nonstick skillet over medium heat. (You can use a regular skillet also; it's just a little more difficult to clean.) Add 1 tablespoon of the oil, and turn the pan to coat the bottom evenly with the oil. Add about ¾ cup of the batter to the pan, spread the batter into a thin layer 6 or 7 inches in diameter, and cook, undisturbed, until you can see the outer edges of the pancake begin to brown, about 2 minutes. While the pancake cooks, place two slices of pork belly over the raw side of the pancake and press them in gently. Using a large spatula, work around the edges of the pancake to loosen it from the pan, then carefully turn the pancake and flatten it gently with the spatula, pressing it down if it bubbles on one side. Add another tablespoon of the oil and cook another 1 to 2 minutes, until the pancake is golden brown on the second side.

Transfer the pancake to a paper towel–lined plate to drain for a moment or two, then serve hot, pork side up, cut into wedges. Repeat with the remaining batter, using as much oil as necessary each time to keep a ⅛-inch layer on the bottom of the pan, until all the batter has been used. See the note on page 169 for serving tips.

continued

QUICK GARLIC CONFIT

Our confited garlic is simmered in oil on the stovetop, which gives it a roasted flavor. It's also convenient for us, because it's much faster—and each clove holds its shape better than when oven-roasted. Place a head's worth of peeled garlic cloves in a small saucepan, and add enough canola oil to cover the cloves completely (about ¾ cup). Heat the pan over medium heat, and cook the garlic at a bare simmer (you may have to adjust the temperature) for 10 to 15 minutes, or until the garlic is evenly tanned and soft inside. (Lighter cloves cooked over lower heat will have a bit less flavor than darker cloves. Note that burnt garlic will turn bitter, though.) Using a fork, transfer the roasted cloves to a paper towel–lined plate to cool. Once the garlic has cooled, you can use it for flavoring meats; soups; stews; Funky, Spicy, Porky Pancakes (page 171); or the sauce for Black Sesame Noodles (page 239). To store extra garlic, cool the garlic and oil separately, then return the garlic to the oil and refrigerate, covered, for up to 2 weeks.

braised pork belly

Be sure to purchase pork belly with the skin removed or remove it yourself. (You can use it for the Pickled Pork Rind, page 277.)

MAKES ABOUT ½ POUND

1 pound skinless pork belly
½ large onion, chopped
1 small carrot, cut into ½-inch pieces
1 large celery rib, cut into ½-inch pieces
½ cup garlic cloves
2 tablespoons Korean bean paste

1. **PREHEAT THE OVEN.** Preheat the oven to 350 degrees F.

2. **BRAISE THE PORK.** In an ovenproof 3-quart soup pot with a lid, combine the pork, onion, carrot, celery, garlic, and bean paste. Add enough water to cover the meat, cover, and cook for about 2 hours, or until the pork is tender enough to pierce easily with a fork but not falling apart.

3. **SLICE THE PORK.** Let the pork belly cool to room temperature in the liquid (or cool, then refrigerate in the liquid overnight), then cut into ⅛-inch slices (from any end) for the pancake. (If the pork seems difficult to cut, chill it for 1 to 2 hours, covered, and try slicing it again.)

classic Korean flavor all in one bite

TARO PANCAKES

green curry, apple chutney

Since Revel opened, we have included a wide variety of vegetables in our pancakes. While almost anything can be used, a really wet vegetable makes the pancakes too heavy and almost mushy, which means drier root vegetables (which also retain some texture when cooked) are often our favorites. The taro and yucca in these pancakes fit the bill. Created by Nikki, a former Revel cook with a Thai background, these are paired with a gentle, floral green curry paste we make in-house. It's become a favorite.

Note that both taro root and yucca root, which may be new to your kitchen, have to be peeled before they are grated. Taro has a barky exterior that must be cut or peeled off, while yucca has a tough, waxy edge that is easiest to cut off with a small, sharp knife. If the yucca has brown spots on the inside or isn't pure white once you peel it (or smells like mothballs), it's going bad. Shred the taro and yucca on the largest holes of a traditional box grater, like you would carrots.

For the best use of time, start soaking the mung beans for the batter according to the directions on page 169 first and make the curry paste and garnishes for the pancake while they soak.

MAKES 4 (6- TO 7-INCH) PANCAKES

FOR THE BATTER:

1 recipe Mung Bean Pancake Batter (page 169)

¾ cup packed grated taro root

½ cup packed grated yucca root

1 medium shallot, thinly sliced (about ⅓ cup total)

⅓ cup plus 1 tablespoon Revel's Green Curry Paste (page 69) or store-bought Thai-style green curry paste

3 tablespoons soy sauce

1 teaspoon kosher salt

FOR FRYING:

½ cup canola oil, plus more if needed

FOR SERVING:

Coconut Crème Fraîche (recipe follows)

Apple Chutney (recipe follows)

1. MAKE THE BATTER. In a medium mixing bowl, stir together the mung bean batter, taro, yucca, shallot, curry paste, soy sauce, and salt. Use your hands, if necessary, to make sure the root vegetables don't clump together. (If you'd like to make the batter ahead of time, you can make it up to 24 hours ahead and store in the refrigerator, covered, but add the salt just before frying.)

2. FRY THE PANCAKES. Heat an 8-inch nonstick skillet over medium heat. (You can use a regular skillet also; it's just a little more difficult to clean.) Add 1 tablespoon of the oil, and turn the pan to coat the bottom evenly with the oil. Add about ¾ cup of the batter to the pan, spread the batter into a thin layer 6 or 7 inches in diameter, and cook,

continued

undisturbed, until you can see the outer edges of the pancake begin to brown, about 2 minutes. Using a large spatula, work around the edges of the pancake to loosen it from the pan, then carefully turn the pancake and flatten it gently with the spatula, pressing it down if it bubbles on one side. Add another tablespoon of the oil and cook another 1 to 2 minutes, until the pancake is golden brown on the second side.

Transfer the pancake to a paper towel–lined plate to drain for a moment, then serve hot, cut into wedges, with a couple tablespoons of the chutney and about 1 tablespoon of crème fraîche heaped on top. Repeat with the remaining batter, using as much oil as necessary each time to keep a ⅛-inch layer on the bottom of the pan, until all the batter has been used. See the note on page 169 for serving tips.

coconut crème fraîche

Coconut cream is the thick white part in a can of coconut milk, which usually settles to the bottom of the can, so you can scoop it right off if you open the can from the bottom. You can usually get a half cup of the cream out of one (fourteen-ounce) can of regular (not light!) coconut milk, but I often buy two cans in case I get a lower-fat batch. Mixed with crème fraîche, it makes a sweetish, tangy topping that complements this pancake's spice quite well.

MAKES 1 CUP

½ cup crème fraîche
½ cup coconut cream

1. **MIX THE CRÈME FRAÎCHE.** In the bowl of a stand mixer fitted with the whisk attachment, whip together the crème fraîche and coconut cream on medium speed until fluffy and well combined, about 1 minute. Set aside until ready to use.

apple chutney

In the United States, it's relatively common to pair winter root vegetables like rutabaga, parsnips, and celeriac with apples, but not so in Asia. We take that vegetable-apple combination (using Asian root vegetables) and apply it to Korean pancakes here. That's why, while this dish might seem very unusual, it actually tastes very familiar.

If you have extra chutney when you're done with the pancakes, try it over rice or with the barbecued pork belly (see page 203).

MAKES 1½ CUPS

1 medium Granny Smith apple, cored and cut into 1-inch chunks
2 tablespoons plus 1 teaspoon sugar, divided
1 teaspoon canola oil
1 small shallot, thinly sliced

2 tablespoons sake
2 tablespoons rice vinegar
1 teaspoon finely chopped peeled fresh ginger
5 (⅛-inch) slices Fresno chili, halved
Kosher salt

1. **BAKE THE APPLE.** Preheat the oven to 350 degrees F. In a small baking dish, toss the apple with 1 tablespoon of the sugar, and bake for 8 to 10 minutes, until the apple's peel begins to soften. Set aside.

2. **MAKE THE PICKLING MIXTURE.** In a small skillet, heat the oil over medium-low heat, add the shallot, and cook, covered, for 2 or 3 minutes, until the shallot begins to soften. Add the sake and cook for about 1 minute more, stirring, until most of the liquid is gone, then add the vinegar, ginger, chili, salt to taste, and the remaining 1 tablespoon plus 1 teaspoon of sugar, and stir to blend. Transfer the mixture, along with the baked apple, to a small nonreactive container. Let sit for at least 1 hour before serving. Store the chutney in the refrigerator for up to 1 week, covered.

SWEET CORN PANCAKES

summer grilled pickle, corn flakes

At our restaurants, we like our food to reflect the season; these pancakes, made with fresh corn, poblano peppers, and freshly toasted spices, make a great summer meal on their own. You can follow the recipe as it appears below, or, like we do, let your imagination take you where your stomach wants to go, adding ground chorizo, for example, or other leftover grilled vegetables. It's a very flexible batter; as long as it has the consistency of thick corn bread batter, it should do well in the pan. The secret to a great crunch on the second side? Regular old corn flakes.

MAKES 4 (6- TO 7-INCH) PANCAKES

FOR THE BATTER:

1 recipe Mung Bean Pancake Batter (page 169)

2 cups fresh corn kernels (from 2 large or 3 small ears of corn)

1 large poblano pepper, seeded and finely chopped

⅓ cup plus 1 tablespoon medium-grind yellow cornmeal

1 heaping tablespoon finely chopped fresh oregano

1 tablespoon plus 1 teaspoon kosher salt

1 teaspoon ground toasted coriander (see Toasting Spices, page 53)

½ to ¾ teaspoon chipotle chili powder

½ teaspoon ground toasted cumin (see Toasting Spices, page 53)

FOR FRYING:

½ cup canola oil, plus more if needed

2½ cups flaked corn cereal

FOR SERVING:

2 cups Summer Grilled Pickles (page 132)

1. MAKE THE BATTER. In a medium mixing bowl, blend together the mung bean batter, corn, pepper, cornmeal, oregano, salt, coriander, chili powder, and cumin.

2. FRY THE PANCAKES. Heat an 8-inch nonstick skillet over medium heat. Add 1 tablespoon of the oil, and turn the pan to coat the bottom evenly with the oil. Add about 1 cup of the batter to the pan, spread the batter into a thin layer 6 or 7 inches in diameter, then add about a quarter of the cornflakes in an even layer, right on top of the batter. Cook the pancake, undisturbed, until you can see the outer edges of the pancake begin to brown, about 2 minutes. Using a large spatula, work around the edges of the pancake to loosen it from the pan, then carefully turn the pancake and flatten it gently with the spatula, pressing it down. Add another tablespoon of the oil and cook another 1 to 2 minutes, until the pancake is golden brown on the second side.

Transfer the pancake to a paper towel–lined plate to drain for a moment or two, then serve hot, corn flake side up, cut into wedges, with a big scoop of pickles piled on top. Repeat with the remaining batter, using as much oil as necessary each time to keep a ⅛-inch layer on the bottom of the pan, until all the batter has been used. See the note on page 169 for serving tips.

think outside the (cereal) box

dumplings

Everyone always assumes our kids are the most adventurous eaters on the planet because they have chefs for parents. Even though both of them went through (or are, ahem, still going through) an all-white foods phase, there was always one exception: dumplings. They have always eaten dumplings, which means Seif and I have often resorted to tricking them into eating the things wrapped inside—even if the fillings might be speckled with green.

Adults aren't that different; dumplings are the ultimate taste vessel. Traditionally filled with a variety of meats and vegetables in Korea, we extend their role to include grains and cheeses wrapped in intensely flavorful doughs, always veering into totally new territory and folding in flavors from around the globe. On the outside, they look familiar and unassuming, which means that even first-time customers will always order the dumplings. (Not even the ruddy-colored dough wrapper we made for our pork-blood sausage dumplings at Revel scared people.) You'll see we make some of our doughs with the traditional oil method but also with butter or yeast. Start with the Basic Dumpling Dough (following page). Once you get the hang of it, go wild. And if you're really ready for fun, bring some kids along.

BASIC DUMPLING DOUGH

Korean dumplings are cousins to Japanese gyoza and Chinese potstickers, but they are rarely folded into pleats at the top like those are and are often made using a slightly thicker dough. Ours aren't necessarily traditional, but we do start with a soft wheat flour–based dough we roll thin, cut into circles, and fold around savory fillings (like the Shrimp and Bacon Dumplings, page 191) before panfrying. They've been especially popular at Revel, where our dumpling menu is always changing, depending on what's in markets and what bits of inspiration—seaweed! saffron!—we're adding to the dough.

When we opened Revel in 2010, our line cooks made dumpling dough at the end of service each night, as the stove cooled and we began our nightly preparation for the next day. We called it "four dough," referring to the four quarts of flour (about two kilograms) that we would use for the batch. At that time, we kneaded every batch by hand, so the shorter cooks—anyone under six feet tall—would get out milk crates to stand on, so they had enough leverage to knead the giant balls of dough. Each batch made a lot of dumplings, but we still had to make the dough every other night, at least.

Today, we have two prep cooks making "sixteen dough" five days a week in a big Hobart mixer we bought on Craigslist for one thousand dollars. (It's one of the most important machines in the restaurant.) You'll notice our technique follows the traditional Italian method for ravioli, except that dumpling dough is a "hard dough," which means it has less water than Italian-style pasta dough. It's also much more difficult to work and knead when using cold water (which is why we always start with warm water).

Like the pancakes and noodles we create each season, we like adding flavors to our dumpling dough—anything from ground spices and seeds to miso paste and pureed herbs. This is a basic dough for you to start with. In most cases, you can add what you'd like without changing the master recipe, keeping in mind that if you add a liquid, you should subtract it from the total amount of water you use in the initial mixing stages. You can also use this dough in place of any of the other dumpling doughs in this chapter.

We always joke that you could fill dumplings with anything and people would eat them. While it's true to a certain extent, when you decide what to use as a filling for this dough, keep in mind that the best fillings have a balance of moisture—they need to be dry enough to be used easily as a filling but moist enough so that each bite is juicy.

Before you begin, see Dumpling and Noodle Basics (page 75).

MAKES 1½ POUNDS DOUGH, OR ENOUGH FOR 3 TO 4 DOZEN DUMPLINGS,
DEPENDING ON ROLLING TECHNIQUE

3 cups all-purpose flour, plus more for
  kneading and rolling the dough
1 teaspoon kosher salt

1 cup warm water
1 tablespoon canola oil

1. **MAKE THE DOUGH.** In a large bowl, whisk together the flour and salt. Make a small well in the center of the dry ingredients, then add the water and oil to the well. Using your hands or a spoon, mix the ingredients until they cling together in a shaggy mass, then pat the dough together, transfer it to a clean lightly floured surface, and knead until smooth. (See Making Dough by Hand, page 75, for more detailed instructions; see Mixing with a Machine, page 77, if you'd prefer to work with a stand mixer.) Wrap the dough well in plastic and set aside to rest at room temperature for about 30 minutes before rolling it out for dumplings (see Making Dumplings, page 84).

CURRIED DUMPLINGS

beef, potato

When Paolo, a sous chef at Trove, tested the butter dough for kimchi empanadas, the result was quite different from the traditional dumpling recipe—the dough turned flaky, almost like pie pastry. Today, we use his butter dough at Trove, and we stuff the dumplings with pork trotter and caramelized kimchi.

This recipe is a take on that, sent on a detour through Korean curry, where the combination of meat and potatoes is common. The turmeric gives the dough a glorious sunny hue, but be warned: it can turn a pale wooden counter yellow in a heartbeat. Also, because it's made with butter, the dough changes as it cools and gets stiff when refrigerated. It's best to roll out at room temperature.

Before you begin, see Dumpling and Noodle Basics (page 75).

MAKES 3 DOZEN DUMPLINGS

FOR THE FILLING:

1½ cups Korean coarse sea salt
1 russet potato (about 8 ounces)
½ pound ground beef chuck
1½ teaspoons kosher salt
2 cloves garlic, finely chopped
2 teaspoons finely chopped peeled
   fresh ginger
1½ teaspoons Madras curry powder
1 teaspoon finely chopped fresh
   Italian parsley
½ teaspoon ground toasted cumin
   (see Toasting Spices, page 53)
½ teaspoon cayenne pepper

FOR THE DOUGH:

2½ cups all-purpose flour, plus more for
   kneading and rolling the dough
1 teaspoon ground turmeric
1 teaspoon kosher salt
⅓ cup cold water
1 large egg
6 tablespoons (¾ stick) unsalted butter,
   melted and cooled slightly

FOR FRYING:

Canola oil

1. PARBAKE THE POTATO IN SALT. Preheat the oven to 300 degrees F. Pour the sea salt into a baking dish just large enough to fit the potato, then nestle the potato into the salt. Bake for 30 minutes, then remove and allow to cool completely.

2. MAKE THE DOUGH. In a large bowl, first whisk together the flour, turmeric, and salt. Next, in a separate bowl, whisk together the water and egg until uniform in color, then add the melted butter and whisk to blend. Make a small well in the center of the dry ingredients, then add the egg mixture to the well. Using your hands or a spoon, mix the ingredients until they cling together in a shaggy mass, then pat the dough together, transfer it to a clean lightly floured surface, and knead until smooth. (See Making Dough by Hand, page 75, for more detailed instructions; or see Mixing with a Machine, page 77, if you'd prefer to work with a stand mixer.) Wrap the dough well in plastic and set aside to rest at room temperature for about 30 minutes.

3. MAKE THE FILLING. Peel the cooled potato, then grate it on the largest holes of a box grater and transfer the grated potato to a medium mixing bowl. Add the beef, salt, garlic, ginger, curry powder, parsley, cumin, and cayenne. Using gloved hands—really, hands work best—blend the mixture until very well incorporated. Cover and chill until ready to use.

4. MAKE THE DUMPLINGS. Using the instructions in Making Dumplings (page 84), roll, fill, and cut the dumplings.

5. PANFRY THE DUMPLINGS. When all the dumplings are assembled, heat a 10- or 12-inch skillet over medium-high heat. Add 1 to 2 tablespoons of oil (or enough to coat the *entire* bottom of the pan with a thin layer of oil), then add as many dumplings as will fit in the pan without touching, likely about a dozen, flat sides down, brushing off any excess flour before you add them to the pan. Cook, undisturbed, for about 1 minute, or until golden brown on the bottom. Add ¼ cup water to the pan, cover, and cook for 6 to 8 minutes, without turning, adding another 2 or 3 tablespoons water (more for a larger pan) after 3 or 4 minutes, when the first batch of water evaporates. When all the water has evaporated and the bottoms of the dumplings have become a shade darker, transfer them to a plate. Serve immediately, then wipe out the pan and repeat with the remaining dumplings and additional oil.

need a flaky dough? add butter.

CAULIFLOWER AND FARRO DUMPLINGS

dukkah

"How do you come up with this shit?" Seif always says, in his hallmark kitchen language, when I ask him to try a new vegetarian dish. It's the same reaction that we often get from our customers. People are frequently surprised that we have so many vegetarian options with big, bold flavors, unlike the usual steamed or simply seasoned dishes vegetarians are often forced to suffer through. Take these dumplings: deep-fried rather than panfried and made with a dough that's yeast-leavened, they look puffier than our other dumplings. Inside, we blend cooked farro with hazelnut *dukkah*, grilled kale, cauliflower, and a little sharp cheddar.

Don't be intimidated by the number of steps required to make the filling; they go quickly. Before you begin, see Dumpling and Noodle Basics (page 75).

MAKES 3 DOZEN DUMPLINGS

FOR THE FARRO:
2½ cups water
½ cup farro
2 dried guajillo chilies
Cloves from 2 medium heads garlic
5 whole cardamom pods
1 sprig thyme

FOR THE CAULIFLOWER:
1 (1-pound) head cauliflower, cored and cut
  into 1½-inch florets
2 tablespoons canola oil
Kosher salt and freshly ground black
  pepper

FOR THE *DUKKAH*:
Finely grated zest of 1 medium lemon
½ cup finely chopped toasted hazelnuts
2 tablespoons toasted white sesame seeds
2 tablespoons ground toasted cumin (see
  Toasting Spices, page 53)
1 tablespoon ground toasted coriander
  (see Toasting Spices, page 53)

FOR THE DOUGH:
1 cup warm water
½ teaspoon active dry yeast
3 cups all-purpose flour, plus more for
  kneading and rolling the dough
1 teaspoon kosher salt
½ teaspoon ground cumin
½ teaspoon ground cardamom
1 tablespoon canola oil

FOR THE KALE:
1 small bunch green kale, ribs removed,
  cut into 3-inch pieces (for 3 packed cups)
1 tablespoon canola oil
Kosher salt and freshly ground black pepper

FOR THE FILLING:
1 cup (2 ounces) lightly packed grated
  sharp cheddar cheese
1 teaspoon kosher salt

FOR FRYING:
Canola oil

1. **COOK THE FARRO.** In a medium saucepan, combine the water, farro, chilies, garlic, cardamom, and thyme, bring to a boil over high heat, reduce to a simmer, and cook, covered, for 30 minutes. Remove the lid and cook another 30 to 45 minutes, or until the liquid is almost gone and the farro is cooked to the point that the skins burst. (You want it to be more cooked than you'd make it for a salad, because you want the grains to be mashed together a little in the filling.) Drain the farro, pick out and discard the aromatics, and spread the farro on a baking sheet to cool to room temperature. Set aside.

continued

2. **ROAST THE CAULIFLOWER.** Preheat the oven to 400 degrees F. Pile the cauliflower on a baking sheet, drizzle with the oil, toss to coat, and season with salt and pepper. Spread the cauliflower out and roast for about 10 minutes, or until just beginning to brown at the edges but still firm. Set aside to cool.

3. **MAKE THE** *DUKKAH.* Reduce the oven temperature to 300 degrees F. Place the lemon zest in a small ovenproof dish and bake for 10 to 15 minutes, or until shriveled and totally dry, stirring once or twice. Set aside to cool completely, then transfer to a small bowl and stir in the hazelnuts, sesame seeds, cumin, and coriander. Set aside.

4. **MAKE THE DOUGH.** First, in a small bowl, whisk together the warm water and yeast and set aside to allow the yeast to activate. In a large bowl, whisk together the flour, salt, cumin, and cardamom. Make a small well in the center of the dry ingredients, then add the oil and yeast water to the well. Using your hands or a spoon, mix the ingredients until they cling together in a shaggy mass, then pat the dough together, transfer it to a clean lightly floured surface, and knead until smooth. (See Making Dough by Hand, page 75, for more detailed instructions; see Mixing with a Machine, page 77, if you'd prefer to work with a stand mixer.) Wrap the dough well in plastic and set aside to rest at room temperature for about 30 minutes. You'll notice the yeast will activate and the dough will begin to grow; you may need to rewrap the dough if it starts to outgrow the plastic wrap.

5. **GRILL THE KALE.** Preheat a gas or charcoal grill to medium-high heat, about 450 degrees F. In a large bowl, toss the kale with the oil, and season with salt and pepper. Grill the kale for about 1 minute per side, until wilted and charred in spots. (It will take less time if you cover the grill for a moment.) Transfer the kale back to the bowl and set aside to cool, then finely chop.

6. **MAKE THE FILLING.** Chop the cauliflower into ¼-inch pieces, measure out 2 cups of cauliflower, and put them in a large mixing bowl. Add the farro, kale, ½ cup of the *dukkah*, the cheese, and the salt and mix until well blended. Transfer about half of the filling to the bowl of a food processor, pulse until very finely chopped, then mix it back in with the rest of the filling.

7. **MAKE THE DUMPLINGS.** Using the instructions in Making Dumplings (page 84), roll, fill, and cut the dumplings.

8. **DEEP-FRY THE DUMPLINGS.** When all the dumplings are assembled, preheat the oil in a deep fryer or a large, heavy pot filled with about 3 inches of oil to 375 degrees F. When the oil is ready, carefully add 5 or 6 dumplings and fry for 2 to 3 minutes, turning halfway through, until the dumplings are golden brown. (Only add as many dumplings as will fit comfortably in your fryer or pot; the dumplings cook best if they have plenty of space.) Transfer the fried dumplings to a rack to cool for just a moment, then serve immediately, sprinkled with some of the remaining *dukkah*. Repeat with the remaining dumplings.

SHRIMP AND BACON DUMPLINGS

mushroom xo

These dumplings take the traditional shrimp and pork combination and add what we thought would be the obvious missing ingredient: bacon. It adds a punch of extra umami that, combined with our unctuous Mushroom XO Sauce (page 59), gives these dumplings the deepest, richest flavor of any we've had.

These are my kids' favorite too. When I'm home with them, I usually just buy round dumpling wrappers at my local grocery store. The premade wrappers are easier to handle, which means I can get dinner on the table quickly. But when we have time, I let Pike and Rye help me make the dough, and they twist the dumplings into ridiculous shapes, often with the help of whatever toys are their current favorites. Hours later, we find little trails of floury white footprints going up our wooden staircase.

I suggest asking a butcher to grind your pork, bacon, and shrimp for you, if you don't have a meat grinder, but you can also just chop it up very finely (freezing it for thirty minutes to an hour first makes it easier), or cut into half-inch pieces, and then whirl it in a food processor.

Before you begin, see Dumpling and Noodle Basics (page 75).

MAKES 3 DOZEN DUMPLINGS

FOR THE FILLING:

⅛ head Napa cabbage (from a 2-pound cabbage), cored, cut into ¼-inch strips

1½ teaspoons kosher salt

½ pound pork butt, coarsely ground or finely chopped

¼ pound peeled and deveined shrimp, coarsely ground or finely chopped (from ⅓ pound shrimp with shells on)

3 ounces bacon (or 3 thick strips), coarsely ground or finely chopped

2 tablespoons fish sauce

1 tablespoon grated peeled fresh ginger

3 large cloves garlic, very finely chopped

½ teaspoon ground toasted Szechuan peppercorns (see Toasting Spices, page 53)

FOR THE DIPPING SAUCE:

½ cup Mushroom XO Sauce (page 59)

½ cup black vinegar

FOR THE DOUGH:

1 recipe Basic Dumpling Dough (page 184) or store-bought round dumpling wrappers

FOR FRYING:

Canola oil

1. **MAKE THE FILLING.** In a medium mixing bowl, blend the cabbage with the salt. Let sit for about 20 minutes to draw excess water out of the cabbage.

Put the pork, shrimp, bacon, fish sauce, ginger, garlic, and ground peppercorns in a medium mixing bowl. After 20 minutes, rinse the cabbage carefully in cold water, using your hands to make sure the salt is rinsed off every piece. (The cabbage is clean enough when it tastes seasoned, instead of salty.) Squeeze it dry, finely chop it, then add it into the meat mixture. Using gloved hands—really, hands work best—blend the mixture until very well incorporated. Cover and chill until ready to use.

continued

2. MAKE THE DIPPING SAUCE. In a small bowl, blend together the Mushroom XO Sauce and black vinegar, and set aside until ready to serve.

3. MAKE THE DUMPLINGS. Using the instructions in Making Dumplings (page 84), roll, fill, and cut the dumplings.

4. PANFRY THE DUMPLINGS. When all the dumplings are assembled, heat a 10- or 12-inch skillet over medium-high heat. Add 1 to 2 tablespoons of the oil (or enough to coat the *entire* bottom of the pan with a thin layer of oil), then add as many dumplings as will fit in the pan without touching, likely about a dozen, flat sides down, brushing off any excess flour before you add them to the pan. Cook, undisturbed, for about 1 minute, or until golden brown on the bottom. Add ¼ cup water to the pan, cover, and cook for 6 to 8 minutes, without turning, adding another 2 or 3 tablespoons water (more for a larger pan) after 3 or 4 minutes, when the first batch of water evaporates and the skins of the dumplings have started to collapse onto the filling underneath. When all the water has evaporated and the bottoms of the dumplings have become a shade darker, transfer them to a plate. Serve immediately, with the dipping sauce, then wipe out the pan and repeat with the remaining dumplings and additional oil.

LAMB AND EGGPLANT DUMPLINGS

szechuan peppercorns, fenugreek

This recipe is the kind of food I love making—food that's firmly rooted in Korean cuisine, but that has strayed into the unexpected. With the faint citrusy buzz of Szechuan peppercorns and the spiced lamb so common to Mongolia, these dumplings are definitely Asian, but the combination of lamb and eggplant nods to Greece. Serve them with the Mother Sauces (pages 71 to 73).

Before you begin, see Dumpling and Noodle Basics (page 75).

MAKES 4 DOZEN DUMPLINGS

FOR THE FILLING:

3 tablespoons canola oil

1 Chinese eggplant (about 8 ounces), skin on, cut into ½-inch cubes

Kosher salt and freshly ground black pepper

¼ cup soy sauce

1 tablespoon ground toasted cumin (see Toasting Spices, page 53)

1 tablespoon ground toasted Szechuan peppercorns (see Toasting Spices, page 53)

1 teaspoon coarse Korean chili flakes

1 teaspoon onion powder

1 teaspoon garlic powder

1 teaspoon ground ginger

1 teaspoon sesame oil

1 teaspoon sugar

1 pound ground lamb

FOR THE DOUGH:

3 cups all-purpose flour, plus more for kneading and rolling the dough

1 tablespoon ground fenugreek

1 teaspoon kosher salt

1 cup milk, at room temperature

1 tablespoon canola oil

1. **COOK THE EGGPLANT.** Heat a large skillet over medium-high heat. Add the oil, then the eggplant, and season with salt and pepper. Cook for about 5 minutes, stirring occasionally, or until the eggplant is soft and brown in spots and the skin has softened. Set aside to cool.

2. **MAKE THE DOUGH.** In a large bowl, first whisk together the flour, fenugreek, and salt. Make a small well in the center of the dry ingredients, then add the milk and oil to the well. Using your hands or a spoon, mix the ingredients until they cling together in a shaggy mass, then pat the dough together, transfer it to a clean lightly floured surface, and knead until smooth. (See Making Dough by Hand, page 75, for more detailed instructions; see Mixing with a Machine, page 77, if you'd prefer to work with a stand mixer.) Wrap the dough well in plastic and set aside to rest at room temperature for about 30 minutes.

continued

eggplant is the secret to a juicy dumpling

3. **MAKE THE FILLING.** In a medium mixing bowl, stir together the soy sauce, cumin, peppercorns, chili flakes, onion powder, garlic powder, ground ginger, sesame oil, and sugar. Add the lamb and cooled eggplant. Using gloved hands—really, hands work best—blend the mixture until very well incorporated. Cover and chill until ready to use.

4. **MAKE THE DUMPLINGS.** Using the instructions in Making Dumplings (page 84), roll, fill, and cut the dumplings.

5. **PANFRY THE DUMPLINGS.** When all the dumplings are assembled, heat a 10- or 12-inch skillet over medium-high heat. Add 1 to 2 tablespoons of the oil (or enough to coat the *entire* bottom of the pan with a thin layer of oil), then add as many dumplings as will fit in the pan without touching, likely about a dozen, flat sides down, brushing off any excess flour before you add them to the pan. Cook, undisturbed, for about 1 minute, or until golden brown on the bottom. Add ¼ cup water to the pan, cover, and cook for 6 to 8 minutes, without turning, adding another 2 or 3 tablespoons water (more for a larger pan) after 3 or 4 minutes, when the first batch of water evaporates and the skins of the dumplings have started to collapse onto the filling underneath. When all the water has evaporated and the bottoms of the dumplings have become a shade darker, transfer them to a plate. Serve immediately, then wipe out the pan and repeat with the remaining dumplings and additional oil.

barbecue

There is a very good reason why Asian chopsticks are often longer than regular forks or spoons: in most of Asia, eating as a group requires good reach. At Korean dinners, it's very common to see the traditional metal chopsticks striking out in different directions on the table; it's not considered rude at all, the way it can be in America, but instead more convivial. In fact, when Seif and I first began venturing into New York City's K-town for late-night meals together, clinking metal chopsticks as we went for the same *banchan* dish or colliding while cooking barbecue together over a tabletop grill, we were probably having our first intimate experiences. Chopsticks bring people together in ways forks and knives never can.

With the rise of shared plates, the concept of communal eating at a restaurant is more commonplace in America today, but in Korea eating has always been a communal act. At Korean barbecue restaurants, whether they're grilling meat, cutting it, or piling it into tender lettuce rolls, every person at the table is involved. It's a kind of eating rarely seen in the United States. Laughter rolls down the table. Hands get dirty. At the end of each meal, life feels a little more understandable. At Trove, of course, we have tabletop grills in the barbecue section, but even at our other restaurants, the feeling of eating as a group is more pervasive than at other places. (Case in point: stand outside the window at Revelry and watch a group of diners dive into a plate of Mrs. Yang's Spicy Fried Chicken, page 223.) Cook these recipes for a group when you're ready to make friends.

PORK COPPA

sweet chili marinade

Unlike so much of what we serve at our restaurants (which is often Korean food spun firmly away from tradition), chili-marinated grilled pork is quite common in Korea today. We use coppa roast, which is a cut on the inside of the pork butt, because it has an even distribution of fat, meaning you wind up with an extremely tender, flavorful piece of meat. Call your butcher ahead of time to ask for it or simply use pork butt or shoulder instead.

As with our other barbecue, we serve the coppa with lettuce wraps and Revel's Savory Chili Sauce (page 73). In Korea, they often stir-fry it, which is also an option—just be sure to throw the meat in at the very last minute, because the sugar in the marinade makes the meat char quickly. On the grill, that's a good thing—cut the cooked meat into small pieces with scissors, and let them sit on the grill for a moment to char before serving.

If you prefer eating more of a pork steak—cut thick instead of thin—then cut the coppa into three-quarter-inch steaks, marinate for four hours, and grill slightly longer (see The Perfect Temp, page 211).

MAKES 4 SERVINGS

⅓ cup rice vinegar

⅓ cup sugar

¼ cup sake

1 tablespoon finely chopped peeled
  fresh ginger

2 cloves garlic

1 tablespoon canola oil

½ teaspoon kosher salt

½ cup Korean chili paste

1 (2-pound) pork coppa roast, cut
  into ¼-inch slices

1. MARINATE THE MEAT. In a blender or the bowl of a food processor, whirl together the vinegar, sugar, sake, ginger, garlic, oil, and salt until smooth. Transfer the mixture to a medium mixing bowl and whisk in the chili paste until smooth. Add the pork slices, turning each to coat evenly in the marinade. Cover and refrigerate for 2 hours.

2. GRILL THE PORK. Preheat a gas or charcoal grill to medium heat, about 400 degrees F. Transfer the pork to a platter, wiping off excess marinade as you do. Grill the pork for about 5 minutes total, turning once after about 3 minutes, or until nicely marked on each side. Serve immediately.

use this marinade anywhere you want THE Korean flavor

PORK BELLY

tahini, za'atar

In Korea, pork belly is one of the most common cuts you'll see on a barbecue menu; it's cheaper than beef, satisfying in relatively small amounts, and delicious with the simplest sauces. There, you'll often find it served with toasted sesame oil sprinkled with crunchy salt. (At Trove, we do something similar, but we infuse the oil with chilies and garlic first. It may seem strange to dip fatty pork belly into oil, but it really brings out the best in the pork's flavor—and because the salt doesn't melt into the oil, you get a little burst of flavor with each bite.)

Unlike in Korea, where the belly is often simply grilled without any seasoning, we tenderize ours in a garlicky tahini marinade, sprinkle it with za'atar before grilling, and serve it hot, with Revel's Spicy Dipping Sauce (page 72). As with all barbecue, I encourage you to serve this recipe with a mix of other meats in the chapter, along with a platter of lettuce, herbs, and other vegetables (like thinly sliced daikon radish) for rolling.

MAKES 4 SERVINGS

½ cup sake
½ cup tahini
4 cloves garlic

1 pound pork belly, skin removed, cut into 8 slices a little thinner than ½ inch
½ cup Za'atar (page 51)

1. **MARINATE THE MEAT.** In a blender or the bowl of a food processor, combine the sake, tahini, and garlic, and whirl until completely smooth. Transfer the mixture to a sealable container, add the pork, and turn to coat the pork evenly on all sides. Cover and refrigerate for 4 to 6 hours.

2. **GRILL THE PORK.** When you're ready to grill, preheat a gas or charcoal grill to medium heat, about 400 degrees F. (It's best to cook over indirect heat, so the pork doesn't flare up—set your grill up accordingly.) Transfer the pork to a platter, wiping off the excess marinade as you do, and sprinkle each side of each slice of pork with a heaping ½ teaspoon of the za'atar.

Place the pork pieces at an angle on the grill. Cook for 2 minutes, covered, and then rotate the pork 90 degrees. Cook for another 2 minutes, covered, then flip the pork and cook for another 4 minutes total, turning the pork 90 degrees again after 2 minutes. (The pork should be nicely browned but not charred.) Serve immediately.

love your sesame? use tahini.

"THAT" SHORT RIB STEAK

kalbi marinade

Kalbi, which simply translates to "short rib" in Korean, is often synonymous with Korean barbecue. Koreans love the marbling so much—the way juicy, tender meat transects firmer cartilage and bone—that it's become one of the most expensive meats there. Here, it's become increasingly popular, and our restaurants are no exception: we go through about 350 pounds of short ribs each week.

At Joule, we serve kalbi steaks that we bone ourselves for larger portions plated out American style, eaten with a knife and fork, instead of with chopsticks or folded up into lettuce wraps. At first, grilling kalbi was a foreign concept for people who considered short ribs an off-cut that required braising, but it became a star. At Trove, we slice it thin and serve it perfectly marinated for customers to grill themselves at their tables, roll in lettuce, and garnish with the dipping sauces (pages 71 to 73). If you'd like, you could also grill it up for our most popular rice bowl at Revel and Revelry, the short rib rice bowl: when the meat is done, slice it up and serve it over white rice with grilled mustard greens (see Grilling Greens, page 110), simple pickled daikon radish dressed with spicy sambal oelek (see page 129), and a fresh egg yolk.

This sweet and savory marinade is the best way to tenderize and flavor kalbi. Ours gets its sweetness from a base of Asian pear and onion, along with a bit of mirin. Marinate your meat based on how you decide to cook it. If you want to grill thin pieces, they only need two to four hours in the marinade, whereas larger steaks take four to six hours to get tender, with bigger pieces taking even longer.

For a larger crowd, this marinade scales up easily—just double or triple it.

MAKES 4 SERVINGS

¼ cup chopped peeled Asian pear

¼ cup chopped yellow onion

¼ cup mirin

¼ cup sake

2 tablespoons soy sauce

1 (1-inch) section peeled fresh ginger, sliced into ¼-inch-thick coins

2 large cloves garlic

1 pound deboned short rib steaks, left whole or cut into ¼-inch slices

1. **MARINATE THE MEAT.** In a blender or the bowl of a food processor, whirl together the pear, onion, mirin, sake, soy sauce, ginger, and garlic until well blended, pausing to scrape down the sides of the bowl halfway through to reincorporate any stray ingredients. Transfer the marinade to a container large enough to fit the short ribs, add the meat, and turn to coat with the marinade. Cover and refrigerate 2 to 6 hours.

continued

a tough cut of meat you have to braise for hours? not so much.

2. GRILL THE SHORT RIBS. Preheat a gas or charcoal grill to medium heat, 350 to 375 degrees F. Cook, covered, for 4 to 5 minutes per side for whole steaks, or 2 to 3 minutes per side for ¼-inch slices, or until the steak is cooked to your liking. (The marinade burns quickly, so watch any hot spots on your grill carefully.) Let the meat rest (just 1 to 2 minutes for thin strips, or 5 to 7 minutes for steaks, depending on their size), then serve immediately.

BRISKET BUNS

horseradish pickled cucumber

Barbecue is a different thing for almost everyone. In the United States, barbecue varies greatly by region; put a North Carolinian next to a Texan and ask them each to describe barbecue, and you'll get different animals, different cuts, and entirely different sauces. Korean-style barbecue is no different.

We swore, when we opened Joule in 2007, that we'd never have the kind of Asian barbecued pork slider bun that was popping up across the country at the time—David Chang was soaring to popularity in New York, and people asked us almost daily when we'd be doing our own version. For fun, we started doing a complimentary bun bar for our anniversary party each year at Joule instead, with an array of meats and plenty of kimchi and pickles to pile on top. This brisket version, served on Asian-style soft buns, is our way of enjoying the bun craze without having to serve them at any of our restaurants—and it makes a great staff meal.

The brisket itself, though, is something we serve at Trove on its own. Cooked low and slow, the meat becomes falling-apart tender, like its American cousins, and the fat becomes melt-in-your-mouth soft. The sauce—a mix of the mustard, brown sugar, and molasses flavors common to the States plus black vinegar, chili paste, and Szechuan flavors more common to Asia—is perfect slathered on the buns but also great as a dip for plain grilled steak.

Count on babysitting the meat for the better part of the day; it isn't much actual work, but it requires four hours of marination and four hours in the oven.

Look for folded buns in the frozen section at an Asian grocery store; there are usually twelve per package, with instructions for steaming them on the back.

MAKES 4 TO 6 SERVINGS

FOR THE BRISKET:

2 tablespoons dry yellow mustard powder

2 tablespoons black vinegar

¼ cup packed light brown sugar

2 tablespoons molasses

1 tablespoon kosher salt

2 teaspoons toasted Szechuan peppercorns, crushed (see Toasting Spices, page 53)

2 teaspoons toasted coriander seeds, crushed (see Toasting Spices, page 53)

1 teaspoon ground toasted cumin (see Toasting Spices, page 53)

1 teaspoon chipotle chili powder

½ teaspoon garlic powder

½ teaspoon ground ginger

½ teaspoon onion powder

2 pounds flat-end brisket

FOR THE SAUCE:

¼ cup Korean chili paste

¼ cup rice vinegar

3 tablespoons packed light brown sugar

continued

FOR THE CUCUMBERS:

1 (10-ounce) seedless cucumber, halved,
  cut into ⅛-inch slices

½ teaspoon kosher salt

¼ cup buttermilk

3 tablespoons finely grated
  fresh horseradish

2 tablespoons rice vinegar

2 cloves garlic, sliced as thinly as possible

FOR SERVING:

24 Asian folded buns, steamed per
  package directions

1. **RUB THE BRISKET.** In a small bowl, stir together the mustard and black vinegar until no lumps remain. Add the brown sugar, molasses, salt, peppercorns, coriander, cumin, chili powder, garlic powder, ground ginger, and onion powder, and stir to blend. Transfer ¼ cup of the marinade to a separate small bowl, and scrape the rest into a ziplock bag. Add the brisket to the bag, turn the meat in the rub until it's coated on all sides, and refrigerate for 4 hours.

2. **MAKE THE BARBECUE SAUCE.** To the bowl with the reserved marinade, add the chili paste, rice vinegar, and brown sugar, and stir until the sugar is mostly dissolved. Cover and refrigerate until ready to serve.

3. **COOK THE BRISKET.** Preheat the oven to 250 degrees F. Place a rack inside a heavy roasting pan. Line the rack with a sheet of heavy-duty foil (or two sheets of regular aluminum foil) big enough to wrap around the brisket. Transfer the meat from the marinade to the foil and enclose the meat in the foil, crimping the foil to seal it closed on top. Roast for 4 hours, or until it flakes easily with a fork. Remove the meat from the oven and let rest for 30 minutes before serving. (You can also cook the meat 1 to 2 days ahead, then reheat it for 20 minutes in a 325-degree-F oven before serving.)

4. **MAKE THE CUCUMBERS.** About 1 hour before serving, place the sliced cucumbers in a large bowl, sprinkle the salt on top, and mix until well blended. Set the cucumbers aside for 10 minutes; the salt will draw excess water out of the cucumbers. After 10 minutes, rinse the cucumbers in three changes of fresh cold water. (The cucumber is clean enough when it tastes seasoned, instead of salty.) Using your hands, working with a small handful of vegetables at a time, squeeze the water out of the cucumbers and transfer them to the mixing bowl. (You will crush the cucumber slices a little, which is fine.)

   Add the buttermilk, horseradish, rice vinegar, and sliced garlic, and stir to blend. Set aside for about 30 minutes to marinate, or until ready to serve.

5. **ASSEMBLE THE BUNS.** When the brisket is done, cut it into ½-inch slices against the grain, then chop the meat and mix it with about half the sauce. Overstuff each bun with a scoop of sauce (you may not use all the buns), then a scoop of meat, then the cucumbers, and serve immediately.

BEEF TRI-TIP

lemongrass marinade

The iron grill at Revel is a cantankerous old thing that suits us perfectly. Built in the so-called Santa Barbara style, it has a grate that can be raised and lowered with a big crank, so you can both tend to the fire without endangering anything that's cooking and adjust the height of the grill without rearranging the fire. In the summers, when demand is high for seating on our enclosed deck, we put two menus on each table: first, our normal menu, and second, a grill menu, which always has a list of items seared on that grate over an applewood fire. Frequently, there's a theme—a holdover from our days doing "urban barbecues" at Joule's first location. If we're going Vietnamese, we often make a lemongrass marinade with coriander, lime leaves, and fish sauce for our beef.

If you'd like to grill the tri-tip as steaks (instead of as thin slices as described below), cut it lengthwise into two (eight-ounce) steaks, and grill for more like ten minutes at a slightly lower temperature, turning halfway through (see The Perfect Temp, page 211).

MAKES 4 SERVINGS

½ cup sake

¼ cup mirin

2 tablespoons fish sauce

¼ cup chopped fresh lemongrass (from the tender insides of 4 medium stalks)

2 lime leaves

1 (1-inch) section peeled fresh ginger, sliced into ¼-inch-thick coins

1 teaspoon ground toasted coriander (see Toasting Spices, page 53)

1 pound tri-tip steak, cut into ¼-inch slices

1. **MARINATE THE MEAT.** In a blender or the bowl of a food processor, whirl the sake, mirin, fish sauce, lemongrass, lime leaves, ginger, and coriander until well blended, pausing to scrape down the sides of the bowl halfway through to reincorporate any stray ingredients. Transfer the marinade to a container large enough to fit the steak, add the meat, and turn to coat it all in the marinade. Cover and refrigerate for 2 hours.

2. **GRILL THE STEAK.** Preheat a gas or charcoal grill to medium heat, about 400 degrees F. Cook the meat, covered, for 2 to 3 minutes per side (chunks of marinade on the meat are welcome). Serve immediately.

THE PERFECT TEMP

Since many of our barbecue cuts have a marinade that's slightly sweet, they burn if you leave them on the grill too long—which means that for thicker cuts, depending on how well cooked you like your meat, you may want to finish them in the oven. At Joule, we finish our steaks in a preheated 375-degree-F oven for 5 to 10 minutes once they've been marked nicely on the grill.

BANANA LEAF–WRAPPED PORK BUTT

achiote, salted shrimp

Although we serve this at Trove in the style of barbecue, it's actually more of a roast: a hunk of tender pork, slathered in a spicy mixture of chilies, garlic, ginger, and achiote that you slice and serve hot after roasting it wrapped in flavorful banana leaves. Adding salty shrimp and fish sauce complements the earthy flavors of the pork, but don't feel confined to serving it sliced, as directed—it would also make incredible pulled pork for Korean tacos, served with Korean Taco Pickles (page 139), or serve it over rice in Kahlua Pork Stone Pot (page 270).

MAKES 4 SERVINGS

FOR THE RUB:

5 Chinese dried chilies, stems removed

5 large cloves garlic

1 (2-inch) section peeled fresh ginger, sliced into ¼-inch-thick coins

1 tablespoon achiote paste

1 tablespoon salted shrimp

1 tablespoon fish sauce

FOR ROASTING:

1 (1-by-2-foot) piece banana leaf, fully thawed if frozen

1½ pounds pork butt

1. **PREHEAT THE OVEN.** Preheat the oven to 350 degrees F.

2. **MAKE THE ACHIOTE RUB.** In a large mortar and pestle, mash together the chilies, garlic, ginger, achiote, shrimp, and fish sauce until all the chilies are finely ground and the mixture begins to look pasty. (You can also grind the ingredients together in a food processor, if you wish, but I prefer the texture a mortar and pestle offer in this situation.)

3. **WRAP THE PORK.** Place a rack inside a heavy roasting pan. Line the rack with a sheet of heavy-duty foil (or two sheets of regular aluminum foil) big enough to wrap around the pork, then place the banana leaf on top of the foil. Smear the chili mixture on all sides of the pork, then place the pork on top of the banana leaf, in the same orientation as the leaf. Fold the leaf over the pork, tucking in the ends, then fold the foil over the leaf, crimping the foil to seal it closed on top of the pork.

4. **ROAST THE PORK.** Roast the pork for 2½ to 3 hours, or until the pork flakes easily with a fork. Remove from the oven and let rest for 20 minutes, then slice the pork into ½-inch pieces, and serve hot.

mixing achiote with sweet salted shrimp is MONEY

GRILLED CORNISH GAME HENS

korean mojo

With the exception of the fried chicken at Revelry (see page 223), we don't have a chicken dish on a single one of our menus. But when it's marinated with a Korean version of Cuban mojo sauce, then grilled on the bone, chicken has an incredible amount of flavor. At home, we use Cornish game hens because they have a big skin-to-meat ratio, so there's lots of deep char from the grill in every bite, and because if you cut the back out of the hen and flatten the bird out, it usually cooks in under twenty minutes. Garnish the chicken with the orange-sesame salt, fresh orange wedges, and thinly sliced garlic chives.

MAKES 4 SERVINGS

FOR THE MOJO:

14 large cloves garlic (from 2 large heads garlic)
6 Chinese dried chilies, stems removed
2 tablespoons sugar
1 cup orange juice
1 cup soy sauce
1 cup sake

FOR THE HENS:

2 (roughly 1¼-pound) Cornish game hens, thawed completely if frozen, backbones removed
2 tablespoons canola oil

FOR THE ORANGE-SESAME SALT:

2 tablespoons Korean coarse sea salt
1 tablespoon toasted sesame seeds
½ teaspoon finely grated orange zest

1. **MARINATE THE HENS.** In a mortar and pestle, crush the garlic, chilies, and sugar together until the sugar is dissolved and the mixture is pasty. (Depending on the size of your mortar, you may need to do this in two batches. The chilies will be broken up but not totally pulverized.) Transfer the mixture to a ziplock bag, add the orange juice, soy sauce, and sake, and then the hens. Close the bag carefully, place in a large bowl, and refrigerate for about 4 hours.

2. **DRY THE HENS.** Remove the hens from the marinade, pat dry, and let sit at room temperature for about 20 minutes.

3. **MAKE THE ORANGE-SESAME SALT.** In a mortar and pestle, crush the salt until fine. Add the sesame seeds and orange zest, and use your fingertips to mix the ingredients together until the zest is evenly distributed throughout the salt.

4. **GRILL THE HENS.** Preheat a gas or charcoal grill to medium-high heat, 425 degrees F. When hot, rub the hens with the oil. Grill the hens splayed out flat on the grates, skin side down first, for about 20 minutes, turning halfway through and rotating the chickens if necessary so they cook evenly.

5. **SERVE THE HENS.** Transfer the hens to a cutting board, let rest for 5 or 10 minutes, then cut in half and serve hot, garnished with the orange-sesame salt.

BROILED MACKEREL

green curry chimichurri

Mackerel has an undeserved bad reputation for several things. The first is that it's overly fatty, which can be true if it's not cooked properly. If it's broiled, though, much of the fat drains off, so the fishiness can be tamed a bit. Paired with a bright chimichurri, it's one of the things people come back to Joule over and over to eat.

The second is that it's hard to eat, because it has a row of pin bones that run down the length of each fillet. Luckily, we have a way of deboning it that's easy but doesn't sacrifice how the fish looks when it's served.

The last is that the skin is too delicate or that it doesn't crisp up nicely the way, say, salmon skin does. The secret to crisp mackerel skin is quite simple: When you lubricate the skin with oil, it becomes more flexible. And, taking a cue from Chinese crispy pork, a quick mop of sherry vinegar and fish sauce allows the skin to puff and lift off the fish without cracking.

MAKES 4 SERVINGS

FOR THE CHIMICHURRI:

1 bunch cilantro, stems removed, roughly chopped

1 tablespoon Revel's Green Curry Paste (page 69) or store-bought Thai-style green curry paste

1 teaspoon crushed toasted coriander (see Toasting Spices, page 53)

¼ cup canola oil

FOR THE FISH CARAMEL:

¼ cup sugar

2 tablespoons water

¼ cup fish sauce

¼ cup sherry vinegar

FOR THE MACKEREL:

2 (1¼- to 1½-pound) mackerel

Kosher salt and freshly ground black pepper

2 tablespoons canola oil

1 tablespoon sherry vinegar

1 tablespoon fish sauce

4 lime wedges

½ cup loosely packed picked cilantro leaves

1. **MAKE THE CHIMICHURRI.** In a blender, whirl together the cilantro, curry paste, coriander, and oil until smooth. Transfer to a small bowl and set aside.

2. **MAKE THE FISH CARAMEL.** In a large saucepan, stir together the sugar and water with a fork, then place the pan over high heat and bring to a boil. Cook, undisturbed, until the liquid turns a pale golden brown. Carefully whisk in the fish sauce and sherry vinegar. Set aside to cool.

3. **FILLET THE MACKEREL.** Using a thin, sharp knife, make a cut behind the front fin on each side of each fish, slicing at a 45-degree angle toward the head of the fish, so you cut through the fillet and down to the spine behind the fin. Next, make a shallow cut down the length of the fish on one side of the spine. Remove the fillet from that side (leaving the bones attached to the fish), and place the fillet flesh side up on a cutting

continued

board. You'll see a dark stripe down the center of the fillet, which contains the pin bones. (If you touch it, you'll feel small bones poking out.) Make an incision down one side of the stripe about ⅛ inch away from the center of the stripe, angling the blade of the knife toward the center of the stripe where it meets the mackerel's skin, but not going through the skin. Repeat on the other side, effectively cutting out a *V*-shaped wedge of flesh that contains the stripe and all the pin bones. (The skin should remain completely intact.) Peel the flesh out and repeat with the remaining fillets.

4. BROIL THE MACKEREL. Preheat your oven's broiler on high and place an oven rack about 3 inches from the heating unit. Season the flesh sides of each fillet with salt and pepper. Turn the fillets, rub the skin side generously with the oil, and season with salt. Stir together the vinegar and fish sauce in a small bowl, and use a brush to dab the mixture all over the mackerel's skin. Fit an oiled cooling rack inside a baking sheet, and place the fillets flesh side down on the rack. Broil for 4 to 5 minutes, or until the skin is browned and puffed.

5. SERVE THE MACKEREL. Transfer each fillet to a plate, skin side up. Drizzle the fillets with the caramel and top with a spoonful of the chimichurri. Serve hot, garnished with the lime and cilantro.

BLACKENED OCTOPUS

onion ash, black sesame

Traditionally, Korean barbecue isn't quite as single-minded as American barbecue tends to be; there's often a grand mix of different proteins on the table, from land and sea. One of my perennial favorites is octopus, which first gets poached, to render it completely tender, then grilled with a blackening rub that is meant to be a Korean take on traditional Southern American flavors. The rub includes both onion ash, made by blackening onion petals on a hot grill, and black sesame powder, both of which add a fantastic deep charred flavor. (It's also great on pork.) We serve it folded into lettuce leaves and drizzle it with one of our Mother Sauces (pages 71 to 73) at the restaurant, but for an unusual combination, I love chopping it up for warm or cold salad.

At Trove, where customers grill their own meats, we often serve just one octopus tentacle per person, along with other things, like grilled pork belly (see page 203) or grilled tri-tip steak (see page 211). If you want to do that, save the remaining tentacles for Kale Salad (page 97). The blackening rub will be enough for about six tentacles, if you'd like to cook one per person. For a bigger party, cook another octopus and double the rub.

MAKES 4 TO 6 SERVINGS

FOR THE RUB:

1 yellow onion, peeled, halved, and
  separated into petals
2 tablespoons coarse Korean chili flakes
1 tablespoon garlic powder
1 tablespoon ground ginger
1 tablespoon black sesame powder
  (see page 50)
½ teaspoon kosher salt

FOR THE OCTOPUS:

4 to 6 tentacles Poached Octopus
  (page 98)
1 to 2 tablespoons canola oil
Kosher salt and freshly ground black
  pepper

FOR SERVING:

Canola oil
Chunky sea salt

1. **MAKE THE RUB.** Preheat a gas or charcoal grill to high heat, about 500 degrees F. When hot, place the dry onion petals on the grill, cut sides down. Grill for 10 minutes, covered, until the onions have started to blacken. Flip the petals and cook another 10 to 15 minutes, or until each piece is entirely charcoal black and completely dried out. (If you're working with coals or a wood fire, you can put the onions directly into the fire, if you'd like.) Transfer the onions to a plate and let cool.

Adjust the grill's temperature to medium-high, about 450 degrees F, if you plan to grill the octopus immediately. Otherwise, you will need to preheat the grill when you're ready.

continued

use burned onion as a spice

In a small bowl, stir together the chili flakes, garlic powder, ground ginger, sesame powder, and salt. Using your fingers, crumble the dry, shattery edges of the onions into a powdery ash, taking care to only use the parts that are dry and brittle, and avoiding any parts that may still be moist and bendable. Stir 1 tablespoon of the onion ash into the spice mixture.

2. GRILL THE OCTOPUS. Put the tentacles on a plate, and drizzle oil over them (1 tablespoon for 4 tentacles, or closer to 1½ tablespoons for 6 tentacles), turning and tossing to coat each one thoroughly with oil. Season the tentacles with salt and pepper, then sprinkle the blackening rub liberally over each tentacle on all sides, using 1 scant tablespoon of the spice per tentacle.

Grill the tentacles, covered, for 2 minutes per side, or until well blackened on all sides. Serve immediately, drizzled with oil and sprinkled with sea salt, if you want.

MRS. YANG'S SPICY FRIED CHICKEN

peanut brittle

Mrs. Yang is my Korean doppelgänger. I am very rarely called Mrs. Chirchi, but since I kept my last name when I married Seif—the traditional practice in Korea—I always feel very Korean when people address me as "Mrs. Yang." These days, I'm more apt to be called "chef" than anything else, but sometimes, there are moments when I can feel my Korean heritage in my cooking, even if I'm cooking something I've never actually made on Korean soil.

This is not my mother's Korean fried chicken but mine: like I sometimes feel, it is clearly Korean on the outside but quite American on the inside. Like many American versions of fried chicken, it's marinated in buttermilk to keep the boneless thigh meat moist and juicy inside and crisped on the outside—but like classic Korean fried chicken, its addictive spicy sauce is really what draws people back. (Its stickiness, you'll see, comes from whisking caramel into the sauce.) We serve it at Revelry in Portland, where topping it with crumbles of chili-flecked peanut brittle tends to cause little frissons of excitement to ripple across every table that receives it. Make the peanut brittle while you marinate the chicken.

MAKES 6 SERVINGS

FOR THE MARINADE:

3 cups buttermilk

8 cloves garlic

¼ cup roughly chopped peeled
  fresh ginger

1 tablespoon fish sauce

2 Thai chilies

1 teaspoon Chinese five spice powder

1 teaspoon Old Bay seasoning

1 teaspoon Madras curry powder

3 pounds boneless, skinless chicken
  breasts, cut into roughly 2-inch pieces

FOR THE DREDGE:

2 recipes (3 cups) Magic Dredge (page 63)

2 teaspoons Chinese five spice powder

2 teaspoons Old Bay seasoning

2 teaspoons Madras curry powder

FOR THE SAUCE:

¾ cup rice vinegar

½ cup golden raisins

¼ cup packed light brown sugar

¼ cup soy sauce

8 cloves garlic

¼ cup roughly chopped peeled
  fresh ginger

4 oil-packed anchovy fillets

1 cup sugar

½ cup water

½ cup fish sauce

¾ cup Korean chili paste

FOR FRYING:

Canola oil

FOR SERVING:

1 cup Peanut Brittle
  (page 54), chopped

go for subtle curry flavor without straight-up curry sauce

continued

1. **MARINATE THE CHICKEN.** In a blender, whirl together the buttermilk, garlic, ginger, fish sauce, chilies, five spice, Old Bay, and curry until smooth. Transfer the marinade to a ziplock bag, add the chicken, and turn the chicken to coat all the pieces. Refrigerate for 6 to 8 hours.

2. **PREPARE FOR FRYING.** Remove the chicken from the marinade, placing each piece on a wire rack set over a baking sheet to let the excess liquid drip off. Meanwhile, in a medium bowl, combine the Magic Dredge with the five spice, Old Bay, and curry and whisk to blend.

3. **MAKE THE FRIED CHICKEN SAUCE.** In a blender, whirl together the vinegar, raisins, brown sugar, soy sauce, garlic, ginger, and anchovies until smooth. Set aside.

   Next, make a pale caramel with the sugar and water: In a large saucepan, stir together the sugar and water with a fork, then place the pan over high heat and bring to a boil. Cook, undisturbed, until the liquid turns a pale golden brown. Carefully whisk in the fish sauce. Once the fish caramel is well mixed, remove the pan from the heat and stir in the contents of the blender. Whisk in the chili paste and transfer the sauce to a large bowl.

4. **FRY THE CHICKEN.** Preheat the oil in a deep fryer or a large, heavy pot filled with about 3 inches of oil to 375 degrees F. When the oil is ready, dredge about six pieces of chicken in the Magic Dredge mixture and fry until crispy and cooked through, about 5 minutes. (Only add as much chicken as will fit comfortably in your fryer or pot; the chicken pieces will cook best if they have plenty of space.) Transfer the chicken to the bowl with the sauce and toss to coat, then serve piping hot, sprinkled with some of the peanut brittle. Repeat with the remaining chicken. (If you'd like to serve the chicken all at once, keep the just-fried chicken in a 200-degree-F oven until all the chicken is fried, then toss it in the sauce all at once and serve immediately.)

noodles

At Revel, we have a twenty-four-foot maple butcher-block countertop. During service hours, it's the best place to sit in the house, but when the doors are closed, we use the entire surface to roll out noodles.

No matter where in the world they're made, noodles are the perfect blank slate. Almost every culture has their own version of flour dough, folded together and cooked, then served with a sauce—but our perception of, say, pad Thai noodles (see page 245) is quite different from that of tagliatelle. (In terms of value, Americans tend to think of Asian noodles as cheaper than European noodles, even though Asian noodles often take more work to make.) Our restaurants' noodle dishes usually land right in between Italian noodles and Asian noodles; we often use sauces with Asian flavors, but we also often use butter or cream for finishing our noodles to give them their hallmark silky texture. Luckily, food doesn't need distinct boundaries. (We use chipotle peppers in that pad Thai.) If it tastes good, it works, no matter where it's from.

BASIC EGG NOODLES

While we never make plain dough in our restaurants (why skip an opportunity to add flavor to a huge component of a dish?), you may want to use this basic recipe to tinker with at home. In general, you can add anything, keeping in mind that if you add something with a lot of moisture, you'll have to balance that with the dough's dry ingredients, and vice versa; if you add a powder to the dough that's likely to suck up moisture, you might want to consider adding a little water. Sauce as desired—any of the sauces on the following pages are also delicious on plain noodles.

Before you begin, see Dumpling and Noodle Basics (page 75).

MAKES ALMOST 2 POUNDS DOUGH, OR 6 TO 8 SERVINGS

4 cups all-purpose flour, plus more for
   kneading and rolling
1 teaspoon kosher salt

6 large eggs
1 tablespoon canola oil
Rice flour, for dusting

1. **MAKE THE DOUGH.** In a large bowl, whisk together the flour and salt. In a small bowl, whisk together the eggs and oil until uniform in color. Make a small well in the center of the dry ingredients, then add the egg mixture to the well. Using your hands or a spoon, mix the ingredients until they cling together in a shaggy mass, then pat the dough together, transfer it to a clean lightly floured surface, and knead until smooth. (See Making Dough by Hand, page 75, for more detailed instructions; see Mixing with a Machine, page 77, if you'd prefer to work with a stand mixer.) Wrap the dough well in plastic, and set aside to rest at room temperature for about 30 minutes.

2. **ROLL OUT THE DOUGH.** Using a pasta-rolling machine, roll to level 5 and cut into thin or thick noodles, dusting the noodles with rice flour as needed to prevent them from sticking together. (See Making Noodles, page 89.)

3. **COOK THE NOODLES.** Bring a large pot of water to a boil over high heat. When the water is ready, add about half the noodles and cook for 2 to 3 minutes, or until the noodles float to the surface of the water and puff. Drain, then sauce and serve immediately. Repeat with the remaining noodles once the water has come back to a boil.

COLD RED CURRY NOODLES

zucchini pesto, shrimp

You could look at this refreshing summery noodle dish from two angles—first, as a noodlefied example of the classic Korean summertime *banchan* combination of zucchini and salted shrimp, and second, as an Easternized version of a more Italian pasta dish with shrimp, pesto, greens, and peppers. Either way, pairing inherently sweet zucchini with salty shrimp produces a flavor we love.

Because noodles do tend to firm up as they cool, we make our cold noodle dishes with softer noodles—achieved, in this case, by adding a mixture of eggs, egg yolks, and baking powder to the dough. Make sure to toss the cooked noodles immediately with the pesto, or they'll stick together.

Before you begin, see Dumpling and Noodle Basics (page 75).

MAKES 4 SERVINGS

FOR THE DOUGH:

2 cups all-purpose flour, plus more for
  kneading and rolling
½ teaspoon baking powder
½ teaspoon kosher salt
4 large egg yolks
2 large eggs
1 tablespoon Thai-style red curry paste
1 teaspoon canola oil
Rice flour, for dusting

FOR THE SHRIMP:

1 quart water
¼ cup sake
½ small daikon radish (about 4 ounces),
  cut into 1-inch pieces
3 cloves garlic
1 small carrot, cut into 1-inch pieces
1 small celery rib, cut into 1-inch pieces
1 small onion, cut into 1-inch pieces
½ teaspoon whole black peppercorns
½ teaspoon whole coriander seeds
1 sprig fresh thyme
1 bay leaf
2 teaspoons kosher salt
1½ pounds large shell-on shrimp, deveined
  (shells left intact)

FOR THE PESTO:

2 cups packed Thai basil leaves
2 medium zucchini (about 1 pound)
1 cup canola oil
1 tablespoon salted shrimp
1 tablespoon fish sauce
1 tablespoon chopped peeled fresh ginger

FOR SERVING:

½ cup drained pickled grilled Korean
  peppers (see page 129)
1 small head escarole (about 4 ounces),
  chopped (about 2 packed cups)

1. **MAKE THE DOUGH.** In a large bowl, whisk together the flour, baking powder, and salt to blend. In a small bowl, whisk together the egg yolks, whole eggs, curry paste, and oil until uniform in color. Make a small well in the center of the dry ingredients, then add the egg mixture to the well. Using your hands or a spoon, mix the ingredients until they cling together in a shaggy mass, then pat the dough together, transfer it to a clean lightly floured surface, and knead until smooth. (See Making Dough by Hand, page 75,

continued

for more detailed instructions; see Mixing with a Machine, page 77, if you'd prefer to work with a stand mixer.) Wrap the dough well in plastic and set aside to rest at room temperature for about 30 minutes.

2. MAKE A COURT BOUILLON FOR POACHING THE SHRIMP. In a 3-quart pot, combine the water, sake, radish, garlic, carrot, celery, onion, peppercorns, coriander, thyme, bay leaf, and salt and stir to combine. Bring to a boil over high heat, then reduce to a bare simmer and cook for 30 minutes.

3. MEANWHILE, MAKE THE PESTO. Bring a small saucepan of water to a boil over high heat. Add the basil and cook for about 30 seconds, then drain and, when cool enough to handle, squeeze the excess water out of the basil. Transfer it to the bowl of a food processor.

Trim the ends off the zucchini, then cut the skin off the zucchini in strips that go about ½ inch into the zucchini, like you're cutting the kernels off a cob of corn. (It's the skins you want to keep.) Cut the skin strips into ½-inch pieces, discarding the white inner core of the zucchini.

Add the zucchini skins, oil, salted shrimp, fish sauce, and ginger to the food processor with the basil, and whirl until the zucchini is very finely chopped (but not totally smooth). Set aside.

4. POACH AND PEEL THE SHRIMP. Add the shrimp to the simmering court bouillon and cook for 2 minutes. Transfer the shrimp to an ice bath to cool, then peel them and set aside.

5. ROLL OUT THE DOUGH. Using a pasta-rolling machine, roll to level 5 and cut into thin noodles, dusting the noodles with rice flour as needed to prevent them from sticking together. (See Making Noodles, page 89.)

6. COOK AND SERVE THE NOODLES. Using the instructions in Cooking Noodles (see page 91), put about half of the noodles in to cook. When the noodles are done, dunk them in an ice bath until cool, then drain them and transfer to a large bowl. Add about 1 cup of the pesto and toss to coat. Repeat with the remaining noodles, then to the entire batch, add another ½ cup of the pesto, plus the pickled peppers, escarole, and reserved shrimp, and toss to blend, adding more pesto as the noodles soak it up. Serve cold in individual Asian-style noodle bowls.

MUSHROOM NOODLES

bitter greens, sweet miso

Considering how many different types of foods Seif and I make each day, and how much of that ever-evolving flavor we bring home, our two small boys aren't always adventurous in the food department. They're apt to choose plain noodles whenever possible. However, when we make noodles together at home, they tend to be more open-minded—especially when I dress them with a sauce that's part sweet, part sour, like the funky miso sauce we use for a dish we call "mushroom noodle" at Trove. Contrary to what the name suggests, the noodles don't have mushrooms in them (those are mixed in separately), but the dough has a zesty mixture of black and Szechuan peppercorns that gives the noodles a lovely bite. I use a bit less pepper when I make them with my kids, because they inevitably play with the dough, and Szechuan peppercorns and small hands rubbing their eyeballs do not mix well. If you want more heat, drizzle with Chili Oil (page 240).

Before you begin, see Dumpling and Noodle Basics (page 75).

MAKES 6 SERVINGS

FOR THE DOUGH:

2 cups plus 1 tablespoon bread flour

2 cups plus 1 tablespoon all-purpose flour, plus more for kneading and rolling

1 teaspoon kosher salt

2 teaspoons ground toasted Szechuan peppercorns (see Toasting Spices, page 53)

1 teaspoon freshly ground black pepper

1 large egg

⅔ cup water

Rice flour, for dusting

FOR THE SAUCE:

¾ cup mirin

½ cup sake

¼ cup soy sauce

1 tablespoon fermented tofu (solids only)

1 tablespoon fermented soybeans

1 tablespoon Japanese white miso

2 cloves garlic

FOR SERVING:

4 tablespoons canola oil, divided

3 (3.5-ounce) packages *honshimeji* mushrooms, bottoms trimmed off

Kosher salt and freshly ground black pepper

6 tablespoons (¾ stick) unsalted butter, divided

1 head radicchio (about 8 ounces), cored and cut into 1-inch chunks (about 2 heaping cups)

1 head escarole (about 12 ounces), trimmed and cut into 2-inch strips (about 3 heaping cups)

⅓ cup soy-pickled leeks (see page 129)

2 tablespoons sherry vinegar, divided

3 tablespoons wild sesame seeds

use fermented tofu like vinegar for its tanginess

1. **MAKE THE DOUGH.** In a large bowl, whisk together the flours, salt, Szechuan peppercorns, and black pepper to blend. In a small bowl, whisk together the egg and water until uniform in color. Make a small well in the center of the dry ingredients, then add the egg mixture to the well. Using your hands or a spoon, mix the ingredients until they

continued

cling together in a shaggy mass, then pat the dough together, transfer it to a clean lightly floured surface, and knead until smooth. (See Making Dough by Hand, page 75, for more detailed instructions; see Mixing with a Machine, page 77, if you'd prefer to work with a stand mixer.) Wrap the dough well in plastic, and set aside to rest at room temperature for about 30 minutes.

2. **MAKE THE SAUCE.** In a heavy-duty blender or the bowl of a food processor, whirl together the mirin, sake, soy sauce, tofu, soybeans, miso, and garlic until smooth. Set aside.

3. **ROLL OUT THE DOUGH.** Using a pasta-rolling machine, roll to level 5 and cut into thick noodles, sprinkling the noodles with rice flour as needed to prevent them from sticking together. (See Making Noodles, page 89.)

4. **COOK AND SERVE THE NOODLES.** Using the instructions in Cooking Noodles (see page 91), put about half of the noodles in to cook. While the noodles cook, heat a large skillet or wok over medium-high heat. Add 2 tablespoons of the oil, then half of the mushrooms, and season with salt and pepper. Cook, stirring often, for about 2 minutes, or until the mushrooms begin to brown, then add 3 tablespoons of the butter and season with salt. When the butter has melted and is beginning to brown, add about half of the sauce. (Give the sauce a quick stir before adding.) Add the cooked noodles, stir to combine them with the sauce, then add about half of the radicchio, escarole, and leeks. Sprinkle everything with 1 tablespoon of the vinegar, then toss to blend for a minute or so, allowing the greens to wilt. (If the noodles seem to want to stick to the pan, you can add a few tablespoons of the noodle-cooking water and shake the pan to loosen them.) Season with additional salt if necessary, transfer to three Asian-style noodle bowls, and serve piping hot, garnished with 1½ tablespoons of the sesame seeds. Repeat with the remaining ingredients.

BLACK SESAME NOODLES

rotisserie chicken, rapini, chili oil

From a distance, these taupe-colored noodles look like a buckwheat version of pappardelle, but get close enough to smell them, and the rich waft of sesame seeds will tell you they're made with ground black sesame seeds and sesame oil. (In general, I don't tend to use a lot of sesame oil, because the flavor can be overpowering, but here, it's perfect.) Paired with rapini and shredded chicken, and topped with a Szechuan-tinged chili oil, it has all the trappings of a noodle dish you never want to put down.

Note that because you'll be rolling and cutting these noodles by hand, the sheets of dough need to be quite dry before you cut. See Dumpling and Noodle Basics (page 75) and Hand-Cutting Noodles (page 91).

MAKES 6 SERVINGS

FOR THE DOUGH:

4 cups all-purpose flour, plus more for kneading and rolling

¼ cup plus 2 tablespoons black sesame powder (see page 50)

1 teaspoon kosher salt

6 large eggs

1 tablespoon toasted sesame oil

Rice flour, for dusting

FOR THE SAUCE:

1 cup soy sauce

¼ cup rice vinegar

½ cup tahini

10 large cloves confited garlic (see Quick Garlic Confit, page 172)

2 tablespoons roughly chopped peeled fresh ginger

FOR SERVING:

4 tablespoons canola oil, divided

1 bunch rapini (about 1 pound), leaves roughly chopped, stems trimmed and cut into 1-inch pieces (about 8 cups)

Kosher salt and freshly ground black pepper

½ cup (1 stick) unsalted butter, at room temperature

4 cups shredded roast chicken meat (from about ½ of a rotisserie chicken)

Chili Oil (recipe follows), to taste

1. MAKE THE DOUGH. In a large bowl, whisk together the flour, sesame powder, and salt to blend. In a small bowl, whisk together the eggs and sesame oil until uniform in color. Make a small well in the center of the dry ingredients, then add the egg mixture to the well. Using your hands or a spoon, mix the ingredients until they cling together in a shaggy mass, then pat the dough together, transfer it to a clean lightly floured surface, and knead until smooth. (See Making Dough by Hand, page 75, for more detailed instructions; see Mixing with a Machine, page 77, if you'd prefer to work with a stand mixer.) Wrap the dough well in plastic and set aside to rest at room temperature for about 30 minutes.

2. MAKE THE SAUCE. In a heavy-duty blender whirl together the soy sauce, vinegar, tahini, garlic, and ginger until smooth. (Because tahini has quite a bit of oil, it's important to blend it very well in order to emulsify the sauce, which makes the flavor well rounded, rather than salty and harsh.) Set aside.

continued

3. **ROLL OUT THE DOUGH.** Using a pasta-rolling machine, roll to level 5, then cut the dough by hand into 1-inch-thick noodles, dusting the noodles with rice flour as needed to prevent them from sticking together. (See Making Noodles, page 89, and Hand-Cutting Noodles, page 91.)

4. **COOK AND SERVE THE NOODLES.** Using the instructions in Cooking Noodles (see page 91), put about half of the noodles in to cook. While the noodles cook, heat a large skillet or wok over high heat. Add 2 tablespoons of the oil, then half of the rapini, and season with salt and pepper. Cook, stirring often, for about 1 minute, then add half the butter. When it has mostly melted, add about ¾ cup of the sauce. (Give the sauce a quick stir before using it each time.) When the sauce is bubbling, stir in half the chicken, then scoop the noodles out of the cooking water and add them to the pan. Toss to blend, and serve piping hot in Asian-style noodle bowls, garnished with 1 to 2 teaspoons of the chili oil. Repeat with the remaining ingredients.

chili oil

Combine mild Korean chili flakes, hotter dried guajillo chilies, and the slightly numbing effect of Szechuan peppercorns, and you've got an oil you'll want to drizzle on absolutely everything.

MAKES 1 GENEROUS CUP

2 dried guajillo chilies

1 cup canola oil

5 bunches green onions, white parts only, cut into ⅛-inch-thick rounds (about 1 cup)

1 tablespoon ground Szechuan peppercorns

1 tablespoon coarse Korean chili flakes

1. **SOFTEN THE CHILIES.** Place the guajillos in a bowl of boiling water, and let sit for 1 hour to soften, submerging them with a plate to make sure they're completely under water.

2. **FRY THE GREEN ONIONS.** In a large, wide skillet over medium-high heat, heat the canola oil until a small piece of green onion sizzles vigorously when you add it. Add the green onions and fry for about 5 minutes, or until they just begin to brown. Remove the pan from the heat, then use a mesh ladle or slotted spoon to transfer the green onions to a paper towel–lined plate.

3. **MAKE THE OIL.** Remove the guajillos from their soak, discard their stems, and blend them in a food processor or blender until pasty, adding a little water to encourage the mixture to move, if necessary. When the oil stops bubbling, carefully add the guajillo paste, Szechuan peppercorns, and chili flakes and stir to blend. When the mixture has stopped bubbling again and the red turns to a deep dark brown color, add the green onions, transfer to a jar, and set aside to cool to room temperature. Use immediately, or keep covered in the refrigerator for up to 1 month.

SEAWEED NOODLES

dungeness crab, crème fraîche

It has happened, on occasion, that we've run out of the crab required to make these ethereal seaweed-infused noodles, which are a staple at both Revel and Revelry. It qualifies as a crisis, which means we do whatever we can in the middle of service to get good Dungeness crab back into the kitchen. According to Sammie (who worked at Revel before moving on to manage Joule), people order these noodle so often because they have everything one could possibly want in a dish—slight heat from the curry in the broth, sweet hunks of crab, pickled slivered ginger, and the creaminess of crème fraîche. These noodles also happen to be Seif's favorite dish because—with a Korean heart, French and Thai flair, and Pacific Northwest ingredients—it captures what we do in one bowl.

At Revel and Revelry, we roll these noodles thinner than all the others, which gives them their hallmark silky mouthfeel.

We always assemble each serving individually at the restaurant, but at home, it's easier to do in two big batches in a large wok, using half the serving ingredients for each batch.

Before you begin, see Dumpling and Noodle Basics (page 75).

MAKES 6 SERVINGS

FOR THE DOUGH:

4 cups all-purpose flour, plus more for
  kneading and rolling
2 tablespoons nori powder (see Making
  Nori Powder, following page)
1 teaspoon kosher salt
6 large eggs
1 tablespoon canola oil
Rice flour, for dusting

FOR THE SAUCE:

1 cup Revel's Seasoned Soy Sauce
  (page 73)
1 cup sake
½ cup mirin
2 tablespoons stirred jarred crab paste

2 tablespoons Thai-style red curry paste
2 tablespoons tamarind paste
⅓ cup roughly chopped peeled
  fresh ginger
8 cloves garlic

FOR SERVING:

¾ cup (1½ sticks) unsalted butter,
  at room temperature
¾ pound picked Dungeness crabmeat
3 baby bok choy, ends trimmed off
½ cup crème fraîche
½ cup pickled julienned ginger (see
  page 129)
¾ cup lightly packed fresh cilantro leaves
Freshly ground black pepper

1. **MAKE THE DOUGH.** In a large bowl, whisk together the flour, nori powder, and salt to blend. In a small bowl, whisk together the eggs and oil until uniform in color. Make a small well in the center of the dry ingredients, then add the egg mixture to the well. Using your hands or a spoon, mix the ingredients until they cling together in a shaggy mass, then pat the dough together, transfer it to a clean lightly floured surface, and

continued

knead until smooth. (See Making Dough by Hand, page 75, for more detailed instructions; or see Mixing with a Machine, page 77, if you'd prefer to work with a stand mixer.) Wrap the dough well in plastic and set aside to rest at room temperature for about 30 minutes.

2. **MAKE THE SAUCE.** In a blender whirl together the soy sauce, sake, mirin, crab paste, curry paste, tamarind paste, ginger, and garlic until smooth. Set aside.

3. **ROLL OUT THE DOUGH.** Using a pasta-rolling machine, roll to level 6 and cut into thick noodles, dusting the noodles with rice flour as needed to prevent them from sticking. (See Making Noodles, page 89.)

4. **COOK AND SERVE THE NOODLES.** Using the instructions in Cooking Noodles (see page 91), put about half of the noodles in to cook. While the noodles cook, heat a large skillet or wok over medium heat. Add half the butter and about 1¼ cups of the sauce. (Give the sauce a quick stir before using it each time.) When the sauce is bubbling, stir in half of the crab and bok choy leaves, then scoop the noodles out of the cooking water and add them to the pan. Toss to blend, and serve piping hot in Asian-style noodle bowls, garnishing each bowl with a heaping tablespoon of crème fraîche, a clump of pickled ginger, a pinch of the cilantro, and pepper to taste. Repeat with the remaining ingredients.

MAKING NORI POWDER

Because nori is inherently shiny, whirling it into a powder essentially makes glitter that tastes like the ocean. We love it sprinkled over rice, salad, or noodles, but we also use it to make the noodles themselves. Blend four ounces of nori in a heavy-duty blender with one teaspoon tapioca starch until it reaches the consistency of glitter. (Like any glitter, it's impossible to clean up.)

SMOKY PAD THAI

pork belly, yu choy

We designed the blonde-wood noodle bar at Trove, in Seattle's Capitol Hill neighborhood, to be a delicious assault on the senses. Made up of five or six dishes, most of which change with the seasons, the black-lettered menu shows how infinitely flexible noodle dough (and noodle dishes) can be. From leek ash to poppy seeds to black sesame powder, the cooks are constantly inventing new noodle flavors. While you wait, the combined scents of Korean, Thai, Chinese, and Japanese spices waft toward the lipstick-red ceiling.

Our take on pad Thai, spiced with chipotle chili powder and chili-spiked peanuts, is both meatier and greener than tradition dictates—and, because of that chipotle, it has a smoky edge too. Note that adding the chipotle to the sauce at the end allows you to control the spiciness—start with less if you want a milder dish or add more to taste, if you prefer.

We always assemble each serving individually at the restaurant, but at home, it's easier to do in two big batches in a large wok, using half the serving ingredients for each batch.

Look for yu choy in the produce section of a large Asian grocery store; it looks like Chinese broccoli with extra-smooth leaves.

MAKES 4 SERVINGS

FOR THE PORK BELLY:
1 pound pork belly, skin removed
1 tablespoon kosher salt

FOR THE SAUCE:
1 cup sugar
½ cup water
1 cup fish sauce
¾ cup tamarind puree
½ cup plus 1 tablespoon rice vinegar
1½ teaspoons ground toasted coriander (see Toasting Spices, page 53)
3 tablespoons chipotle puree, or more to taste (see Making Chipotle Puree, page 113)

FOR THE CHILI PEANUTS:
1½ cups blister peanuts (or regular shelled peanuts)
2 tablespoons canola oil
1 tablespoon plus 1 teaspoon coarse Korean chili flakes
½ teaspoon kosher salt

FOR SERVING:
4 tablespoons canola oil, divided
2 (16-ounce) packages fresh pad Thai noodles, or 1 (16-ounce) package dried noodles, soaked in cold water for 1 hour and drained before serving
1 cup water
4 cups roughly chopped yu choy (about 8 ounces)
1 small lime, cut into 6 wedges
½ small bunch fresh cilantro

continued

1. **ROAST THE PORK BELLY.** Preheat the oven to 300 degrees F. Line a baking sheet with foil, place the pork belly fat side up on a rack over the foil, and rub the belly on all sides with the salt. Roast for 1½ to 2 hours, or until tender but not yet falling apart. Set aside to cool, then cut into ½-inch slices.

2. **MEANWHILE, MAKE THE PAD THAI SAUCE.** First, make a fish caramel: In a large saucepan, stir together the sugar and water with a fork, then place the pan over high heat and bring to a boil. Cook, undisturbed, until the liquid turns a deep golden brown. Carefully whisk in the fish sauce. Once the fish caramel is well mixed, set aside to cool.

In a heavy-duty blender, whirl together the fish caramel, tamarind, vinegar, and coriander until smooth, and transfer to a small bowl.

Stir the chipotle puree it into the fish sauce mixture, and take a tiny taste. It should be spicy and smoky, but if you like things on the hotter side, add as much of the chipotle puree as you'd like. Set aside.

3. **MAKE THE CHILI PEANUTS.** Place the peanuts in a small baking dish and slide them into the oven next to the pork. Roast for about 20 minutes, or until fragrant and lightly browned.

When the peanuts are toasted, heat the oil and 1 teaspoon of the chili flakes in a small saucepan over medium heat. When the flakes begin to sizzle, add the peanuts, and cook for about 1 minute, stirring. Using a slotted spoon, transfer the peanuts to a paper towel–lined plate, allow them to drain briefly, then toss with the remaining 1 tablespoon chili flakes and the salt until the peanuts are powdered with red. Set aside on the towel until cool.

4. **SERVE THE NOODLES.** Heat a large skillet or wok over medium-high heat. Add 2 tablespoons of the oil, then half the pork slices, and sear the pork on each side for 1 to 2 minutes, until golden brown. (If the pork seems to give off a lot of fat, drain some of it off, so the fat just coats the bottom of the pan.) Add half the noodles, stir to coat them in the oil, then add ½ cup water and half the pad Thai sauce (give it a quick stir first). Cook until the sauce reduces enough to coat the noodles, stirring frequently, about 2 minutes. Add half the yu choy, saute for 1 minute more, and then divide the noodles and pork between two Asian-style noodle bowls. Top each bowl with a handful of peanuts, a lime section, and a few cilantro sprigs, and serve hot. Repeat with the remaining ingredients.

CHOW FUN

lemongrass sausage, pea vines, mint

With their light texture, rice-based chow fun noodles (sometimes spelled *shao fen*) are a natural match for the springy, green flavor of homemade lemongrass sausage. Tossed with a loose mint and cilantro pesto, baby peas, and pea vines, this Trove favorite is the antithesis of a heavy noodle dish. We top it with our version of togarashi, the traditionally Japanese spice mixture that we blend with dried orange zest, to add just a hint of heat.

Look for the wide, flat chow fun noodles in the produce section or the refrigerated section of a large Asian grocery store. Although they're sometimes sold already cut into half-inch strips, look for the kind that are packaged uncut, so you can cut them yourself into slightly wider strips, if possible. (They're impossible to tear apart when cold. If you purchase them refrigerated, reheat them in the microwave for about ten seconds at a time, until the noodles are soft and pliable.)

If you'd like to break up the work for this recipe, make the sausage, pesto, and togarashi up to a day before serving, and refrigerate the first two, covered, until ready to use.

We always assemble each serving individually at the restaurant, but at home, it's easier to do in two big batches in a large wok, using half the serving ingredients for each batch.

MAKES 4 SERVINGS

FOR THE SAUSAGE:

1 pound ground pork

2 tablespoons finely chopped fresh lemongrass (from the tender insides of 2 medium stalks)

1 tablespoon chopped garlic (from 3 to 4 cloves)

1 tablespoon grated peeled fresh ginger

2 teaspoons salted shrimp

2 teaspoons ground toasted coriander (see Toasting Spices, page 53)

1 teaspoon fish sauce

1 teaspoon finely chopped shallot

FOR THE PESTO:

1 cup roughly chopped mustard greens (including stems)

½ cup packed fresh mint leaves

¼ cup packed cilantro (including stems)

½ cup mirin

½ cup sake

¼ cup fish sauce

2 teaspoons canola oil

1 teaspoon sherry vinegar

⅛ teaspoon ground toasted caraway seeds (see Toasting Spices, page 53)

⅛ teaspoon crushed red pepper flakes

FOR THE NOODLES:

1 (32-ounce) package chow fun noodles (uncut if available)

½ cup canola oil

4 cups packed young pea vines, cut into 3-inch pieces, if long

1 cup baby peas (fresh or frozen)

Orange Togarashi (page 51), for garnish

continued

chipotle introduces smoky flavor to Asian cuisine

1. **MAKE THE SAUSAGE.** In a large bowl, mix together the pork, lemongrass, garlic, ginger, salted shrimp, coriander, fish sauce, and shallot. Using gloved hands—really, hands work best—blend the mixture until very well incorporated. Set aside.

2. **MAKE THE PESTO.** In a blender or the bowl of a food processor, whirl together the mustard greens, mint, and cilantro until chopped. Add the mirin, sake, fish sauce, oil, vinegar, caraway, and red pepper flakes, and blend until evenly green, with no large pieces remaining, pausing to scrape down the sides of the bowl if necessary. Transfer the sauce to a small bowl (or 2-cup glass measuring cup with a spout, for easy measuring later).

3. **PREPARE THE NOODLES AND GET READY TO COOK.** When you're ready to cook, trim the rounded ends off the patty of chow fun, then cut into ¾-inch strips and transfer the noodles to a large bowl, breaking them into long individual strips if you can. (They'll continue to break apart in the pan. If they seem particularly stuck together, put them in the microwave for about 10 seconds at a time, until they're soft enough to peel apart, or give them 30 seconds or so in a steamer.) Gather the sausage, togarashi, pesto, oil, pea vines, peas, and noodles in a spot near the stove. (You'll be making the noodles in four quick batches, so it's nice to have everything nearby.)

4. **FRY THE SAUSAGE AND NOODLES.** Heat a large skillet or wok over medium-high heat. When hot, working quickly, add about 2 tablespoons of the canola oil to the pan, then scatter a quarter of the sausage over the pan in big bite-size chunks. Let the sausage cook for about 3 minutes, turning once or twice, then add a quarter of the noodles and cook, stirring, for another 2 minutes, until the noodles are soft and the pork is cooked through. Stir the pesto, then add about a ½ cup of the pesto, and a quarter of the pea vines and peas, and toss just until combined. Transfer the noodles to Asian-style noodle bowls, sprinkle with togarashi, and serve immediately. Repeat with the remaining ingredients, wiping out the pan (or using a different pan) when necessary between batches.

SPICY RICE CAKES

chorizo, fermented chinese mustard greens

One of our restaurants' most popular noodle dishes isn't made with what you might think of as noodles. It's made with rice cakes—not the crisp, dry kind made with puffed rice but thin, ovoid discs of glutinous rice that most Asian grocery stores stock with the refrigerated noodles. (Their shape is meant to mimic that of coins, so in Korea, they symbolize wealth.) In Korean food, you'll see them most in soups and stews, but everyone also has their own version of rice cakes cooked in a simple spicy sauce. At Joule, we serve them in a spicy *gochujang* sauce (nicknamed "crack sauce" by our customers), with housemade chorizo and fermented Chinese mustard greens—on an average night, one in every three customers will order it. At Trove, we make a curried version with lamb that's equally popular. Trove and Joule both receive eighty pounds of rice cakes each week, and sometimes, we run out.

What makes our rice cakes so special is textural contrast. The way we cook them, the rice cakes are simultaneously crisp on the outside and chewy on the inside—and that chewiness, which is rare in traditional savory American food, is almost addictive.

This dish is certainly best when you make everything from scratch, but you can also purchase a pound of premade chorizo and prepackaged fermented mustard greens. Then it becomes easy to make for a weeknight dinner—something that's not always possible when you have to think about fermenting the greens *a week* before you want to serve the rice cakes.

We always assemble each serving individually at the restaurant, but at home, it's easier to do in two big batches in a large wok, using half the serving ingredients for each batch.

MAKES 4 SERVINGS

FOR SERVING:

- 1 package rice cakes (about 4 cups)
- 4 tablespoons canola oil, divided, plus more as needed
- 1 cup Fermented Chinese Mustard Greens (page 61), finely chopped
- 1 recipe Sweet and Spicy All-Purpose Sauce (page 48)
- 1 cup water, divided
- 4 green onions (green parts only), thinly sliced

FOR THE CHORIZO:

- 1 tablespoon rice vinegar
- 1 tablespoon soju
- 2 cloves garlic, finely chopped
- 2 tablespoons plus 1 teaspoon coarse Korean chili flakes
- 1 tablespoon hot smoked Spanish paprika (*pimentón de la vera*)
- ¾ teaspoon kosher salt
- ½ teaspoon freshly ground black pepper
- ½ teaspoon ground toasted cumin (see Toasting Spices, page 53)
- ½ teaspoon ground toasted coriander (see Toasting Spices, page 53)
- 1 pound ground pork

continued

1. **SOAK THE RICE CAKES.** Put the rice cakes into a large bowl, breaking them up as you go if they seem stuck together. Add water to cover and let sit for about 1 hour.

2. **MAKE THE CHORIZO.** In a small bowl, stir together the vinegar, soju, and garlic. Add the chili flakes, paprika, salt, pepper, cumin, and coriander, and stir until well blended. Transfer 2 tablespoons of this spice mixture to a large bowl and add the pork. (For spicier chorizo, you could add more spice mixture, but remember that the dish will be simmered in a chili paste–based sauce.) Using gloved hands—really, hands work best—blend the mixture until very well incorporated. Cover and refrigerate until ready to use. (You can make the meat mixture up to 3 days before serving and store in the refrigerator, covered, until you add it to the pan.)

3. **COOK AND SERVE THE RICE CAKES.** Drain the rice cakes. Decide whether you want to cook the dish in two batches by cooking in two pans at once, or by cooking in one pan, cleaning it out quickly, and repeating with the remaining ingredients. For cooking in one pan: Heat a large skillet or wok over medium-high heat. Add 2 tablespoons of the oil, then pat about half the chorizo into a ¾-inch-thick patty on one side of the pan. Add half the rice cakes to the rest of the pan, breaking up the rice cakes with your hands as you drop them in. (Depending on the size of your pan, you may need to add a bit more oil. There should be enough oil that you see it bubbling around the edges of the ingredients in the pan.) Cook for 3 minutes undisturbed, or until the chorizo is cooked on the bottom side and the rice cakes have begun to brown lightly. Turn all the ingredients, breaking up the rice cakes and chorizo a little with a wooden spoon and adding more oil, if necessary, to keep a thin layer across the bottom of the pan. Cook 3 minutes more. Add half the mustard greens, about half the sauce, and ½ cup of the water, stir to combine, and cook for another 3 to 5 minutes, or until the sauce has thickened, the chorizo is cooked through, and the rice cakes begin to separate from each other. Divide between two Asian-style noodle bowls and serve immediately, garnished with half of the green onions. Repeat with the remaining ingredients.

not your typical rice cake from the streets of Korea

rice and grains

The first time they met, my dad reminded Seif that Korea has two millennia of consistent cultural history compared to the United States's two hundred or so years. In Korea, there's really no such thing as multiple cultures. People are all from the same ethnic pot, with very few outliers. There is often just one way of doing things, whether in cooking or otherwise. For generations, people have known that if you put the tip of your index finger on the surface of dry rice in a pot, you need to add water up to the first crease on the inside of your finger. As a kid, new to America, that made me feel different. I was torn between hewing to the deeply rooted traditions of Korea's past and embracing America's spicy cultural mash-up.

But today, being me—someone who brings a totally goofy mixture of Korean and American cultures to each dish I make—is what makes us successful. Doing what I do now enables me to feel at home here while embracing my past at the same time. I still use my finger almost every day to cook rice. (In fact, because rice is such a humble, simple food, it seems strange to write a whole chapter on it.) But now, I feel free to intertwine different flavors into the foods of my childhood. Our more complex rice dishes are often the edible portrayals of my history. The rice bowls at Revel and Revelry—unexpected takes on Korean *bibimbap*, if you're thinking very broadly, based on everything from curried lamb (see page 273) to our local geoduck (see page 275)—make me proud to be a Korean American.

SIMPLE WHITE RICE

I grew up in a household where my mom was always making what we call mixed rice—rice made with a variety of different grains, and often with red or black beans. She used a pressure cooker, usually, and we must have gone through two or three cups of rice every single day. Pure white rice was reserved for birthdays and holidays, though. In Korea, it connotes purity, abundance, and celebration. There's deep symbolism in serving it, even. The top of every pot always goes to the most esteemed guests, which often means your parents. That's because no matter how you cook your rice, it is always true that the very top part is the best—sweeter than the other grains, and slightly tacky but not ever sticky or wet. (If you take the time to notice it, you'll realize the rest of the pot pales in comparison.) We had a cook at Revel who famously always took the top spoonful from our giant batches, because he said it was the happiest he felt every day.

They say perfect rice takes a lifetime to achieve. But while Koreans use the same short-grain rice sushi chefs use, we don't tend to be quite as fussy. What's important is how much water you use.

The part most home cooks get wrong is that when you double the amount of rice you're cooking, you don't need to double the water. You want one and one-quarter to one and one-half cups of water for each cup of rice (depending in part on how sticky you want your rice to be), but you skew to the lower end when you cook more. (The backs of American-made rice bags often advocate for using one and one-half to one and three-quarters cups of water per cup of rice, which results in mushy grains.) Growing up, my mom always measured the water with her finger, so that's the way I still do it when I cook rice in a pot—you just put your index finger on the surface of the grains in the pot and add water up to the first line on the inside of your finger. It's the same no matter how much rice you make.

We use a rice cooker for both rices and grains at all our restaurants. Because it turns off as soon as the rice has reached a certain temperature, it's foolproof. If you're going to be cooking rice frequently, it may make sense to invest in a good one—but in the meantime, you can make wonderful rice with just rice, water, and a pot that leaves plenty of room for steam.

MAKES 8 CUPS

3 cups short-grain white rice, rinsed and drained three times
About 1 quart water

1. **MAKE THE RICE.** In a large saucepan, combine the rice and water (see Rice Cooking Tips, page 260). Bring the water to a boil over high heat, then reduce the heat to the lowest setting, cover, and cook, undisturbed, for 20 minutes, or until all the water is absorbed. Remove the rice from the heat, let rest for 15 minutes, then fluff and serve.

RICE COOKING TIPS

rinse your rice

Rice has a fine layer of starch on the outside of each grain that can make it sticky as it cooks. Although different cultures have different norms, we wash our rice in three changes of water to rid the grains of the starch. To rinse it, put the rice in the pot you plan to cook it in, then fill the pot about halfway with water. Swirl the rice and water around with your hands, then drain the water off. You're not looking for the water to be clear—that takes a while—but it should look significantly less milky after three rinses. Cook the rice immediately after rinsing.

give your rice space

Since rice expands greatly when it cooks, never fill a pot more than a third full with raw rice.

let it rest and give it a turn

Rice grains continue changing after they've absorbed their cooking water. Allowing the rice to rest for 10 to 15 minutes after cooking is ideal. Once it's steamed, turn the rice so that the grains on the bottom, which have more moisture and get compacted by the rice on the top, have a chance to dry out and fluff up.

don't mash it

We use a paddle to scoop our rice because it doesn't squish the grains. When you serve rice, think about using more of a crowbar motion, prying the rice out, instead of scooping it out by smearing the spoon into the grains. A flat spatula works better than a spoon.

reheating rice

The best way to reheat rice is in a microwave. Although the time will vary based on your machine, always reheat it with a lid, and let it sit for a minute or two afterward, so the steam created by recooking can reach all the grains.

troubleshooting

If you feel like your rice is undercooked, add 2 tablespoons of water and simmer with the lid on for a few more minutes. If the rice seems too wet, you can fluff it, put it in a wide bowl so more steam escapes, and then serve it immediately—wet rice doesn't sit well.

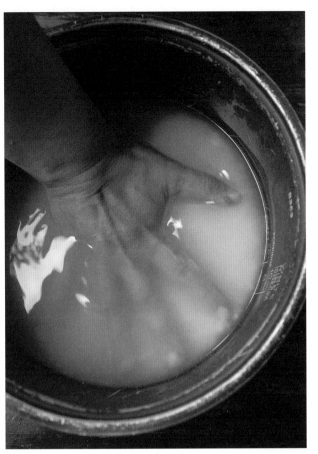

RED QUINOA RICE

dried dates

Although we serve our rice bowls at Revel and Revelry over white rice most often, we sometimes sneak in different grains. This is our take on quinoa, made with dates to give it sweetness.

MAKES 4 GENEROUS CUPS

2 tablespoons unsalted butter

1 medium shallot, sliced into rings

1 cup red quinoa

1 cup medium- or short-grain rice, rinsed and drained three times

1 quart water

5 pitted Korean dried dates (jujubes), slivered

1 teaspoon kosher salt

1. **MAKE THE QUINOA.** In a large saucepan over medium heat, melt the butter. When melted, add the shallot and cook, stirring frequently, until translucent, about 3 minutes. Add the quinoa and rice and cook for another 2 minutes, stirring, until the rice begins to look slightly toasted. Stir in the water, dates, and salt, bring to a simmer, then reduce the heat to the lowest setting, cover, and cook for about 15 to 20 minutes, or until the water is absorbed and the quinoa and rice are cooked (see Cooking Grains, page 266). Remove the grains from the heat, let sit for 10 minutes, then fluff and serve.

JASMINE RICE

coconut milk, turmeric

In general, jasmine rice does a great job of soaking up flavor if it's cooked in something other than water—think chicken stock, dashi, or in this case, coconut milk. Serve it as is, with the toasted coconut on top, or leave the coconut off and use it as a base for our Lamb Curry Rice Bowl (page 273).

MAKES 8 CUPS

1 quart water

3 cups jasmine rice, rinsed and drained three times

1 cup coconut milk

1 (¼-inch) slice peeled turmeric

1 cup toasted large unsweetened coconut flakes (see Toasting Coconut, page 300)

1. **MAKE THE RICE.** In a medium saucepan, combine the water, rice, coconut milk, and turmeric. Bring the mixture to a simmer, then reduce the heat to the lowest setting, cover, and cook for about 30 minutes, or until the water is absorbed and the rice is cooked (see Rice Cooking Tips, page 260). Remove the rice from the heat, let sit for 10 minutes, then fluff and serve, garnished with the toasted coconut.

DIRTY FARRO

chicken liver, togarashi

Dirty rice—rice cooked with various bits of meat, often from pork or chicken organs—has long been synonymous with Creole cooking in the United States, but Chinese, Thai, and even Nigerian cooking traditions all have their own versions of fried rice made with liver. Our version matches the intensity of chicken liver with farro, a grain that also has big flavor. Instead of stir-frying the farro with the meat, we essentially whirl the liver into a sauce, which gets cooked as it hits the hot farro. The orange in the togarashi is a surprising match; it acts the same way fruit jam does with, say, a chicken liver pâté.

MAKES 6 TO 8 SERVINGS

FOR THE FARRO:
4 cups farro
7½ cups water
1 teaspoon kosher salt

FOR THE LIVER:
8 ounces chicken livers
1 cup sake
¼ cup julienned peeled fresh ginger

FOR SERVING:
¼ cup Orange Togarashi (page 51)

1. **COOK THE FARRO.** In a medium saucepan, combine the farro, water, and salt. Bring to a boil, then reduce to a simmer and cook, covered, until the farro is tender and the water is almost absorbed, about 45 minutes. Drain off any excess water.

2. **MARINATE THE LIVERS.** While the farro cooks, in a medium bowl, stir together the livers, sake, and ginger. Cover and marinate in the refrigerator for 30 minutes.

3. **BLEND THE LIVERS.** After 30 minutes, drain the sake off the livers, then blend the livers and ginger together in a food processor until smooth.

4. **ASSEMBLE THE FARRO.** Right after you drain the farro, stir in the liver mixture, cover, and let sit for 5 minutes. (The steam from the farro cooks the livers.) Serve warm, with the togarashi sprinkled on top.

chicken liver is the best way to dirty up rice and grains

KOREAN TREASURE RICE

shiitake, burdock, walnuts

In Korea, there's a traditional special-occasion dish whose name translates to "healthy mix rice." It's served in a big stone pot, usually posed as a table centerpiece and decorated with, say, a circle of gingko nuts, or something else that makes it pretty. It always has grains, nuts, mushrooms, and dates, but beyond that, like so many traditions around the world, the recipe varies by household. This is my own version, which I make with Medjool dates (rather than Korean jujubes) because they break down and become almost jammy. It's the ultimate recharging dish in the winter, meant to be deeply satisfying but also nutritious when the juiciest produce isn't in season. Eat the rice alone as a meal in itself, for breakfast or lunch.

Look for mixed-grain rice in the rice section of a large Asian grocery store. It should have a mix of grain types—different-colored rice, oats, millet, barley, and sometimes beans.

MAKES ABOUT 6 CUPS

2 cups mixed-grain rice, rinsed and
  drained three times
1 ounce dried shiitake mushrooms
  (about 1 cup)
1 quart water

½ cup Medjool dates, pitted and halved
1 (2-inch) piece burdock root, peeled and
  cut into ⅛-inch slices
½ cup walnuts, chopped

1. **SOAK THE RICE.** Put the rice in a medium mixing bowl. Add cold water to cover, and soak for 30 minutes.

2. **SOAK THE MUSHROOMS.** Put the mushrooms in a small bowl. In a small saucepan, bring the 1 quart of water to a boil, then pour the hot water over the mushrooms. Let the mushrooms soak, submerging them with a plate if necessary, for about 30 minutes, or until soft.

3. **MAKE THE RICE.** Drain the rice and add it to a large saucepan, then drain the mushroom soaking liquid directly into the pot with the rice. Trim off and discard the mushroom stems, then quarter the mushrooms and add them to the pot, along with the dates, burdock, and walnuts. Bring the rice to a simmer, then reduce the heat to the lowest setting, cover, and cook for about 1 hour, or until the water is absorbed and the grains are cooked (see Cooking Grains, page 266). Remove the rice from the heat, let sit for 10 minutes, then fluff and serve.

the ultimate granola-bar rice

BLACK RICE

dried shrimp

Dried shrimp—not the tiny kind dried to a crisp, but the softer thumb-size dried variety that are most akin to jerky—are often used for making stock across Asia, or for eating out of hand as a snack. If you cook them with rice, the entire pot takes on a sweet, briny flavor. I love putting them in black rice (also called forbidden rice) because between the deep purplish color the rice takes on and the fun of digging to see who gets to eat the shrimp, it makes me cool with our kids.

MAKES 6 CUPS

3 cups Two-Ingredient Dashi Stock
  (page 58)
2 cups short-grain black rice, rinsed and
  drained three times

¼ cup dried shrimp
1 (3-by-5-inch) strip kombu

1. **MAKE THE RICE.** In a medium saucepan, combine the dashi, rice, shrimp, and kombu. Bring the mixture to a simmer, then reduce the heat to the lowest setting, cover, and cook for about 30 minutes, or until the water is absorbed and the rice is cooked (see Rice Cooking Tips, page 260). Remove the rice from the heat, let sit for 10 minutes, then fluff and serve.

COOKING GRAINS

While we don't usually rinse grains, in general, we treat them like rice—give them plenty of room to cook and plenty of time to rest when they're finished cooking. The water amount varies depending on how hearty the grain is. When you are making grains that take a long time to cook, like brown rice, they tend to require more water.

CHARRED SHIITAKE MUSHROOM RICE BOWL

chinese broccoli, togarashi walnuts

When Seif first started cooking, he worked at a restaurant in Urbana, Illinois, that sold at least a case of white zinfandel wine every night. The sell-out dish was Amaretto chicken, but the place was most widely known for a meaty monster sandwich called the Train Wreck. The chef there, a big guy named Steve who started cooking in the military when he was drafted for Vietnam, told Seif that if he had his career to start over again, he'd go work for Alain Ducasse. Because of that, Seif went to Portland for culinary school and then on to work for Ducasse.

Sometimes, when some of our most popular dishes fly off the line, we have a moment to stop and look at each other and realize how far we've come. Our horizons have expanded so much, but the variety of people we feed has changed too. The closest thing Seif's first restaurant had to a vegetarian dish was Cobb salad. This vegetarian rice bowl—a hearty, deeply satisfying combination of charred mushrooms, broccoli, onions, and spicy toasted walnuts—is a long way from Urbana.

You'll have extra walnuts, which is a good thing. They're great on salads or eaten straight out of hand as a snack.

MAKES 4 SERVINGS

FOR THE WALNUTS:

2 tablespoons Japanese white miso
2 tablespoons canola oil
2 cups walnut halves
¼ cup Orange Togarashi (page 51)

FOR THE SAUCE:

¼ cup black sesame seeds
¼ cup canola oil
¼ cup rice vinegar
1 tablespoon hoisin sauce
2 large cloves garlic

FOR THE VEGETABLES:

1 large bunch Chinese broccoli (about 1
   pound), thick stems peeled
8 ounces large cipollini onions, ends
   trimmed, halved
8 ounces fresh shiitake mushrooms (about
   4 cups), stems removed, halved
4 tablespoons canola oil, divided
Kosher salt and freshly ground black pepper

FOR SERVING:

8 cups Simple White Rice (page 258)
4 fresh egg yolks

1. **PREPARE THE WALNUTS.** Preheat the oven to 350 degrees F. Line a baking sheet with parchment paper.

In a medium bowl, whisk together the miso and oil until blended. Add the walnuts and toss to coat them evenly in the miso mixture, then sprinkle the togarashi over the walnuts, stirring as you go, tossing until most surfaces of every nut are covered. Spread out on the prepared baking sheet and bake the walnuts for 10 minutes, then set aside to cool.

continued

2. **MAKE THE BLACK SESAME SAUCE.** In a heavy-duty blender, whirl together the sesame seeds, oil, vinegar, hoisin, and garlic until smooth on the highest speed. (You may have to stop and scrape down the sides a few times.)

3. **PREPARE THE VEGETABLES FOR GRILLING.** Preheat a gas or charcoal grill to medium-high heat, about 425 degrees F. Fill a medium saucepan with water and bring to a boil for blanching the broccoli.

Cut the broccoli in half where the stalks meet the leaves. Cut any stalks thicker than about ½ inch in diameter in half lengthwise, then cut each stalk and the leafy tops into 2-inch sections. When the water is boiling, add the stalks, and cook for 2 minutes. Add the tops, cook for 1 minute more, then drain the greens in a colander and set aside to cool slightly.

In separate medium bowls, mix the onions and mushrooms with 1 tablespoon each of the oil, and season each with salt and pepper. Set aside.

In a large bowl, toss the broccoli pieces with the remaining 2 tablespoons oil and season with salt and pepper.

4. **GRILL THE VEGETABLES.** When the grill is hot, add the onions to the grill, then the mushrooms, then the broccoli, spreading out any large broccoli leaves as you go. Grill the broccoli for about 2 to 3 minutes per side, until wilted and charred in spots. (It will take less time if you cover the grill for a moment.) Transfer the broccoli back to a large bowl, then turn the onions and mushrooms and cook them another 2 to 3 minutes, until well browned and soft, then transfer them to a different medium bowl. Scrape the black sesame sauce into the bowl with the onions and mushrooms, and toss to coat.

5. **SERVE THE RICE BOWLS.** Fill individual Asian-style noodle bowls with 1½ to 2 cups of rice each, then top with some of the onion and mushroom mixture, the broccoli, and the walnuts. Nestle an egg yolk on top, and serve immediately.

rice bowls are made to be mash-ups —
don't be afraid to go wild

KALUA PORK STONE POT

swiss chard, salted shrimp

In our restaurants, as in Korea, rice bowls like *bibimbap* are served year-round. In the winter, though, serving them in their traditional large stone pot adds a new level of warmth—and if you make them with a saucy topping that leaks down into the rice and mixes with the grains against the hot stone as you eat it, you wind up with a surprise layer of crunchy caramelized rice at the end. The longer you leave the rice undisturbed at the bottom of the bowl, the crispier it gets.

    Cook the Banana Leaf–Wrapped Pork Butt for a full three hours, so it becomes shreddable. If you want to time it all just right, start the rice when the pork comes out of the oven. You can make the vinaigrette, pull the pork, and grill the chard while the rice cooks, so that when the rice is done, you can fluff it up and serve it piping hot. If you have the Korean stone pots typical of *bibimbap*, or four smaller cast-iron pans, make it a stone pot: About ten minutes before you're ready to serve, heat the pots in a preheated 450-degree-F oven (for the stone) for ten minutes or on the stovetop over high heat (for the cast iron) until the pan is hot but not smoking. Pile the rice directly into the oiled hot vessels, as directed below, and serve (carefully).

MAKES 4 TO 6 SERVINGS

FOR THE CHARD:

1 bunch Swiss chard (about 8 ounces)
¼ cup canola oil
Kosher salt and freshly ground black pepper
1 recipe Salted Shrimp Vinaigrette
  (page 47)

FOR SERVING:

Sesame oil, as needed
8 cups Simple White Rice (page 258)
1 recipe Banana Leaf–Wrapped Pork
  Butt (page 213), pulled into big
  bite-size chunks
4 to 6 fresh egg yolks

1. GRILL THE CHARD. Preheat a gas or charcoal grill to medium-high heat, about 450 degrees F. Place the chard leaves on a baking sheet, brush both sides evenly with a thin layer of the oil, and season with salt and pepper. Grill the chard for 1 to 2 minutes per side, until the leaves are wilted and charred in spots and the stems have begun to soften. (It will take less time if you cover the grill for a moment.) Transfer the chard to a cutting board. Remove from the leaves from the stems, chop the leaves into roughly 2-inch pieces, and transfer the chopped leaves to a medium bowl. Chop the stems into 1-inch sections and add to the leaves. Whisk the vinaigrette and add to the chard, tossing until the leaves are all coated.

2. SERVE THE STONE POT. If you're using stone pots or cast-iron pans, carefully rub the insides liberally with sesame oil. Fill them (or individual Asian-style noodle bowls) with 1½ to 2 cups of rice each, then top with some of the chard and pork. Nestle an egg yolk on top, and serve immediately.

LAMB CURRY RICE BOWL

charred cucumber relish, kale

Start with a Moroccan tagine. Take a hard right at Thai curry, bend left at Greece, and wave at Korea, and you have this rice bowl—a rich lamb curry tinged with sweetness, served over rice with a tangy cucumber salad and crisp grilled kale.

Think of fermented tofu as an ingredient to reach for when you want to add a salty, sour, and tangy note. Here, because the dish plays on a classically Greek combination of ingredients, it almost takes the place of feta cheese. If you can't find top round or prefer lamb that's a little less lean, use cubes of leg meat.

MAKES 4 TO 6 SERVINGS

FOR THE CURRY:

⅓ cup thinly sliced fresh lemongrass (from the tender insides of 2 or 3 large stalks)

10 large cloves garlic

1 (2-inch) section peeled fresh ginger, sliced into ¼-inch-thick coins

⅓ cup mirin

1 tablespoon fish sauce

1 tablespoon salted shrimp

1 tablespoon coarse Korean chili flakes

1 teaspoon ground coriander

FOR THE LAMB:

2 tablespoons canola oil

1½ pounds top round of lamb, cut into 2-inch cubes

Kosher salt

½ cup sake

1 cup dried chickpeas, soaked in 2 cups water overnight

1 quart water

FOR THE CUCUMBER RELISH:

2 long English cucumbers

¼ cup canola oil, plus more for oiling the cucumbers

½ cup fermented tofu (solids only)

¼ cup rice vinegar

¼ cup packed finely chopped fresh mint

2 tablespoons julienned peeled fresh ginger

FOR THE KALE:

1 large (or 2 small) bunches green kale (about 12 ounces), ribs removed, cut into 3-inch pieces (about 8 loosely packed cups)

¼ cup canola oil

Kosher salt and freshly ground black pepper

FOR SERVING:

8 cups Jasmine Rice (page 262)

4 to 6 fresh egg yolks

1. **MAKE THE CURRY.** In a blender or the bowl of a food processor, whirl together the lemongrass, garlic, ginger, mirin, fish sauce, salted shrimp, chili flakes, and coriander until finely chopped. Set aside.

2. **MAKE THE LAMB.** Heat a large, heavy pot over medium-high heat. Add the oil, season the lamb with salt, then add the lamb. Cook the lamb for about 10 minutes, or until lightly browned on all sides, only turning the pieces once they release easily from the pan. Add the curry mixture and cook, stirring, until the curry begins to stick to the side of the pan and brown, about 5 minutes more. Add the sake and cook, scraping the brown bits off the sides and bottom of the pan, for another minute or so. Drain and add the chickpeas and water, bring to a boil, reduce to a simmer, and cook the lamb for

continued

about 1 hour, or until fork-tender. (You can use the lamb as is, or, if you want a thicker sauce, use a slotted spoon to transfer the lamb and chickpeas to a large bowl, boil the sauce for about 10 minutes, until it reduces to about ¾ cup, then add the lamb and chickpeas back in, stirring to coat them in the sauce.)

3. **WHILE THE LAMB COOKS, MAKE THE CUCUMBER RELISH.** Preheat a gas or charcoal grill to medium-high heat, about 450 degrees F. While the grill heats, slice the cucumbers in half lengthwise and scoop out the seeds (a spoon, ice cream scoop, or melon baller works well), then pat the cut sides dry with paper towels. Rub the cucumbers very lightly on both sides with oil. Grill the cucumbers for a few minutes, cut side down first, until nicely marked on both sides, then transfer them to a cutting board. Set aside to cool. Keep the grill on.

In a medium bowl, mash together the tofu, vinegar, oil, mint, and ginger until the tofu breaks apart. Cut the grilled cucumbers on the bias into ½-inch slices, and fold the cucumbers into the tofu mixture. Set aside.

4. **GRILL THE KALE.** In a large bowl, toss the kale pieces with the oil and season with salt and pepper. Grill the kale for about 1 minute per side, until wilted and charred in spots. (It will take less time if you cover the grill for a moment.) Transfer the kale back to the bowl.

5. **SERVE THE RICE BOWLS.** Fill individual Asian-style noodle bowls with 1½ to 2 cups of rice, then top with some of the kale, lamb curry, and cucumber relish. Nestle an egg yolk on top, and serve immediately.

GEODUCK FRIED RICE

seaweed dust, pickled pork rind

Geoduck (pronounced GOO-ey-duck) is one of the Pacific Northwest's prized bivalves. It's a giant clam with a large protruding siphon—an intimidating creature if there ever was one. But ultimately, it's quite easy to prepare, and when you serve it raw, sliced paper thin, it tastes like the breath of the sea. Because it's quite expensive, we always use the whole creature at Joule. Here, we make a compound butter out of the geoduck's belly and use that to make what's essentially butter fried rice. You could use a larger geoduck than we call for here and put more of it on the fried rice, if you prefer. In either case, savor the brininess. We always think of geoduck as the ultimate luxury.

MAKES 4 TO 6 SERVINGS AS A MEAL, OR 8 TO 10 AS A SMALLER COURSE

FOR THE RICE:

1 tablespoon canola oil

2 cups medium-grain rice, rinsed and drained three times

2½ cups water

1 (2-by-3-inch) strip kombu

FOR SERVING:

1 (1-pound) geoduck

½ cup (1 stick) unsalted butter, at room temperature

1 small leek (white part only), halved and cut into half moons

¼ cup drained and chopped Pickled Pork Rind (recipe follows)

Kosher salt

4 teaspoons nori powder (see Making Nori Powder, page 244), divided

¼ cup chopped fresh chives

1. **COOK THE RICE.** In a medium saucepan over medium heat, heat the oil. Add the rice and cook, stirring, for 1 to 2 minutes. (It will begin cooking but not actually toast.) Add the water and kombu, bring the mixture to a simmer, then reduce the heat to the lowest setting, cover, and cook for about 20 minutes, or until the water is absorbed and the rice is cooked (see Rice Cooking Tips, page 260). Remove the rice from the heat, let sit for 10 minutes, then fluff the rice and transfer it to an oiled or parchment-lined baking sheet. Let the rice cool to room temperature, then refrigerate until the rice is dry enough to separate the grains with your hands, 2 to 4 hours. (You can make the rice ahead to this point, cover, and refrigerate up to 48 hours.)

use old rice — or make lightly toasted medium-grain rice to make it extra special

continued

2. **PREPARE THE GEODUCK.** When you're ready to serve the rice, bring a large pot of water to a boil. Dip the entire geoduck in the boiling water once—just a dip, not an extended bath—and transfer it to a cutting board. Using a small knife, detach the siphon from the animal where it meets the shell. Set the shell and its innards aside.

Working from the cut end of the siphon, gently peel off and discard the siphon's outer skin. Using a sharp knife, cut the siphon first in half lengthwise. Rinse out any sand that may be visible, then slice into paper-thin half moons. (The thinner the better here. If the geoduck is fresh, the slices will begin to curl up as soon as you cut them.) Set the shellfish aside.

3. **MAKE THE BELLY BUTTER.** Run a small knife between the shell and the insides of the geoduck. Remove the meat and innards from the shell, rinse to remove any sand or grit, and then remove the stomach, which is the cream- or pinkish-colored, roughly

egg-shaped orb in the center of the animal. In the bowl of a food processor, pulse the belly until finely chopped. Add the butter, and pulse until uniformly pale green. Transfer the butter to a small bowl and reserve. (A 1-pound geoduck typically yields a roughly 4-ounce belly, but if you're using a larger creature, weigh it and use double the amount in butter. Use any leftover butter for frying eggs or toss it with hot noodles.)

4. FRY THE RICE. Cook the rice in two batches: Heat a large skillet over medium heat. When hot, add half of the butter and half of the leek. Once the butter has melted, cook and stir the leek for about 1 minute, then add half the rice, half the pork rind, and salt. Cook, stirring with a spoon and digging through any rice grains that seem to be clumped together, for 2 to 3 minutes, or until just beginning to toast but not actually browning. Stir in 2 teaspoons of the nori powder and half the geoduck, just to warm, and pile immediately into two Asian-style noodle bowls. Repeat with the remaining ingredients, keeping the first batch hot while you work, then serve immediately, garnished with the chives.

pickled pork rind

Because different butchers may send you home with different things, be sure to check out your pork rind before you begin; it should be soft and clean. You want the pork skin but not the pork fat, so scrape any visible excess fat off gently with the back of a spoon. Much of the fat that clings to the actual skin will cook away as you braise it.

Note that because pork rind from different parts of the pig has different thicknesses, it's important to find pork *belly* skin; other parts of the pig have skin that can be tough or leathery. If you can't find pork skin that you know is specifically from the belly of a pig, buy a whole piece of pork belly (which should have the skin intact) and cut off the skin. You can cut the fleshy part into bacon.

MAKES ABOUT ½ CUP

1 (3-by-4-inch) piece pork rind (about 2 ounces), preferably from the belly, excess fat scraped off with a spoon
2 cups water

2 cups sake
1 tablespoon kosher salt
½ teaspoon pink curing salt (see page 62)

1. COOK THE PORK RIND. In a medium saucepan, combine the pork rind, water, sake, kosher salt, and curing salt. Bring to a simmer and cook for 75 to 90 minutes, or until the skin is soft enough that you can easily pull a small piece off the corner with a fork. (It will shrink significantly in size.) Let the pork cool in the liquid until it is comfortable to handle, then slice it into 2-by-⅛-inch strips. Spread the strips out on the cutting board to cool. (The pork will gelatinize as it cools, so if you leave the pork in a bundle, it will all stick together.)

hot pots
and stews

Instead of saying "hello" in Korea, we say "did you eat?" It's a good reflection of how important food is there. Knowing whether someone has eaten tells you two things: first, whether someone has enough money to eat; and second, whether before doing anything else, you need to find that person some food. If a friend is hungry, you feed them. Hot pots are the physical incarnation of that dictum. Served in large bowls (usually in the center of the table on a butane burner), they're meted out with a big ladle into separate bowls for each person and served with rice and *banchan*. In Korea, it's often the type of meal you share with people when you want to impress them and get to know them, because it's warming and sharable and intensely satisfying. No one goes home hungry.

When Revel opened, we were flooded with customers. We hated the idea of turning people away—for the obvious financial reasons, but also because of my innate Korean values—so we expanded by putting portable burners on the countertop in our workspace and using them to make hot pots. That simple expansion allowed us to feed more people during Seattle's wet winters. And as restaurant owners, it helped us learn how important it is to remember, with each dish that crosses the pass, that cooking with love and care is just as important as cooking with the best ingredients you can find.

SPICY PORK RIB HOT POT

tomatillo, potato, perilla

Potatoes and wild sesame seeds, which are rounder and more herbaceous tasting than their more widely used cousins, are what gives Korea's most typical pork soup, *gamjatang*, its identity—a spicy bowl with deep pork flavor and herbal overtones that combine to make something far more than the sum of its parts. It's the ultimate dish of comfort, built quickly and simmered long and slow.

If you order it in Korea, you'll usually find fairly bony pieces of pork, but we use spare ribs, because they're nice and meaty. Sesame leaves are palm-size greens that look like shiso or stinging nettle but have a much softer, vanilla-tinged flavor with hints of licorice. Also known as perilla leaves, they're one of the only indigenous herbs used in Korean cooking. We finish our stew with wild sesame oil for additional herbal flavor. (Look for sesame leaves in the herb section of a large Asian grocery store, and the wild sesame oil and seeds near their more well-known relatives.)

You can cool the stew and refrigerate it overnight after cooking the potatoes, if you'd like, and add the remaining ingredients before serving it a day or two later.

MAKES 4 TO 6 SERVINGS

4 cups water, divided

¼ cup roughly chopped peeled fresh ginger

2 tablespoons coarse Korean chili flakes

2 tablespoons fish sauce

6 large cloves garlic

2 tablespoons canola oil

2 pounds pork baby back or St. Louis ribs, cut into 2-rib sections

1 tablespoon kosher salt

8 ounces tomatillos, husks removed, quartered

½ cup sake

8 ounces small yellow potatoes, such as German Butterball, quartered

4 ounces collard greens (about 4 large leaves), ribs removed, leaves cut into 3-inch strips

6 fresh sesame leaves, roughly chopped

2 tablespoons wild sesame seeds, toasted and crushed (see Toasting Nuts and Seeds, page 288)

2 tablespoons wild sesame oil

1. **MAKE THE SPICE MIXTURE.** In a blender, whirl 1 cup of the water with the ginger, chili flakes, fish sauce, and garlic until completely smooth. Set aside.

2. **SEAR THE PORK.** In a large, heavy pot with a lid over medium-high heat, heat the oil. Add the pork, then season with the salt and cook until the pork is nicely browned on both sides, 6 to 8 minutes total, turning only when the pork releases easily from the pan.

wild sesame oil is the next hot thing

3. **BUILD THE HOT POT.** Add the tomatillos first, and cook, stirring occasionally, for 2 minutes. Add the sake and cook for another few minutes, stirring, until the sake just glazes the bottom of the pan. Add the spice liquid and the remaining 3 cups water, bring a boil, then reduce to a strong simmer and cook, covered, for about 1 hour. (You can also cook the mixture in the oven at 375 degrees F, if you prefer.) Add the potatoes, and cook another 20 minutes. Set aside until ready to serve.

4. **SERVE THE HOT POT.** When ready to serve, bring the soup back to a boil, add the greens, and cook for 3 to 5 minutes, or until soft but still bright green. Stir in the sesame leaves and seeds, and serve piping hot, drizzling each bowl with a bit of sesame oil.

OXTAIL STEW

leek, glass noodles

In our restaurants, hot pots are more like stews than soups—or, really, just braises served with their liquid. In other words, there's not as much juicy business as you might expect. We serve them with rice, which soaks up the best parts from the bottom of each bowl, but ultimately, when you order a hot pot at Revel, you're ordering an entrée. This is our version of braised oxtail.

The Chinese method of red cooking, or red braising, is at heart about cooking meat with a little bit of sugar. The sugar caramelizes on the surface of the meat, which pumps up the naturally sweet flavor that comes with searing the surface of any protein. Once the browned bits of the oxtail simmer for a couple hours, the entire broth takes on a rich, sweet flavor that the glass noodles soak up as they cook. You can cool the stew and refrigerate it overnight after cooking the oxtail, if you'd like, and add the remaining ingredients before serving it a day or two later.

Note that if you buy small (six- to eight-inch), tender Chinese mustard in the spring, it probably doesn't need to be chopped.

MAKES 4 SERVINGS

2 pounds beef oxtail (4 to 6 sections)

¼ cup sugar

1 tablespoon kosher salt

½ teaspoon freshly ground black pepper

2 tablespoons canola oil

6 large cloves garlic, halved lengthwise

2 red Fresno chilies, stems removed, halved lengthwise

½ cup sake

1 quart water

½ cup soy sauce

½ cup rice vinegar

1 small leek (white and light-green parts), cut into 1-inch half-moons

4 ounces glass noodles

1 bunch Chinese mustard greens (about 8 ounces), roughly chopped (about 3 cups)

1. PREPARE THE OXTAIL. Put the oxtail in a colander in the sink and run under cold water for 5 to 10 minutes, turning occasionally. Pat the oxtail dry.

In a small bowl, blend together the sugar, salt, and pepper. Pat this mixture into the oxtail on all sides.

2. SEAR THE OXTAIL. Preheat the oven to 375 degrees F. Heat a large, heavy pot with a lid over medium-high heat. Add the oil, then the coated oxtail, and cook attentively for 5 or 6 minutes, turning each piece as it caramelizes on the bottom. (You want the pieces to get good and dark on all sides but don't want them to actually burn.)

3. BUILD THE STEW. Add the garlic and chilies, and stir for 1 to 2 minutes, scraping some of the browned bits up off the bottom of the pan. Add the sake and cook for another few minutes, stirring, until the sake just glazes the bottom of the pan. Add the water, soy sauce, and vinegar, stir to combine, and bring back to a boil. Cover the pot and transfer it to the oven, and cook for 2 hours, or until the oxtail meat comes off the bone easily when you tug at it.

glass noodles don't fill you up like regular noodles

4. SERVE THE STEW. Carefully transfer the pot back to the stovetop, maintaining a strong simmer. Add the leek and cook for about 3 minutes, then add the noodles, stirring them in as they soften on top of the liquid, and cook another 5 minutes. Just before serving, stir in the mustard greens, cook for 1 to 2 minutes, and serve.

PORK KIMCHI RAGOUT

butternut squash soojebi

From a distance, the rich, spicy pork ragout that forms the body of this dumpling stew looks like a thinnish Italian bolognese poured over gnocchi. Get closer, though, and the smell will tell you it's Korean; rich with ground pork, Korean bean paste, and traditional cabbage kimchi, it's the ultimate Korean comfort food.

Soojebi (SOO-je-BI) is a Korean noodle, but not a noodle in the traditional sense—sooje translates roughly to "handmade," and like the hand-torn noodles of many cultures, these are meant to be irregular and a little chewier than most. In my book, they're more like dumplings. They're often made with a regular flour dough, like Chinese hand-shaved noodles, but in the fall and winter, I love making them with butternut squash, which gives the whole dish an earthier flavor.

Serve the soojebi as soon as they're finished cooking, in big bowls, with the pumpkin seed and cabbage gremolata piled on top. Or do what I do at home: skip the noodle altogether, make the ragout, let it hang out in the fridge for a day or two, then eat it cold for breakfast.

MAKES 4 SERVINGS

FOR THE DUMPLINGS:

1 (8-ounce) section butternut squash
  (from the long part)
1 teaspoon canola oil
½ teaspoon kosher salt,
  plus more for seasoning
½ cup all-purpose flour,
  plus more as needed
1 tablespoon plus 1 teaspoon cornstarch

FOR THE RAGOUT:

2 cups chopped kimchi (about 1 pound),
  such as Spicy Napa Kimchi (page 151)
1 tablespoon canola oil

½ pound ground pork
3 tablespoons Korean bean paste
1½ cups dry sake
8 cups Two-Ingredient Dashi Stock
  (page 58)

FOR THE GREMOLATA:

1 (2-ounce) wedge green cabbage, cut into
  ½-inch slices through the core
¼ cup pumpkin seeds, toasted and
  finely chopped (see Toasting Nuts and
  Seeds, following page)
½ teaspoon kosher salt

1. **ROAST THE SQUASH FOR THE SOOJEBI.** Preheat the oven to 400 degrees F. Place the squash in a small baking dish, rub with the oil, and season with salt. Cover the dish with foil, sealing it at the edges, and roast for about 45 minutes, until completely soft and yielding when poked with a fork. Remove from the oven and set aside to cool. When cool enough to handle, scoop the squash out of the peel, transfer it to the bowl of a food processor, and whirl until completely smooth. Measure out ½ cup of the squash puree, and transfer it to a medium mixing bowl. Set aside to cool completely.

continued

2. START THE RAGOUT. In a blender or the bowl of a food processor, puree the kimchi. (Traditionally, Korean pork and kimchi stew has bigger pieces of kimchi, but for this, I like to make the pieces finer. Experiment as you wish. I make it differently every time.) Set aside.

3. MAKE THE RAGOUT. Heat a 5-quart soup pot over medium heat. Add the oil, then the pork and the bean paste. Cook, stirring frequently, for 6 to 8 minutes, or until the pork is cooked and crumbled and the bean paste begins to caramelize on the bottom of the pan. Add the kimchi and cook, stirring, for another 5 or 6 minutes, until the kimchi begins to look brown (as opposed to red) and the pan begins to dry out. Add the sake, and cook for another few minutes, scraping the pan to lift up any good caramelized bits and stir them into the ragout. When the pan is beginning to dry out again, add the dashi. Bring the mixture to a simmer, cook for another minute, then remove the pot from the heat and set aside.

4. MAKE THE GREMOLATA. Preheat a gas or charcoal grill to medium-high heat, about 450 degrees F. When hot, add the dry cabbage slices and cook, covered, for about 5 minutes, turning once, or until the cabbage is charred black and brittle in some places on both sides but still green near the core. Transfer the cabbage to a cutting board to cool, then finely chop it, discarding the core. Put the cabbage in a small bowl and stir in the toasted pumpkin seeds and salt, and set aside.

5. MAKE THE DUMPLINGS. Add the ½ teaspoon salt, flour, and cornstarch to the bowl with the squash, and immediately mix with a fork until you have a soft, wet dough. Taking care not to overwork the dough, stir in another tablespoon of flour, and perhaps another, adding flour only until the dough stops sticking to the fork. (The less flour the dough has, the lighter the dumplings will be.) Transfer the dough to a clean lightly floured surface, cut it in half, roll it into two ½-inch-thick logs, and use a small knife to cut the dough into ½-inch slices, which will flatten as you cut them. Using your hands, separate the pieces of dough, dusting each with flour just enough to work with them, and use a floured thumb to squish each into a roughly ¼-inch-thick flat, long oval. (Honestly, their shape doesn't really matter. You should get about 4 dozen *soojebi*, each strip about 1 to 2 inches long.) When all the pieces have been floured and squished, bring the ragout back up to a simmer.

6. COOK THE DUMPLINGS. Drop the *soojebi* into the pot one by one, taking care to shake the dumplings off and add as little extra flour as possible. Cook for 5 minutes, then scoop the ragout into bowls and serve immediately, garnished with the gremolata.

TOASTING NUTS AND SEEDS

Spread nuts or seeds out on a rimmed baking sheet. Toast for 8 to 10 minutes in a preheated 350-degree-F oven, or until fragrant, crackling, and browned. (Timing will depend on the size of what you're toasting.) Let cool before using.

SEAFOOD HOT POT

anchovy, rapini

Even if Seif has never met you before, he can make you feel like you've known him for years. At first, for me, having restaurants was about being a chef—about me and my food. But as Seif and I worked at it longer, he really brought hospitality into the picture. He's always been the one who talks to customers for hours and really makes them feel welcome, even when they're complete strangers. That outgoing ebullience was not part of my nature. But now, I've learned how to cook in such a way that I can convey the same feeling. My food has more soul now than it did at the beginning, because I cook to make people feel welcome, and to make them happy. Today, we train our staff to cook with genuine care and love. When we get ready to close the doors each night, we don't tend to turn people away when they come in at the last minute, because they've come for a reason.

Nothing makes people feel more welcome late at night than hot pot. This is our favorite seafood version. Classic Korean seafood stews are meant to have a clear broth. But with a broth that's a heady mix of spicy anchovy-miso paste and quick homemade dashi, this Asian-inspired take on cioppino is anything but traditional. Don't limit yourself to the seafood listed below; the goal is to show off what's fresh and delicious.

A large, shallow casserole dish with a lid works best for this hot pot, because the fish cooks more evenly if you can arrange it in just one or two layers.

MAKES 4 SERVINGS

FOR THE ANCHOVY PASTE:

1 (4-ounce) jar or 2 (2-ounce) tins anchovies, drained

3 tablespoons Japanese white miso

1 large garlic clove

1 Fresno chili, chopped

¼ cup roughly chopped peeled fresh ginger

FOR THE HOT POT:

4 cups Two-Ingredient Dashi Stock (page 58)

2 pounds seafood (such as white-fleshed fish, clams, crab, mussels, squid, shrimp, or scallops), or more if you're using a lot of stuff with shells

1 (1-pound) bunch rapini

FOR SERVING:

2 lemons, halved

1 bunch green onions (green parts only), thinly sliced

1 Fresno chili, thinly sliced

1. **MAKE THE ANCHOVY PASTE.** In the bowl of a food processor, whirl together the anchovies, miso, garlic, chili, and ginger until pasty. Set aside.

2. **PREPARE THE INGREDIENTS.** In a medium saucepan, bring the dashi to a boil. Prepare the seafood, as needed, with white fish sliced in roughly 3-inch squares and all shellfish cleaned. Cut the rapini in half where the stems meet the leaves.

continued

3. **GRILL THE LEMONS.** Preheat a gas or charcoal grill to medium-high heat, about 450 degrees F. When hot, grill the lemons, cut side down, for about 2 minutes, or until well marked.

4. **BUILD THE HOT POT.** Meanwhile, layer the seafood into a large, wide casserole dish with a lid while it's still cold: Place any white fish on the bottom first, followed by the rapini stems, then the rapini greens, then the shellfish. Add a heaping ¼ cup of the anchovy paste, then the dashi, place the casserole over high heat, and bring to a simmer. Reduce the heat to low and simmer for about 10 minutes, stirring once or twice and rearranging things as the clams and mussels open, or until the seafood is just cooked through. Taste the broth and add as much additional anchovy paste as you'd like.

5. **SERVE THE HOT POT.** Garnish with the green onions and chilies. You can serve the hot pot in one giant bowl with a ladle, or scoop into four separate bowls. Serve with the grilled lemons, which can be squeezed right over the stew before eating.

using preserved fish, like anchovies,
accentuates the fish flavor

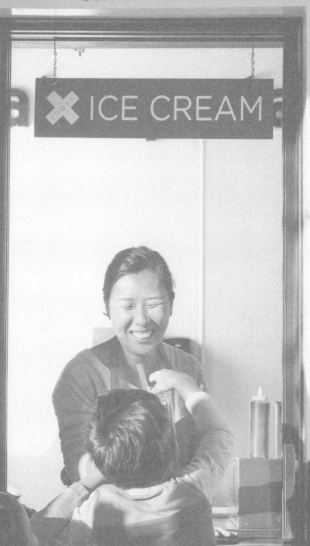

desserts

For the first two years we owned a restaurant, we didn't necessarily think we'd make it. By year five, we realized something we were doing was working, but we still braced ourselves against the knowledge that it could end at any time. We wondered what the future might look like. But by about the seventh year, suddenly, we began thinking that as long as we worked hard, we might have found a formula that makes our restaurants successful. There is no magic formula, of course—just using plain, old-fashioned common sense with respect to taking care of your guests and your crew and always remembering to taste what you are making. Today, the standard that we set for ourselves is higher than ever and requires more work than ever. But it was a pretty sweet realization that when you make restaurants and cooking your life, you get to live to the fullest and enjoy the sweet successes.

When we first opened Joule, I was the one who made all our desserts. I wasn't really trained in pastry, so the menu had to be full of things I could make without too much difficulty. I took a savory approach, incorporating a lot of spices and smoky flavors into each dessert. Today, you'll see a lot of ingredients not usually associated with sweet dishes in our desserts—things like miso, smoked tea, curry powder, and turmeric. We have favorites, of course—the Joule Box (page 299) has been on our menu since we opened—but mostly, we use the dessert menu as a playground for improvisation. Because new things can only work if you try them.

MISO CARAMEL CHOCOLATE TORTE

passion fruit fluff

The goal of this torte—known in our restaurants (in a slightly different form) as the "mother lode" brownie—is simply to put the very best things about dessert all in one bite. The torte itself is a lightly chili-tinged version of a basic flourless chocolate cake. (If you don't eat it immediately, you'll notice the spice comes out nicely in the days following baking.) Because the torte puffs in the oven, it leaves an indentation in the center as it cools, which is perfect for filling with our miso caramel (think salted caramel, but with more depth). Just before serving, top the cake with tangy passion fruit fluff—gloriously puffy, shiny marshmallow that you can brown with a kitchen torch, if you have one. Sprinkle each serving with crunchy sea salt, if you'd like.

Look for passion fruit puree in the frozen fruit section of a gourmet grocery store. In our kitchens, we use a brand called Perfect Puree, which is available for order online.

MAKES 8 TO 12 SERVINGS

FOR THE CAKE:

Baking spray, for the pan

10 ounces semisweet chocolate, finely chopped

¼ cup (½ stick) unsalted butter, cut into pieces, at room temperature

2 teaspoons Korean chili paste

1⅓ cups sugar

6 large eggs

FOR THE CARAMEL:

1 cup sugar

¼ cup water

⅓ cup cream

6 tablespoons (¾ stick) unsalted butter, cut into pieces, at room temperature

1 tablespoon Japanese white miso

FOR THE FLUFF:

3 large egg whites

2 cups plus 2 tablespoons sugar, divided

⅓ cup water

½ cup passion fruit puree (thawed, if frozen)

1. PREPARE THE PAN. Spray the bottom of a 9-inch round cake pan with baking spray. Line the pan with a round of parchment paper, then spray the paper. Preheat the oven to 350 degrees F.

2. MAKE THE CAKE. In a double boiler set over low heat, melt the chocolate, butter, and chili paste together until smooth. (A mixing bowl set over a pan with an inch of simmering water in it also works fine.) Once the chocolate has melted completely, whisk in the sugar until no dry spots remain. Remove the top pan from the heat and whisk the eggs in one at a time, making sure to incorporate each egg completely before adding the next. Pour the batter into the pan, tap the pan on the counter to release any bubbles,

continued

and bake for 30 to 40 minutes, or until the cake has puffed up evenly and a cake tester comes out clean. (The top of the cake shouldn't crack.) Set aside to cool to room temperature, then refrigerate or freeze the cake until cool.

3. **WHILE THE CAKE BAKES, MAKE THE CARAMEL.** In a medium saucepan, blend the sugar and water together with a fork until the sugar is moistened. Place the pan over medium-high heat and cook, undisturbed, until the sugar caramelizes and turns a medium amber color. Reduce the heat to low and carefully add in the cream in a slow, steady stream, whisking to incorporate it as you go, then add the butter and miso. Whisk until both the butter and the miso have disappeared completely, then remove the pan from the heat and let cool to room temperature. (The caramel should still be pourable.)

4. **ADD THE CARAMEL TO THE CAKE.** When the cake is completely cool, pour the caramel onto the top. It should almost fill the depression in the center of the cake, but you may need to use a knife or a small offset spatula to push the caramel all the way to the cake's edges. Freeze the cake until the caramel is firm, at least 2 hours, or refrigerate overnight. (You can make the cake, freeze or refrigerate it until the caramel hardens, then wrap it in plastic and store, frozen, for up to 2 weeks.)

5. **MAKE THE FLUFF.** In the bowl of a stand mixer fitted with the whisk attachment, whip the egg whites on medium speed until frothy. With the mixer running, add 2 tablespoons of the sugar in a slow, steady stream, increase the speed to medium-high, and whisk until the whites form soft peaks, 2 to 3 minutes more. When the whites are ready, turn off the mixer.

Meanwhile, in a medium saucepan, stir together the remaining 2 cups of sugar and the water with a fork until the sugar is moistened, then place the pan over high heat and bring to a boil. Cook, undisturbed, until the liquid reaches 265 degrees F on an instant-read thermometer. While the sugar syrup cooks, in a separate small saucepan, bring the passion fruit puree to a boil. When the syrup reaches 265 degrees F, carefully add the puree to the syrup.

Turn the stand mixer back on at medium speed. With the mixer running, pour the puree mixture down the side of the bowl in a slow, steady stream. When all of the puree mixture has been added, increase the speed to high and whip for 3 to 4 minutes, or until the mixture is stiff and shiny. Set aside. (The fluff will keep at room temperature for 3 to 4 hours before serving.)

6. **SERVE THE CAKE.** To serve, top the cake with the fluff, then slice the cake into 8 to 12 pieces, and serve cold. Note that the caramel on the cake begins to melt at room temperature, so it's best to keep the cake chilled.

JOULE BOX

coconut tapioca, grapefruit brûlée, lime

One of just two recipes we've kept on Joule's menu since its original incarnation, the Joule Box is one of the only dishes we've ever given a proper name. But because we initially served it in such a specific way—sweet coconut pudding, tender tapioca pearls, crunchy ruby grapefruit, and a flurry of lime zest nestled into a rectangular baking dish—it's not a name we've ever thought of changing. And really, no matter how we serve it, the Joule Box has the same effect on customers as a real jewel box might. Seif likes to watch people dig into it, because every time—whether they're new to Joule or not—they light up like they've been given a gift. It's a surprisingly fun way to finish a big meal. And ultimately, it makes people happy, which is what we're after.

Because it doesn't quite work to brown the grapefruit in the oven with the pudding underneath, we recommend using a kitchen-specific or butane torch. (We buy the kind available at most hardware stores.) If you don't have one, simply skip the torching step.

MAKES 8 SERVINGS

FOR THE TAPIOCA:

½ cup tapioca pearls

2 quarts plus 2 cups water, divided

1 (13.5-ounce) can coconut milk

½ cup sugar

1 teaspoon kosher salt

FOR THE PUDDING:

1 large egg

2 large egg yolks

2 tablespoons cornstarch

2 cups coconut milk

½ cup sugar

Pinch kosher salt

FOR SERVING:

Sections from 2 red grapefruits
  (about 24 supremes)

¼ cup turbinado sugar

¼ cup toasted large unsweetened
  coconut flakes

1 large lime, for zesting

1. **SOAK THE TAPIOCA.** In a small bowl, combine the tapioca with 2 cups of the water. Set aside for about 30 minutes. (The tapioca will soak up the water.)

2. **SWEETEN THE COCONUT MILK.** In a small saucepan, stir the can of coconut milk, sugar, and salt together. Bring to a simmer, stirring until the sugar melts completely, then transfer to a wide, shallow container and refrigerate until cold, about 30 minutes.

3. **MAKE THE COCONUT PUDDING.** In a medium bowl, whisk together the egg, egg yolks, and cornstarch and set aside. In a medium saucepan, stir together the coconut milk, sugar, and salt. Warm the mixture over medium-high heat, stirring until the sugar dissolves, then cook until you see bubbles around the edges, 1 to 2 minutes more. Remove the milk mixture from the heat and add it to the egg mixture in a slow, steady

continued

stream, whisking constantly as you add it. Return the mixture to the saucepan, place over low heat, and cook, whisking constantly and vigorously, until the mixture comes to a boil, then let it burble for 1 minute more. Quickly transfer the mixture to a nonreactive container, cover the surface directly with plastic wrap, set aside to cool to room temperature, then refrigerate. (The pudding can be made 1 to 2 days ahead, as long as you whip it just before serving.)

4. **COOK THE TAPIOCA.** Fill a large saucepan with the remaining 2 quarts of water and bring to a boil. Drain the excess water off the tapioca, then add the tapioca pearls to the boiling water and cook until clear, 8 to 10 minutes. Using a fine-mesh strainer, drain the tapioca and rinse under cold water until the water runs clear, then stir the tapioca into the cold coconut milk mixture.

5. **SERVE THE PUDDING.** Fill eight small bowls with the tapioca mixture. Add a big scoop of the pudding to the center of each, then top the pudding with 3 or 4 grapefruit supremes. Sprinkle the grapefruit on each serving with 1 to 2 teaspoons of the turbinado sugar. Using a kitchen torch, burn the top edges of each grapefruit until golden brown. Garnish each dish with a quarter of the toasted coconut flakes and finely grated lime zest.

TOASTING COCONUT

Coconut's natural oils come out best when it's toasted, so it pays to take the time to make it evenly brown on all sides. To toast it, spread it out in a thin layer on a baking sheet and bake it for 10 to 15 minutes in a preheated 350-degree-F oven, stirring it and rotating the pan occasionally to ensure even coloring.

a beautiful confluence of sweet, tart, nutty, sour, and bitter flavors

UPSIDE-DOWN FIG MOCHI CAKE

bleu cheese whip

We never wanted to do a cheese and fruit platter at our restaurants, but this cake, made with *mochiko* (sweet rice flour), is the dessertish incarnation of one, with soft figs and bleu cheese. It's the best of all worlds, because you get the chewiness of Korean rice flour treats but the rich egginess of a traditional European cake. Like any upside-down cake, the process is straightforward: the fruit goes into the bottom of the pan, and you top it with a simple cake batter, but finishing the cake with light bleu cheese whipped cream makes it totally unique.

While we like the texture of Mission figs best, you can also make it with dried apricots.

Serve the cake warm, with cracked pepper. Because the texture of the cake can be starchy once cooled, reheat leftovers for about ten minutes in a 300-degree-F oven.

MAKES 8 OR 9 SERVINGS

FOR THE FIG MIXTURE:
12 ounces (about 2 cups) dried
 Mission figs, stems trimmed, sliced
 into ½-inch rounds
Baking spray
2 tablespoons unsalted butter, softened
⅓ cup plus 1 tablespoon packed light
 brown sugar
½ teaspoon kosher salt

FOR THE CAKE:
1 cup sweet rice flour
⅔ cup sugar

2 teaspoons baking powder
½ teaspoon kosher salt
2 large eggs
2 tablespoons unsalted butter, melted
2 teaspoons vanilla extract
1 cup whole milk

FOR THE BLEU CHEESE WHIP:
¼ cup crumbled bleu cheese
 (such as bleu d'Auvergne)
¼ cup confectioners' sugar
1 teaspoon vanilla extract
¾ cup heavy cream

1. SOAK THE FIGS. Put the figs in a small bowl and cover with very hot tap water. Let soak for 10 minutes, then drain, squeezing out any excess water.

2. PREPARE THE PAN. Coat an 8-by-8-inch pan with a thin layer of baking spray. Line the pan with parchment paper, so the paper comes up and over the sides of the pan, and spray the parchment. Preheat the oven to 375 degrees F.

3. MAKE THE FIG MIXTURE. In the bowl of a stand mixer fitted with the paddle attachment, whip the butter, brown sugar, and salt together for 1 minute on medium speed, until evenly sandy. Add the drained figs to the mixture and stir by hand until the figs are all coated in sugar, then spread the figs into a single layer on the bottom of the prepared pan. Transfer the pan to the refrigerator to chill while you make the batter.

4. MAKE THE CAKE. In a medium bowl, whisk together the flour, sugar, baking powder, and salt to blend. In a large bowl, whisk together the eggs, melted butter, and vanilla, then whisk in the milk. Add the dry ingredients to the wet and stir until well blended. Pour the batter over the chilled figs and bake for 30 to 35 minutes, or until golden brown and set in the center. Set aside to cool for about 20 minutes. (You can make the cake a day ahead; just let it cool to room temperature, and then refrigerate it overnight before serving.)

5. MAKE THE BLEU CHEESE WHIP. In the bowl of a stand mixer fitted with the paddle attachment, stir together the bleu cheese, sugar, and vanilla on medium speed just to blend. Switch to the whisk attachment, add the cream, and whip on high speed for 2 to 3 minutes, or until smooth and thick, stopping to scrape down the sides of the bowl as needed. Set aside.

6. SERVE THE CAKE. To serve, invert the cake onto a cutting board, remove the paper, then cut the cake into 8 rectangles or 9 squares. Place each piece on a plate, and serve topped with a dollop of bleu cheese whip.

a sweet rice cake will impress your Korean
neighbor AND your American neighbor

MILK CHOCOLATE BINGSOO

black sesame mousse, peanut brittle

Shave ice desserts, or *bingsoo*, are big in Korea. They are served both in fancy hotels and from street carts, usually layered with something creamy, something syrupy, sometimes sweet red beans, plus a fruity or crunchy topping—which is why we put the ice cream "truck" in at Trove. (If we could have this much fun playing with savory foods, we thought, imagine what we could do with sweets!)

Peanut butter is not indigenous to Korean cuisine in any way. But by combining a flaky chocolate granita and black sesame mousse, our *bingsoo* actually begins tasting a little like peanut butter. Because chocolate gets creamy when you turn it into a granita, the overall effect is like peanut butter cup ice cream, in *bingsoo* form.

It's important to nail the water content of the granita. Our pastry chef, Renee, relies on an "egg test" to determine how much water to add, as you'll see in the instructions below.

MAKES 4 SERVINGS

FOR THE GRANITA:

¾ cup whole milk

2 tablespoons packed light brown sugar

2 tablespoons malt powder

2 tablespoons light corn syrup

Pinch kosher salt

2 ounces milk chocolate, finely chopped

2 ounces dark chocolate, finely chopped

About 1½ cups cold water

1 large egg, in its shell

FOR THE MOUSSE:

2 tablespoons cold water

1 teaspoon gelatin powder

⅔ cup black sesame powder (see page 50)

½ cup whole milk

¼ cup light corn syrup

6 ounces white chocolate, finely chopped, or about 1 cup white chocolate chips

½ teaspoon kosher salt

½ cup cold heavy cream

FOR SERVING:

2 cups Peanut Brittle (page 54), chopped

1. **MAKE THE GRANITA.** In a small saucepan, heat the milk, brown sugar, malt powder, corn syrup, and salt over medium-high heat, stirring to encourage the sugar to dissolve, until the mixture boils. Transfer the mixture to a tall (such as quart-size) heatproof container, add the chocolates, and stir until completely melted. When there are no flecks of chocolate left, stir in 1 cup of the cold water.

Next, do the egg test, which allows you to add water until the chocolate mixture is at the correct density for freezing: Carefully place an egg (in its shell) into the chocolate mixture. Add some of the remaining water, stirring it in a little at a time, until only a dime-size portion of the egg's top peeks through the liquid. (You probably won't need all the liquid.) When you're done, remove the egg, rinse it off, and save it for another use.

Transfer the chocolate mixture to a large, shallow pan and freeze for about 4 hours, scraping the granita mixture with a fork to break it up every 30 minutes after the first

2 hours. (You can make the granita up to this point and keep it frozen for a few days before serving. Scrape it again before you use it.)

2. MAKE THE MOUSSE. Put the water in a large mixing bowl. Sprinkle the gelatin bit by bit into the water, stir with a spoon to blend, and set aside. (The gelatin will soak up the water and begin to look like applesauce.)

In a small saucepan, heat the sesame powder, milk, and corn syrup together over high heat, stirring occasionally, until the mixture boils. Pour the mixture into the bowl with the gelatin, whisk to blend, then add the white chocolate and salt and let sit for 3 minutes. Transfer the mixture to the bowl of a blender, and blend the mixture until smooth. Whisk in the cold cream by hand, then strain the mixture through a fine-mesh strainer into a container. Press a sheet of plastic wrap directly onto the surface of the mousse and refrigerate until the mixture is thick all the way through, about 1½ hours.

3. BUILD THE BINGSOO. In each of four serving bowls or glasses, put about ½ cup of mousse on the bottom, followed by 1 cup of the granita, then a ¼ cup sprinkling of peanut brittle. Serve immediately.

acknowledgments

This book is a product of so many things—my upbringing, my training, my marriage, my parenthood, and my work as a restaurateur. But I could never have done it alone.

To 엄마 and 아빠: Sorry that I never learned to call you 어머니 and 아버지. I blame it on the fact that I left Korea when I was sixteen, and sometimes still speak like that. Mom, you told me, instead of asking me, that I should write good things about you and Dad in the cookbook. I got upset with you for always trying to dictate my life, even still, at thirty-eight. But the truth is, I became exactly the person you always molded me to be. I am hardworking because you told me it's the virtue that would make me successful. I try to be caring and helpful because your selflessness toward your children rubbed off on me, no matter what country you were in. Now I tell my kids how I know what's best for them, just like you tell me, and when they ask for candy after they've brushed their teeth, I really do know best. Thank you.

To our restaurant family: Whether I like it or not, the cycles of restaurant family members are inherently shorter than in other workplaces. But the intense relationship that we get to have when we work together allows us to call ourselves family. I ask for so much, and you give so much in return. I meet a lot of you as green cooks, and there's a lot to teach you, but you make me a better chef. Grease is stronger than blood. Thank you.

To the little boys: When people often ask me how I juggle restaurants with the kids, I have one very simple answer: both are crazy, but one balances the other. It may sound strange, but Pike and Rye, you actually keep me sane. Thank you.

To the big boy: You taught me how to be myself and to trust myself. You showed me how to be generous and kind. You told me life is supposed to be fun and that we gotta just enjoy the ride. It's an incredible thing to say that I share everything with you. Seif, I love you so much for an amazing ten years of married life and partnership. (And thank you for not giving up on teaching me to understand hip-hop.)

Of course, none of it would have happened without the creative minds at Sasquatch Books. Thanks to our editor, Susan Roxborough, who was willing to take on a different kind of cookbook, and to Em Gale and Dana Youlin for seeing it through. To the team at Electric Coffin, for adding the same kind of ingenious design elements they've used at our Seattle restaurants, and to designer Anna Goldstein and photographer Charity Burggraaf, for grasping our vision and making it better. And to our recipe testers: Dan Horner, Erica Goldsmith, Maddie Smith, Ryan Newell, Aaron Erbeck, Chris Horton, Allison Howe, Ben Humphrey, Anne Prins, Rebekah Denn, David Dickey, and Ryan Rogers.

And to Jess Thomson, my coauthor, for adding fat and the necessary bones. It's been an incredible experience to cook side by side with you, to ride the train together, to invade your backyard with my kids, and to talk about my life. Thank you for making this book so dirty.

—Rachel

index

conversions

volume

UNITED STATES	METRIC	IMPERIAL
¼ tsp.	1.25 ml	
½ tsp.	2.5 ml	
1 tsp.	5 ml	
½ Tbsp.	7.5 ml	
1 Tbsp.	15 ml	
⅛ c.	30 ml	1 fl. oz.
¼ c.	60 ml	2 fl. oz.
⅓ c.	80 ml	2.5 fl. oz.
½ c.	125 ml	4 fl. oz.
1 c.	250 ml	8 fl. oz.
2 c. (1 pt.)	500 ml	16 fl. oz.
1 qt.	1 l	32 fl. oz.

length

UNITED STATES	METRIC
⅛ in.	3 mm
¼ in.	6 mm
½ in.	1.25 cm
1 in.	2.5 cm
1 ft.	30 cm

weight

AVOIRDUPOIS	METRIC
¼ oz.	7 g
½ oz.	15 g
1 oz.	30 g
2 oz.	60 g
3 oz.	90 g
4 oz.	115 g
5 oz.	150 g
6 oz.	175 g
7 oz.	200 g
8 oz. (½ lb.)	225 g
9 oz.	250 g
10 oz.	300 g
11 oz.	325 g
12 oz.	350 g
13 oz.	375 g
14 oz.	400 g
15 oz.	425 g
16 oz. (1 lb.)	450 g
1½ lb.	750 g
2 lb.	900 g
2¼ lb.	1 kg
3 lb.	1.4 kg
4 lb.	1.8 kg

temperature

OVEN MARK	FAHRENHEIT	CELSIUS	GAS
Very cool	250–275	130–140	½–1
Cool	300	150	2
Warm	325	165	3
Moderate	350	175	4
Moderately hot	375	190	5
	400	200	6
Hot	425	220	7
	450	230	8
Very Hot	475	245	9

about the authors

RACHEL YANG

Rachel and her husband, Seif Chirchi, own and operate Joule, Revel, and Trove restaurants in Seattle, and Revelry in Portland, under the Relay Restaurant Group umbrella. Their food is based on a wildly creative vision that combines their shared love of bold, unexpected Asian flavors with classic, rigorous technique. The duo holds three James Beard Award nominations for Best Chef Northwest in 2015, 2016, and 2017. Both Rachel and Seif remain working chefs who still cook on the line most nights in one of their signature open kitchens. Their two young sons, Pike and Rye, can often be found in the family's restaurants as well.

JESS THOMSON

Jess is an award-winning freelance food and travel writer, and the author of seven cookbooks, many written with Seattle-area restaurateurs, plus her recent memoir, *A Year Right Here: Adventures with Food and Family in the Great Nearby*. Her work has appeared in *Food & Wine*, *Cooking Light*, *Seattle*, *Sunset*, and *Edible Seattle* magazines, in the *New York Times*, and in multiple issues of the yearly *Best Food Writing* book collection. She lives in Seattle with her husband and eight-year-old son.

Printed in China

Published by Sasquatch Books
21 20 19 18 17   9 8 7 6 5 4 3 2 1

Library of Congress Cataloging-in-Publication
 Data is available.

ISBN: 978-1-63217-078-1

Editor: Susan Roxborough
Production editor: Em Gale
Cover design: Sasquatch Books with Electric Coffin
Cover illustrations:
   Octopus © Nikiparonak/Shutterstock.com
   Dumplings © Epine/Shutterstock.com
   Dinosaur © CSA Images/iStockPhoto.com
Interior design: Anna Goldstein
Handwritten notes: Hannah Viano
Photography: Charity Burggraaf
Food styling: Rachel Yang
Prop styling: Charity Burggraaf and Rachel Yang
Copyeditor: Dana Youlin

Sasquatch Books
1904 Third Avenue, Suite 710 | Seattle, WA 98101
(206) 467-4300 | custserv@sasquatchbooks.com
www.sasquatchbooks.com